THE CULTURAL ORIGINS
OF HUMAN COGNITION

THE CULTURAL
ORIGINS OF
HUMAN COGNITION

Michael Tomasello

HARVARD UNIVERSITY PRESS

Cambridge, Massachusetts

London, England   1999

Library of Congress Cataloging-in-Publication Data

Tomasello, Michael.
The cultural origins of human cognition / Michael Tomasello.
p.   cm.
Includes bibliographical references and index.
ISBN 0–674–00070–6
1. Cognition and culture.   2. Cognition in children.   I. Title.
BF311.T647   1999
153—dc21   99-35902

ACKNOWLEDGMENTS

Individual human beings are able to create culturally significant artifacts only if they receive significant amounts of assistance from other human beings and social institutions. In my case, I was able to write this book—whatever its faults and however limited its cultural significance—only because I received direct assistance from the following people and institutions (and, of course, indirect assistance from all the other people over the past 2,500 years of Western civilization who have thought and written about the basic puzzles of human cognition).

Financial support for a one-year leave of absence, during which the majority of the book was written, was provided by the Guggenheim Foundation, by Emory University (Dr. Steven Sanderson, Dean of Emory College), and by the Max Planck Gesellschaft. Support for my empirical research over the past decade or so has been provided by the Spencer Foundation, the National Science Foundation (Animal Behavior Section), and the National Institute of Child Health and Human Development. I express my deepest gratitude to all of these people and institutions. I am ever hopeful that they feel they got their money's worth.

I have benefited immensely from discussions of many of the issues in this book with a number of friends and colleagues. Of special importance are discussions I have had with Philippe Rochat, Josep Call, Malinda Carpenter, Nameera Akhtar, Gina Conti-Ramsden, Elena Lieven, Tricia Striano, Holger Diessel, Nancy Budwig, and Ann Kruger. All of these people also read some or all of a draft of the manuscript and provided extremely useful commentary. I am also grateful to Michael Cole and Katherine Nelson, who reviewed the manuscript for Harvard University Press and provided very helpful and timely feedback as well.

Finally, I would like to thank Katharina Haberl and Anke Förster for all of their editorial and other assistance on the home front in Leipzig, and Elizabeth Knoll and Camille Smith for all of their editorial and other assistance at Harvard University Press.

CONTENTS

1

A PUZZLE AND A HYPOTHESIS

All the greatest achievements of mind
have been beyond the power of unaided individuals.

—Charles Sanders Peirce

Somewhere in Africa, sometime about 6 million years ago, in a routine evolutionary event, a population of great apes became reproductively isolated from its conspecifics. This new group evolved and split into still other groups, leading eventually to several different species of bipedal ape of the genus *Australopithecus*. All of these new species eventually died out except one that survived until about 2 million years ago, by which time it had changed so much that it needed not just a new species designation but a new genus designation, *Homo*. Compared with its australopithecine forebears—who were four feet tall with ape-sized brains and no stone tools—*Homo* was larger physically, had a larger brain, and made stone tools. Before long, *Homo* began to travel the globe widely, although none of its early forays out of Africa succeeded in establishing any populations that survived permanently.

Then, somewhere still in Africa, sometime about 200,000 years ago, one population of *Homo* began on a new and different evolutionary trajectory. It began living in new ways in Africa and then spread out across the world, outcompeting all other populations of *Homo* and leaving descendants that are known today as *Homo sapiens* (see Figure 1.1). The individuals of this new species had a number of new physical characteristics, including somewhat larger brains, but

most striking were the new cognitive skills and products they
created:

- They began to produce a plethora of new stone tools adapted to
  specific ends, with each population of the species creating its
  own tool-use "industry"—resulting eventually in some populations creating such things as computerized manufacturing
  processes.
- They began to use symbols to communicate and to structure
  their social lives, including not only linguistic symbols but also
  artistic symbols in the form of stone carvings and cave paint-
  ings—resulting eventually in some populations creating such
  things as written language, money, mathematical notation,
  and art.
- They began to engage in new kinds of social practices and orga-
  nizations, including everything from the burying of the dead
  ceremonially to the domestication of plants and animals—resulting eventually in some populations creating such things as for-
  malized religious, governmental, educational, and commercial
  institutions.

The basic puzzle is this. The 6 million years that separates human
beings from other great apes is a very short time evolutionarily, with
modern humans and chimpanzees sharing something on the order
of 99 percent of their genetic material—the same degree of related-
ness as that of other sister genera such as lions and tigers, horses and
zebras, and rats and mice (King and Wilson, 1975). Our problem is
thus one of time. The fact is, there simply has not been enough time
for normal processes of biological evolution involving genetic variation and natural selection to have created, one by one, each of the
cognitive skills necessary for modern humans to invent and maintain complex tool-use industries and technologies, complex forms of
symbolic communication and representation, and complex social or-
ganizations and institutions. And the puzzle is only magnified if we
take seriously current research in paleoanthropology suggesting that
(a) for all but the last 2 million years the human lineage showed no

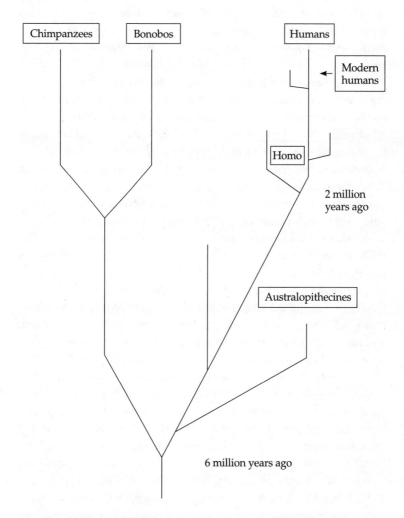

Figure 1.1 A simplified depiction of the time scale of human evolution.

signs of anything other than typical great ape cognitive skills, and (b) the first dramatic signs of species-unique cognitive skills emerged only in the last one-quarter of a million years with modern *Homo sapiens* (Foley and Lahr, 1997; Klein, 1989; Stringer and McKie, 1996).

There is only one possible solution to this puzzle. That is, there is only one known biological mechanism that could bring about these kinds of changes in behavior and cognition in so short a time— whether that time be thought of as 6 million, 2 million, or one-quarter of a million years. This biological mechanism is social or cultural transmission, which works on time scales many orders of magnitude faster than those of organic evolution. Broadly speaking, cultural transmission is a moderately common evolutionary process that enables individual organisms to save much time and effort, not to mention risk, by exploiting the already existing knowledge and skills of conspecifics. Cultural transmission includes such things as fledgling birds mimicking their species-typical song from parents, rat pups eating only the foods eaten by their mothers, ants locating food by following the pheromone trails of conspecifics, young chimpanzees learning the tool-use practices of the adults around them, and human children acquiring the linguistic conventions of others in their social groups (Mundinger, 1980; Heyes and Galef, 1996). However, despite the fact that all of these processes may be grouped under the general rubric of cultural transmission, the precise behavioral and cognitive mechanisms involved in the different cases are numerous and diverse, including everything from parents eliciting fixed action patterns from their offspring to transmission of skills by imitative learning and instruction—which suggests the possibility of significant subtypes of cultural transmission processes (Tomasello, 1990; 1994). One reasonable hypothesis, then, is that the amazing suite of cognitive skills and products displayed by modern humans is the result of some sort of species-unique mode or modes of cultural transmission.

The evidence that human beings do indeed have species-unique modes of cultural transmission is overwhelming. Most importantly, the cultural traditions and artifacts of human beings accumulate modifications over time in a way that those of other animal species do not—so-called cumulative cultural evolution. Basically none of the most complex human artifacts or social practices—including tool industries, symbolic communication, and social institutions—were invented once and for all at a single moment by any one individual or group of individuals. Rather, what happened was that some individual or group of individuals first invented a primitive version of the artifact or practice, and then some later user or users made a modification, an "improvement," that others then adopted perhaps without change for many generations, at which point some other individual or group of individuals made another modification, which was then learned and used by others, and so on over historical time in what has sometimes been dubbed "the ratchet effect" (Tomasello, Kruger, and Ratner, 1993). The process of cumulative cultural evolution requires not only creative invention but also, and just as importantly, faithful social transmission that can work as a ratchet to prevent slippage backward—so that the newly invented artifact or practice preserves its new and improved form at least somewhat faithfully until a further modification or improvement comes along. Perhaps surprisingly, for many animal species it is not the creative component, but rather the stabilizing ratchet component, that is the difficult feat. Thus, many nonhuman primate individuals regularly produce intelligent behavioral innovations and novelties, but then their groupmates do not engage in the kinds of social learning that would enable, over time, the cultural ratchet to do its work (Kummer and Goodall, 1985).

The basic fact is thus that human beings are able to pool their cognitive resources in ways that other animal species are not. Accordingly, Tomasello, Kruger, and Ratner (1993) distinguished human cultural learning from more widespread forms of social learning, identifying three basic types: imitative learning, instructed learning, and collaborative learning. These three types of cultural learning are made possible by a single very special form of social cognition, namely, the ability of individual organisms to understand conspecifics as beings *like themselves* who have intentional and mental lives like their own. This understanding enables individuals to imagine themselves "in the mental shoes" of some other person, so that they can learn not just *from* the other but *through* the other. This understanding of others as intentional beings like the self is crucial in human cultural learning because cultural artifacts and social practices—exemplified prototypically by the use of tools and linguistic symbols—invariably point beyond themselves to other outside entities: tools point to the problems they are designed to solve and linguistic symbols point to the communicative situations they are designed to represent. Therefore, to socially learn the conventional use of a tool or a symbol, children must come to understand why, toward what outside end, the other person is using the tool or symbol; that is to say, they must come to understand the intentional significance of the tool use or symbolic practice—what it is "for," what "we," the users of this tool or symbol, do with it.

Processes of cultural learning are especially powerful forms of social learning because they constitute both (a) especially faithful forms of cultural transmission (creating an especially powerful cultural ratchet) and (b) especially powerful forms of social-collaborative creativeness and inventiveness, that is, processes of sociogenesis in which multiple individuals create something together that no one individual could have created on its own. These special powers come directly from the fact that as one human being is learning "through" another, she identifies with that other person and his intentional and sometimes mental states. Despite some observations suggesting that some nonhuman primates in some situations are capable of understanding conspecifics as intentional agents and of learning from them in ways that resemble some forms of human cultural learning, the overwhelming weight of the empirical evidence suggests that only human beings understand conspecifics as intentional agents like the self and so only human beings engage in cultural learning (Tomasello, 1996b, 1998; Tomasello and Call, 1997; see Chapter 2). It is also worth noting in this connection that there is a very specific and biologically based syndrome in human ontogeny, namely autism, in which the most severely afflicted individuals are incapable both of understanding other persons as intentional/mental agents like the self and also of engaging in species-typical skills of cultural learning (Hobson, 1993; Baron-Cohen, 1993; Sigman and Capps, 1997; Carpenter and Tomasello, in press).

The complete sequence of hypothesized evolutionary events is thus: human beings evolved a new form of social cognition, which enabled some new forms of cultural learning, which enabled some new processes of sociogenesis and cumulative cultural evolution. This scenario solves our time problem because it posits one and only one biological adaptation—which could have happened at any time in human evolution, including quite recently. The cultural processes that this one adaptation unleashed did not then create new cognitive skills out of nothing, but rather they took existing individually based cognitive skills—such as those possessed by most primates for dealing with space, objects, tools, quantities, categories, social relationships, communication, and social learning—and transformed them into new, culturally based cognitive skills with a social-collective dimension. These transformations took place not in evolutionary time but in historical time, where much can happen in several thousand years.

Cumulative cultural evolution is thus the explanation for many of human beings' most impressive cognitive achievements. However, to fully appreciate the role of cultural-historical processes in constituting modern human cognition we must look at what happens during human ontogeny. Most importantly, cumulative cultural evolution ensures that human cognitive ontogeny takes place in an environment of ever-new artifacts and social practices which, at any one time, represent something resembling the entire collective wisdom of the entire social group throughout its entire cultural history. Children are able to participate fully in this cognitive collectivity from about nine months of age when they, for the first time, begin to make attempts to share attention with, and to imitatively learn from and through, their conspecifics (see Chapter 3). These newly emerging joint attentional activities represent nothing other than the ontogenetic emergence of the uniquely human social-cognitive adaptation for identifying with other persons and so understanding them as intentional agents like the self. This new understanding and these new activities thus form the basis for children's initial entry into the world of culture. The outcome is that each child who understands her conspecifics as intentional/mental beings like herself—that is, each child who possesses the social-cognitive key to the historically constituted cognitive products of her social group—can now participate in the collectivity known as human cognition, and so say (following Isaac Newton) that she sees as far as she does because she "stands on the shoulders of giants." Importantly, we may contrast this species-typical situation with that of both:

- children with autism, who grow up in the midst of cumulative cultural products but are not able to take advantage of the collective wisdom embodied in them because, for biological reasons, they do not possess the requisite social-cognitive skills; and
- an imaginary wild child who grows up on a desert island with a normal brain, body, and sense organs, but with no access to tools, other material artifacts, language, graphic symbols, writing, Arabic numerals, pictures, people who could teach her things, people whose behavior she could observe and imitate, or people with whom she could collaborate.

For the child with autism there are cognitive shoulders to stand on, if only she could, whereas for the imaginary wild child there are no cognitive shoulders to stand on. In either case the result is, or would be, the same: something other than species-typical cognitive skills.

But growing up in a cultural world has cognitive implications that go beyond even this. Growing up in a cultural world—assuming possession of the social-cognitive key giving access to this world—actually serves to create some unique forms of cognitive representation. Most important to this process, human children use their cultural learning skills to acquire linguistic and other communicative symbols. Linguistic symbols are especially important symbolic artifacts for developing children because they embody the ways that previous generations of human beings in a social group have found it useful to categorize and construe the world for purposes of interpersonal communication. For example, in different communicative situations one and the same object may be construed as a dog, an animal, a pet, or a pest; one and the same event may be construed as running, moving, fleeing, or surviving; one and the same place may be construed as the coast, the shore, the beach, or the sand—all depending on the communicative goals of the speaker. As the child masters the linguistic symbols of her culture she thereby acquires the ability to adopt multiple perspectives simultaneously on one and the same perceptual situation. As perspectively based cognitive representations, then, linguistic symbols are based not on the recording of direct sensory or motor experiences, as are the cognitive representations of other animal species and human infants, but rather on the ways in which individuals choose to construe things out of a number of other ways they might have construed them, as embodied in the other available linguistic symbols that they might have chosen, but did not. Linguistic symbols thus free human cognition from the immediate perceptual situation not simply by enabling reference to things outside this situation ("displacement"; Hockett, 1960), but rather by enabling multiple simultaneous representations of each and every, indeed all possible, perceptual situations.

Later, as children become more skillful with their native language, additional possibilities for construing things in different ways open up. For example, natural languages contain cognitive resources for partitioning the world into such things as events and their participants—who may play many and various roles in these events—and for forming abstract categories of event and participant types. Moreover, natural languages also contain cognitive resources for construing whole events or situations in terms of one another, that is, for creating the various kinds of analogies and metaphors that are so important in adult cognition—such as seeing the atom as a solar system, love as a journey, or anger as heat (Lakoff, 1987; Gentner and Markman, 1997; see Chapter 5). Also, children's growing skills of linguistic communication enable them to participate in complex discourse interactions in which the explicitly symbolized perspectives of interactants clash and so must be negotiated and resolved. These kinds of interactions may lead children to begin to construct something like a theory of mind of their communicative partners, and, in some special cases of pedagogical discourse, to internalize adult instructions and so begin to self-regulate and to reflect on their own thinking—perhaps leading to some types of metacognition and representational redescription (Karmiloff-Smith, 1992). The internalization of discourse interactions containing multiple, conflicting perspectives may even be identified with certain types of uniquely human, dialogical thinking processes (Vygotsky, 1978).

In this book—for which the foregoing may be seen as a kind of précis—I attempt to spell out this general line of argumentation in some detail. That is, my specific hypothesis is that human cognition has the species-unique qualities it does because:

- *Phylogenetically:* modern human beings evolved the ability to "identify" with conspecifics, which led to an understanding of them as intentional and mental beings like the self.
- *Historically:* this enabled new forms of cultural learning and sociogenesis, which led to cultural artifacts and behavioral traditions that accumulate modifications over historical time.
- *Ontogenetically:* human children grow up in the midst of these socially and historically constituted artifacts and traditions, which enables them to (a) benefit from the accumulated knowledge and skills of their social groups; (b) acquire and use perspectivally based cognitive representations in the form of linguistic symbols (and analogies and metaphors constructed from these symbols); and (c) internalize certain types of discourse interactions into skills of metacognition, representational redescription, and dialogic thinking.

I should emphasize at the outset that my focus is only on the species-unique aspects of human cognition. Of course human cognition is in large measure constituted by the kinds of things that appear as chapter headings in traditional Cognitive Psychology textbooks: perception, memory, attention, categorization, and so on. But these are all cognitive processes that human beings share with other primates (Tomasello and Call, 1997; Tomasello, 1998). My account here simply presupposes them, and then focuses in Vygotskian fashion on the kinds of evolutionary, historical, and ontogenetic processes that might have transformed these fundamental skills into the special version of primate cognition that is human cognition. I should also emphasize that I will deal with the biological and historical processes involved in the evolution of human cognition only briefly and somewhat indirectly—mainly because the events of interest took place deep in the evolutionary and historical past and our information about them is very poor (Chapter 2). On the other hand, I will focus in some detail on human cognitive ontogeny—about which we know a good deal through several decades of direct observation and experimentation—and the processes by which human children actively exploit and make use of both their biological and cultural inheritances (Chapters 3–6).

Unfortunately, in today's intellectual climate my argument may be taken by some theorists to be an essentially genetic one: the social-cognitive adaptation characteristic of modern humans is a kind of "magic bullet" that differentiates human beings from other primate species. But this is an erroneous view that basically ignores all of the social-cultural work that must be done by individuals and groups of individuals, in both historical and ontogenetic time, to create uniquely human cognitive skills and products. From an historical perspective, a quarter of a million years is a very long time during which much may be accomplished culturally, and anyone who has spent time with young children knows how many learning experiences may take place within the course of several years—or even several days or several hours—of continuous, active engagement with the environment. Any serious inquiry into human cognition, therefore, must include some account of these historical and ontogenetic processes, which are enabled but not in any way determined by human beings' biological adaptation for a special form of social cognition. Indeed, my central argument in this book is that it is these processes, not any specialized biological adaptations directly, that have done the actual work in creating many, if not all, of the most distinctive and important cognitive products and processes of the species *Homo sapiens*. And it is worth noting in this context that taking these processes seriously enables us to explain not only the universal features of uniquely human cognition—such as the creation and use of material, symbolic, and institutional artifacts with accumulated histories—but also the particularities of particular cultures, each of which has developed for itself via these same historical and ontogenetic processes a variety of culturally unique cognitive skills and products during the past several dozen millennia of human history.

2

BIOLOGICAL AND CULTURAL INHERITANCE

But there is nothing odd about the product of a given process contributing to, or even becoming an essential factor in, the further development of that process.

—George Herbert Mead

The overarching fact of the organic world is evolution by means of natural selection. A key element in this process is biological inheritance, by means of which an organism inherits the basic *Bauplan* of its forebears, along with its implications for perceptual, behavioral, and cognitive functioning. But for all mammalian species, including all primate species, much of the ontogeny by means of which this *Bauplan* comes into being takes place while the developing organism is interacting with its environment. The relatively long period of immaturity in which this interaction takes place is of course a very risky life-history strategy, as it means that offspring are totally dependent on one or more parents for food and protection from predators for some time. The compensating advantage of a long immaturity is that it enables ontogenetic pathways that incorporate significant amounts of individual learning and cognition, which typically result in more flexible behavioral and cognitive adaptations. Flexible behavioral/cognitive adaptations closely attuned to the local environment are especially useful for organisms whose populations live in diverse environmental niches, or whose environmental niches change relatively rapidly over time (Bruner, 1972).

In some animal species, the developing organism individually ac-quires information not only from its physical environment but also from its social environment—or from aspects of its physical environ-ment that have been modified in important ways by conspecifics. For example, as alluded to above, some bird species acquire their species-typical song by listening to the song of their parents, and some insects are able to find food on their first day in the external environment because they know instinctively how to follow the pheromone trails laid down by conspecifics (Mundinger, 1980; Heyes and Galef, 1996). In its broadest definition, as used by many evolutionary biologists, this process is called cultural transmission, or cultural inheritance, and it produces cultural traditions. Recent recognition of the importance of cultural transmission for many ani-mal species has led to the creation of Dual Inheritance Theory, in which the mature phenotypes of many species are seen to depend on what they inherit from their forebears both biologically and cul-turally (Boyd and Richerson, 1985; Durham, 1991).

Human beings, of course, are the prototypical species for Dual In-heritance Theory, as normal human development depends crucially on both biological and cultural inheritance. My particular claim is that in the cognitive realm the biological inheritance of humans is very much like that of other primates. There is just one major differ-ence, and that is the fact that human beings "identify" with con-specifics more deeply than do other primates. This identification is not something mysterious, but simply the process by which the human child understands that other persons are beings like her-self—in a way that inanimate objects are not, for example—and so she sometimes tries to understand things from their point of view. During early ontogeny, in a process that will be spelled out in more detail in later chapters, the child comes to experience herself as an intentional agent—that is, a being whose behavioral and attentional strategies are organized by goals—and so she automatically sees other beings with whom she identifies in these same terms. Later in ontogeny, the child comes to experience herself as a mental agent—that is, a being with thoughts and beliefs that may differ from those of other people as well as from reality—and so from that time on she will see conspecifics in these new terms. For purposes of exposition I refer to this process generally as "understanding others as intentional (or mental) agents (like the self)."

This one cognitive difference has many cascading effects because it makes possible some new and uniquely powerful forms of cultural inheritance. Understanding other persons as intentional agents like the self makes possible both (a) processes of sociogenesis by means of which multiple individuals collaboratively create cultural artifacts and practices with accumulated histories, and (b) processes of cultural learning and internalization by means of which developing individuals learn to use and then internalize aspects of the collaborative products created by conspecifics. This means that most, if not all, of the species-unique cognitive skills of human beings are not due to a unique biological inheritance directly, but rather result from a variety of historical and ontogenetic processes that are set into motion by the one uniquely human, biologically inherited, cognitive capacity.

Biological Inheritance

Human beings are primates. They have the same basic sense organs, the same basic body plan, and the same basic brain plan as all other primates. Therefore, if we are attempting to characterize the evolutionary bases of human cognition, we must begin with primates in general. In the current context there are two questions of central importance: (a) How does the cognition of primates differ from that of other mammals? and (b) How does the cognition of humans differ from that of other primates? My answers to these two questions will be based on the research of Tomasello and Call (1997), who provide more detailed analyses of the relevant empirical studies and theoretical arguments, as well as a more complete set of references. It must be acknowledged at the outset, of course, that other answers to these questions are also possible (see, for example, Byrne, 1995, for some different views).

Mammalian and Primate Cognition

All mammals live in basically the same sensory-motor world of permanent objects arrayed in a representational space; primates, including humans, have no special skills in this regard. Moreover, many mammalian species and basically all primates cognitively represent the categorical and quantitative relations among objects as well. These cognitive skills are evidenced by their ability to do such things as:

- remember "what" is "where" in their local environments, e.g., which fruits are in which trees (at what times);
- take novel detours and shortcuts in navigating through space;
- follow the visible and invisible movements of objects (i.e., pass rigorously controlled Piagetian object permanence tests—some Stage 6);
- categorize objects on the basis of perceptual similarities;
- understand and thus match small numerosities of objects;
- use insight in problem solving.

And much evidence suggests that mammals do not acquire these skills in some behavioristic connecting of stimuli and responses, or via some simple form of rote memory, but rather actually come to comprehend and cognitively represent spaces and objects (and categories and quantities of objects) in ways that enable creative inferences and insightful problem solving.

Similarly, all mammals live in basically the same social world of individually recognized conspecifics and their vertical (dominance) and horizontal (affiliative) relationships, and they have the ability to predict the behavior of conspecifics in many situations based on a variety of cues and insights. These cognitive skills are evidenced by their ability to do such things as:

- recognize individuals in their social groups;
- form direct relationships with other individuals based on such things as kinship, friendship, and dominance rank;

- predict the behavior of individuals based on such things as their emotional state and their direction of locomotion;
- use many types of social and communicative strategies to out-compete groupmates for valued resources;
- cooperate with conspecifics in problem-solving tasks and in forming social coalitions and alliances;
- engage in various forms of social learning in which they learn valuable things from conspecifics.

And again much evidence suggests that mammalian individuals do not act blindly socially, but rather actually comprehend and cognitively represent what they are doing when they interact with their groupmates in these various complex ways.

There is one exception to this overall cognitive similarity among mammals, however, and that concerns primates' understanding of relational categories, which manifests itself in both the social and physical domains. In the social domain, primates, but not other mammals, understand something of the third-party social relationships that hold among other individuals; for example, they understand such things as the kinship and dominance relations that third parties have with one another. Thus, primates are selective in choosing their coalition partners, selecting as an ally, for instance, an individual who is dominant to their potential adversary—indicating their understanding of the relative dominance ranks of these two individuals. They also seek retribution for attacks against themselves not just on the attacker, but also in some circumstances on the attacker's kin—in this case evidencing an understanding of third-party kinship relations. And there is even some evidence that primates understand whole categories of third-party social relationships across different individuals, for example, many different instances of the relationship "mother-child" (Dasser, 1988a, 1988b). Other mammals do not display these kinds of understandings (Tomasello and Call, 1997). The hypothesis is thus that while all mammals recognize individuals and form relationships with them, only primates understand external social relationships in which they themselves are not directly involved.

In the physical domain, primates are especially skillful as compared with other mammals in dealing with relational categories. For example, primates are relatively skillful in tasks in which they must choose from an array the pair of objects whose members have the same relationship to one another as the members of some experimental sample (e.g., the members of the chosen pair are identical to one another, rather than different, just as are the members of the experimental sample; Thomas, 1986). Interestingly, however, primate individuals take many hundreds of trials, sometimes thousands of trials, to master these tasks, which contrasts markedly with their seemingly effortless understanding of third-party social relationships—which also involve the understanding of relational categories. Following Humphrey's (1976) general line of reasoning, therefore, one hypothesis is that primates evolved the ability to understand categories of third-party social relationships, and in the laboratory we may sometimes tap into this skill using physical rather than social objects if we train individuals for long enough. Indeed it is difficult to think of specific problems in the physical world with which the understanding of relational categories would be of direct help, whereas in the social world there are many kinds of situations in which the understanding of third-party social relationships and categories would immediately make for more effective social action.

The understanding of relational categories in general, then, is the major skill that differentiates the cognition of primates from that of other mammals. This hypothesis is important in the current context because the understanding of relational categories is a potential evolutionary precursor—a kind of halfway house—for the uniquely human cognitive ability to understand the intentional relations that animate beings have to the external world and the causal relations that inanimate objects and events have with one another.

Human Understanding of Intentionality and Causality

It is widely believed that nonhuman primates have an understanding of the intentionality of conspecifics and the causality of inanimate objects and events. I do not believe that they do, and I have argued and reviewed evidence extensively for this negative conclusion (Tomasello, 1990, 1994, 1996b; Tomasello, Kruger, and Ratner, 1993; Tomasello and Call, 1994, 1997). However, it must be emphasized— again and again if necessary—that my negative conclusion about nonhuman primate cognition is quite specific and delimited. Nonhuman primates definitely do have an understanding of all kinds of complex physical and social events, they possess and use many kinds of concepts and cognitive representations, they clearly differentiate between animate and inanimate objects, and they employ in their interactions with their environments many complex and insightful problem-solving strategies (as reviewed above). It is just that they do not view the world in terms of the kinds of intermediate and often hidden "forces," the underlying causes and intentional/mental states, that are so important to human thinking. Briefly said: nonhuman primates are themselves intentional and causal beings, they just do not understand the world in intentional and causal terms.

In the social realm, the evidence concerning nonhuman primate understanding of the intentionality/mentality of other animate beings comes from both experimental and naturalistic studies. First, Premack and Woodruff (1978) had the chimpanzee Sarah choose pictures to complete video sequences of intentional human actions (e.g., she had to choose a picture of a key when the human in the video was trying to exit a locked door). Her success in the task led to the inference that she knew the human's goal in the depicted actions. However, Savage-Rumbaugh, Rumbaugh, and Boysen (1978) produced similar results using as stimuli simple associates; for example, their apes also chose a picture of a key when shown a picture of a lock with no human action occurring at all. This raises the possibility that what Sarah was doing was something cognitively much simpler. (Premack, 1986, reported that in a subsequent study he could not train Sarah to discriminate videos of humans engaged in intentional versus nonintentional actions, and Povinelli et al., 1998, report some similar negative findings, with the results of Call and Tomasello, 1998, being mixed.) The other main experimental study is that of Povinelli, Nelson, and Boysen (1990), who found that chimpanzees preferred to ask for food from a person who had witnessed its hiding over someone who had not witnessed its hiding—the inference being that they could discriminate a "knowledgeable" from an "ignorant" human. The problem in this case is that the apes in this study only learned to do this over many scores of trials with feedback on their accuracy after every trial (Heyes, 1993; Povinelli, 1994). And this is also a problem for the study of Woodruff and Premack (1979) in which chimpanzees learned after many trials with feedback to direct humans to the box without food so they could obtain the one with food (what some call deception). The problem is thus that the chimpanzees in these studies did not seem to bring a knowledge of others' intentionality or mentality to the experiment, but rather learned how to behave to get what they wanted as the experiment unfolded. In a study in which learning during the experiment was all but ruled out, Call and Tomasello (1999) found that chimpanzees showed no understanding of the false beliefs of others.

Because all of these experiments are artificial in various ways, other investigators have turned to the natural behavior of nonhuman primates for positive evidence of the understanding of intentionality, mostly involving social strategies that supposedly rely on the manipulation of conspecifics' mental states in a deceptive fashion. The problem in this case is that almost all of the reported observations are anecdotes that lack the appropriate control observations to rule out competing explanations (Byrne and Whiten, 1988). But even in reliable (replicable) cases it is not clear what is going on cognitively. For example, de Waal (1986) observed a female chimpanzee on repeated occasions hold out her hand to another in an apparent appeasement gesture, but when the other approached she attacked him. This might be a case of human-like deception: the perpetrator wanted the other to believe that she had friendly intentions when in fact she did not. It is just as likely, however, that the perpetrator wanted the other individual to approach her (so she could attack), and so performed a behavior that had in the past led conspecifics to approach in other contexts. This use of an established social behavior in a novel context is clearly a very intelligent and perhaps insightful social strategy for manipulating the behavior of others, but it is not clear that it involves the understanding and manipulation of the intentional or mental states of others.

I should also point out some social behaviors that nonhuman primates in their natural habitats do not perform (some apes raised in human cultural environments do some of them—see discussion below). In their natural habitats, nonhuman primates:

- do not point or gesture to outside objects for others;
- do not hold objects up to show them to others;
- do not try to bring others to locations so that they can observe things there;
- do not actively offer objects to other individuals by holding them out;
- do not intentionally teach other individuals new behaviors.

They do not do these things, in my view, because they do not understand that the conspecific has intentional and mental states that can potentially be affected. The most plausible hypothesis is thus that nonhuman primates understand conspecifics as animate beings capable of spontaneous self-movement—indeed, this is the basis for their social understanding in general and their understanding of third-party social relationships in particular—but do not understand others as intentional agents in the process of pursuing goals or mental agents in the process of thinking about the world. Nonhuman primates see a conspecific moving toward food and may infer, based on past experience, what is likely to happen next, and they may even use intelligent and insightful social strategies to affect what happens next. But human beings see something different. They see a conspecific as trying to obtain the food as a goal, and they can attempt to affect this and other intentional and mental states, not just behavior.

In the physical realm, Visalberghi has recently observed some limitations in primates' skills at adapting to novel foraging tasks in which some understanding of causality is required. The basic task involves the subject using a stick to push food out of a clear tube. In one set of tasks, the tools are varied, with some being too short, or too fat, or not rigid enough to work properly. The basic idea is that if an individual understands the physical causality involved in how the stick works to extract the food from the tube—physical force transferred from self to stick to food—it should be able to predict just from perceptual inspection of a tool, without extensive trial and error, whether or not the tool will effect the required causal sequence. Both apes and capuchin monkeys succeed with the novel tools in this task, but only after much trial and error. In a recent task variation, these species were given a clear tube with a small trap under one part of the tube. If subjects appreciate the causal force of gravity and the physics of holes and sticks moving objects, they should learn to avoid this trap as they attempt to push the food through the tube (i.e., they should always push the food out the end away from the trap). But neither capuchins nor chimpanzees learned to do this quickly; for example, all four chimpanzee subjects behaved at chance levels for seventy or more trials. In a final twist, after the animals had learned through trial and error to avoid the trap, the tube was flipped over—so that the trap was on top of the tube and posed no danger. Subjects of both species (the chimpanzees in a study by Reaux, 1995) still pushed the food away from the trap, not understanding its new harmless status. Two- to three-year-old children behave much more flexibly and adaptively on these tube problems—seeming to understand something of the causal principles at work—from the very earliest trials (see Visalberghi and Limongelli, 1996, for a review).

The conclusion is thus that nonhuman primates have many cognitive skills involving physical objects and events—including an understanding of relational categories and basic antecedent-consequent event sequences—but they do not perceive or understand underlying causes as mediating the dynamic relations among these objects and events. They thus do not show the kind of flexibility of behavior and understanding of general causal principles characteristic of human children, from a fairly young age, as they try to solve physical problems. Nonhuman primates understand many antecedent-consequent relations in the world, but they do not seem to understand causal forces as mediating these relations.

By way of summary, I would like to be fully explicit about what differentiates intentional/causal cognition from other types of cognition. Foundationally, this form of thinking requires an individual to understand the antecedent-consequent relations among external events in the absence of its own direct involvement, which is something that primates are clearly able to do. But, in addition, the understanding of intentionality and causality requires the individual to understand the mediating forces in these external events that explain "why" a particular antecedent-consequent sequence occurs as it does—and these mediating forces are typically not readily observable. This understanding seems to be unique to humans. Thus, for humans, the weight of the falling rock "forces" the log to splinter; the goal of obtaining food "forces" the organism to look under the log. And, importantly, in both of these cases there may be other antecedent events that may bring about the same result so long as the same mediating "force" is involved. This is an important point because it demonstrates that the key component in all of this is not a specific antecedent event (as in associative learning) but the underlying causal or intentional force, which may be induced by many different antecedent events. This can be clearly seen in Figure 2.1, which depicts one physical causal situation (different physical events that create a force that causes a fruit to drop) and one social causal situation (different social events that create a psychological state that causes an individual to flee). Obviously, the specific way these forces work are very different in the causality of inanimate objects and the intentionality of animate beings, but the overall structure of the reasoning processes involved is of the same general nature: antecedent event > mediating force > consequent event.

In terms of evolution, then, the hypothesis is that human beings built directly on the uniquely primate cognitive adaptation for understanding external relational categories, they just added a small but important twist in terms of mediating forces such as causes and intentions. This scenario gains some of its plausibility from the fact that it provides for continuity between uniquely primate and uniquely human cognitive adaptations. Moreover, my hypothesis is that, just as primate understanding of relational categories evolved first in the social domain to comprehend third-party social relationships, human causal understanding also evolved first in the social domain to comprehend others as intentional agents. There is currently no way of knowing if this is true, of course, but many of the people of the world, when they are in doubt as to the physical cause of an event, often invoke various types of animistic or deistic forces to explain it; perhaps this is the default approach. And so, my hypothesis is that the uniquely human ability to understand external events in terms of mediating intentional/causal forces emerged first in human evolution to allow individuals to predict and explain the

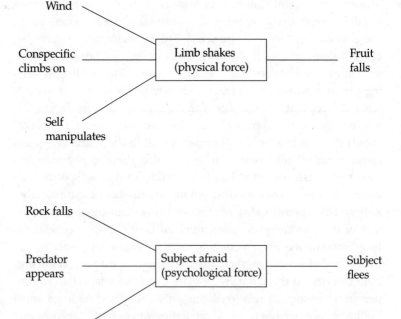

Figure 2.1 A graphic depiction of one physical event *(top)* and one social event *(bottom)*. In both cases many different antecedent events may create the force that causes the consequent event.

behavior of conspecifics and has since been transported to deal with the behavior of inert objects.

We have no idea when this might have occurred, but one possibility is that it was characteristic of modern humans as they first evolved somewhere in Africa some 200,000 years ago, and this may even explain why they outcompeted other hominids as they migrated all over the globe. The competitive advantages of intentional/causal thinking are mainly two. First, this kind of cognition enables humans to solve problems in especially creative, flexible, and foresightful ways. Thus in many cases intentional/causal understanding enables an individual to predict and control events even when their usual antecedent is not present—that is, if there is some other event that may serve to instigate the mediating force. For example, an individual might create a novel way to distract a competitor away from something over which they are competing (e.g., by placing food in the opposite direction), or a novel tool for generating the force needed to move an obstacle. Conversely, if an event occurs in a circumstance in which the mediating force is somehow blocked, it could be predicted that its usual consequent will not follow. For example, an individual could block the visual access of a competitor to the object of their competition, or could prevent a stone from rolling down a hill by placing another stone under it. Humans causal and intentional understanding thus have immediate consequences for effective action, as they open up the possibility of finding novel ways to either manipulate or suppress mediating forces.

The second advantage of intentional/causal understanding derives from its powerful transforming role in processes of social learning. That is, understanding the behavior of other persons as intentional and/or mental directly enables certain very powerful forms of cultural learning and sociogenesis, and these forms of social learning are directly responsible for the special forms of cultural inheritance characteristic of human beings. But to appreciate this claim, we must look more closely at the cultural transmission processes characteristic of our nearest primate relatives and then compare these to the human case.

Nonhuman Primate Culture

There are many different forms of cultural inheritance and transmission depending on the precise social learning mechanisms involved. Among the most commonly cited are:

- *Exposure:* youngsters may be exposed to new learning experiences because they stay physically close to conspecifics, without learning anything from the behavior of conspecifics directly—as when a youngster follows its mother and so stumbles upon water, thereby learning the water's location.
- *Stimulus enhancement:* youngsters may be attracted to objects with which others are interacting, and then learn things on their own about those objects—as when a young chimpanzee is attracted to a stick its mother has discarded, and the attraction sets in motion certain individual learning experiences with the stick.
- *Mimicking:* youngsters have adaptive specializations for reproducing the actual behavior of conspecifics, although without an appreciation for its instrumental efficacy and typically within a very narrowly specialized behavioral domain—as when some bird species acquire their species-typical vocalizations (or as in the prelinguistic babbling of human infants).
- *Imitative learning:* youngsters actually reproduce the behavior or behavioral strategy of the demonstrator, for the same goal as the demonstrator.

To fully account for the differences of social learning between human and nonhuman primates we will actually need to distinguish a few additional processes, but they are best explained in context.

Macaque Potato Washing

The most often cited case of a nonhuman primate cultural tradition is that of Japanese macaque potato washing (Kawamura, 1959; Kawai, 1965). The story is this. In 1953 an eighteen-month-old female named Imo was observed to take pieces of sweet potato, given to her and the rest of the troop by researchers, and to wash the sand off them in some nearby water. About three months after she began to wash her potatoes the practice was observed in Imo's mother and two of her playmates (and then their mothers). During the next two years, seven other youngsters also began to wash potatoes, and within three years of Imo's first potato washing about 40 percent of the troop was doing the same. The fact that it was Imo's close associates who learned the behavior first, and their associates directly after, was thought to be significant in suggesting that the means of propagation of this behavior was some form of imitation in which one individual actually copied the behavior of another.

The interpretation of these observations in terms of culture and imitation has two main problems, however. The first problem is that potato washing is much less unusual a behavior for monkeys than was originally thought. Brushing sand off food turns out to be something that many monkeys do naturally, and indeed this had been observed in the Koshima monkeys prior to the emergence of washing. It is thus not surprising that potato washing was also observed in four other troops of human-provisioned Japanese macaques soon after the Koshima observations (Kawai, 1965)—implying at least four individuals who learned on their own. Also, in captivity individuals of other monkey species learn quite rapidly, on their own, to wash their food when provided with sandy fruits and bowls of water (Visalberghi and Fragaszy, 1990). The second problem has to do with the pattern of the spread of potato-washing behavior within the group. The fact is that the spread of the behavior was relatively slow, with an average time of over two years for acquisition by the members of the group who learned it (Galef, 1992). Moreover, the rate of spread did not increase as the number of users increased. If the mechanism of transmission were imitation, an increase in the rate of propagation would be expected as more demonstrators became available for observation over time. In contrast, if processes of individual learning were at work, a slower and steadier rate of spread would be expected—which was in fact observed. That Imo's friends and relatives were first to learn the behavior may be due to the fact that friends and relatives stay close to one another, and thus Imo's friends may have followed her to the water more often during feeding than other group members, increasing their chances for individual discovery.

Chimpanzee Tool Use

Perhaps the best species to examine in the current context is humans' closest primate relative, the chimpanzee, which is by far and away the most cultural of nonhuman primates (McGrew, 1992, 1998; Boesch, 1996, in press). Chimpanzees in their natural habitats have a number of population-specific behavioral traditions that virtually all group members acquire and that persist across generations, including such things as food choice, tool use, and gestural signaling. For a variety of reasons, genetic explanations for these population differences of behavior are unlikely (e.g., populations living close together are no more similar than populations living far apart), and so they have been widely talked about as chimpanzee cultural traditions (e.g., Wrangham et al., 1994).

The best-known example is chimpanzee tool use. For example, chimpanzees in some populations of eastern Africa fish for termites by probing termite mounds with small, thin sticks. Some other populations of chimpanzees in western Africa, however, simply destroy termite mounds with large sticks and attempt to scoop up the insects by the handful. Field researchers such as Boesch (1993) and McGrew (1992) have claimed that specific tool-use practices such as these are "culturally transmitted" among the individuals of the various communities. But there is a competing explanation that is also quite plausible. The fact is that the termite mounds in western Africa are much softer, owing to larger amounts of rain, than those of eastern Africa. The strategy of destroying the mound with a large stick is thus available only to the western populations. Under this hypothesis, then, there would be group differences of behavior superficially resembling human cultural differences, but with no type of social learning involved at all. In such cases the "culture" is simply a result of individual learning driven by the different local ecologies of the different populations—and so this process is called simply *environmental shaping*.

Although environmental shaping is probably a part of the explanations for group differences of behavior for all primate species, including humans, extensive ecological analyses by Boesch et al. (1994) make this an unlikely explanation for all of the differences of behavior among different chimpanzee groups. Experimental analyses also confirm that more than environmental shaping is at work in chimpanzee tool use. Tomasello (1996a) reviewed all of the experimental studies of chimpanzee social learning of tool use and concluded that chimpanzees are very good at learning about the dynamic affordances of objects that they discover through watching others manipulate them, but they are not skillful at learning from others a new behavioral strategy per se. For example, if a mother rolls a log and eats the insects underneath, her child will very likely follow suit. This is simply because the child learned from the mother's act that there are insects under the log—a fact she did not know and very likely would not have discovered on her own. But she did not learn from her mother how to roll a log or to eat insects; these are things she already knew how to do or could learn how to do on her own. (Thus, the youngster would have learned the same thing if the wind, rather than her mother, had caused the log to roll over and expose the ants.) This has been called *emulation learning* because it is learning that focuses on the environmental events involved—the changes of state in the environment that the other produced—not on a conspecific's behavior or behavioral strategy (Tomasello 1990, 1996a).

Emulation learning is a very intelligent and creative learning process that, in some circumstances, is a more adaptive strategy than imitative learning. For example, Nagell, Olguin, and Tomasello (1993) presented chimpanzees and two-year-old human children with a rake-like tool and an out-of-reach object. The tool could be used in either of two ways leading to the same result of obtaining the object. For each species one group of subjects observed a demonstrator employ one method of tool use (less efficient) and another group of subjects observed the other method of tool use (more efficient). The result was that whereas human children in general copied the method of the demonstrator in each of the two observation conditions (imitative learning), chimpanzees did lots of different things to obtain the object, and these were of the same type no matter which demonstration they observed (emulation learning). The interesting point is that many children insisted on this reproduction of adult behavior even in the case of the less efficient method—leading to less successful performance than the chimpanzees in this condition. Imitative learning is thus not a "higher" or "more intelligent" learning strategy than emulation learning; it is simply a more social strategy—which, in some circumstances and for some behaviors, has some advantages. This emulation-learning explanation also applies to other studies of chimpanzee social learning of tool use such as those of Whiten et al., (1996) and Russon and Galdikas (1993).

Chimpanzees are thus very intelligent and creative in using tools and understanding changes in the environment brought about by the tool use of others, but they do not seem to understand the instrumental behavior of conspecifics in the same way as do humans. For humans the goal or intention of the demonstrator is a central part of what they perceive, and indeed the goal is understood as something separate from the various behavioral means that may be used to accomplish the goal. Observers' ability to separate goal and means serves to highlight for them the demonstrator's method or strategy of tool use as an independent entity—the behavior she is using in an attempt to accomplish the goal, given the possibility of other means of accomplishing it. In the absence of this ability to understand goal and behavioral means as separable in the actions of others, chimpanzee observers focus on the changes of state (including changes of spatial position) of the objects involved during the demonstration, with the actions of the demonstrator being, in effect, just other physical motions. The intentional states of the demonstrator, and thus her behavioral methods as distinct behavioral entities, are simply not part of their experience.

Chimpanzee Gestural Signaling

The other well-known case is the gestural communication of chimpanzees. Although there are few systematic studies of chimpanzee gestures in the wild, by all indications there are some population-specific behaviors that might be called cultural (Goodall, 1986; Tomasello, 1990; Nishida, 1980). In captivity much more systematic work has been done in which the specific gestures used by specific individuals over time have been documented—allowing for inferences about the social learning processes involved. In a series of studies, Tomasello and colleagues have asked whether youngsters acquire their gestural signals by imitative learning or by a process of *ontogenetic ritualization* (Tomasello et al., 1985; 1989; 1994; 1997). In ontogenetic ritualization a communicatory signal is created by two organisms shaping each other's behavior in repeated instances of a social interaction. For example, an infant may initiate nursing by going directly for the mother's nipple, perhaps grabbing and moving her arm in the process. In some future encounter the mother may anticipate the infant's impending behavioral efforts at the first touch of her arm, and so become receptive at that point—leading the infant on some future occasion still to abbreviate its behavior to a touch on the arm while waiting for a response ("arm-touch" as a so-called intention movement). Note that there is no hint here that one individual is seeking to reproduce the behavior of another; there is only reciprocal social interaction over repeated encounters that results eventually in a communicative signal. This is presumably the way that most human infants learn the "arms-over-head" gesture to request that adults pick them up, that is, first as a direct attempt to crawl up the adult's body, and then, as the adult anticipates their desire and picks them up, as an abbreviated, ritualized version of this crawling activity performed for communicative purposes only (Lock, 1978).

All of the available evidence suggests that ontogenetic ritualization, not imitative learning, is responsible for chimpanzees' acquisition of communicative gestures. First, there are a number of idiosyncratic signals that are used by only one individual (see also Goodall, 1986); these signals could not have been learned by imitative processes and so must have been individually invented and ritualized. Second, longitudinal analyses have revealed by both qualitative and quantitative comparisons that there is much individual variability, both within and across generations, in chimpanzee gestural signaling—suggesting something other than imitative learning, which generally produces homogeneity of behavior. It is also important that the gestures that are used in common by many youngsters are gestures that are also used quite frequently by captive youngsters raised in peer groups with no opportunity to observe older conspecifics. Finally, in an experimental study, Tomasello and colleagues (1997) removed an individual from the group and taught her two different arbitrary signals by means of which she obtained desired food from a human. When she was then returned to the group and used these same gestures to obtain food from a human, there was not one instance of another individual reproducing either of the new gestures—even though all of the other individuals were observing the gesturer and highly motivated for the food.

The clear conclusion is thus that chimpanzee youngsters acquire the majority, if not the totality, of their gestures by individually ritualizing them with one another. The explanation for this learning process is analogous to the explanation for emulation learning in the case of tool use. Like emulation learning, ontogenetic ritualization does not require individuals to understand the behavior of others as separable into means and goals in the same way as does imitative learning. Imitatively learning an "arm-touch" as a solicitation for nursing would require that an infant observe another infant using an "arm-touch" and know what goal it was pursuing (viz., nursing)—so that when it had the same goal it could use the same behavioral means. Ritualizing an "arm-touch," in contrast, only requires the infant to anticipate the future behavior of a conspecific in a context in which it (the infant) already has the goal of nursing. Ontogenetic ritualization is thus, like emulation learning, a very intelligent and creative social learning process that is very important in all social species, including humans. But it is not a learning process by means of which individuals attempt to reproduce the behavioral strategies of others.

Chimpanzee Teaching

These two domains thus provide us with two very different sources of evidence about nonhuman primate social learning. In the case of tool use, it is very likely that chimpanzees acquire the tool-use skills to which they are exposed by a process of emulation learning. In the case of gestural signals, it is very likely that they acquire their communicative gestures through a process of ontogenetic ritualization. Both emulation learning and ontogenetic ritualization require skills of cognition and social learning, each in its own way, but neither requires skills of imitative learning in which the learner (a) comprehends both the demonstrator's goal and the strategy being used to pursue that goal, and then (b) in some way aligns this goal and strategy with her own. Indeed, emulation learning and ontogenetic ritualization are precisely the kinds of social learning one would expect of organisms that are very intelligent and quick to learn, but that do not understand others as intentional agents with whom they can align themselves.

The other main process involved in cultural transmission as traditionally defined is teaching. Whereas social learning comes from the "bottom up," as ignorant or unskilled individuals seek to become more knowledgeable or skilled, teaching comes from the "top down," as knowledgeable or skilled individuals seek to impart knowledge or skills to others. The problem in this case is that there are very few systematic studies of teaching in nonhuman primates. The most thorough study is that of Boesch (1991) in which chimpanzee mothers and infants were observed in the context of tool use (nut cracking). Boesch discovered that mothers do a number of things that serve to facilitate the infant's activities with the tool and nuts, such as leaving them idle so the infant can use them while she goes to gather more nuts (which she would not do if another adult were present). But the interpretation of the mother's intention in such cases is far from straightforward. Moreover, in the category of "active instruction," in which the mother appears to be actively attempting to instruct her child, Boesch observed only two possible instances (over many years of observation). These two instances are also difficult to interpret in the sense that the mother may or may not have had the goal of helping the youngster learn to use the tool. On the other hand, although there is much variability across different societies, adult humans in all cultures actively instruct their young on a regular basis in one way or another (Kruger and Tomasello, 1996). Along with imitative learning, the process of active instruction is very likely crucial to the uniquely human pattern of cultural evolution as well.

Enculturated Apes

It may be objected that there are a number of very convincing observations of chimpanzee imitative learning in the literature, and indeed there are some. It is interesting, however, that basically all of the clear cases concern chimpanzees that have had extensive human contact. In many cases this has taken the form of intentional instruction involving human encouragement of behavior and attention, and even direct reinforcement for imitation for many months; for example, Hayes and Hayes (1952) provided their chimpanzee Vicki with seven months of systematic training, and Custance, Whiten, and Bard (1995) provided their two chimpanzees with four months of systematic training. This raises the possibility that imitative learning skills may be influenced, or even enabled, by certain kinds of social interaction during early ontogeny.

Confirmation for this point of view is provided in a study by Tomasello, Savage-Rumbaugh, and Kruger (1993). This study compared the imitative learning abilities of mother-reared captive chimpanzees, enculturated chimpanzees (raised like human children and exposed to a language-like system of communication), and two-year-old human children. Each subject was shown twenty-four different and novel actions on objects, and each subject's behavior on each trial was scored as to whether it successfully reproduced (1) the end result of the demonstrated action, and/or (2) the behavioral means used by the demonstrator. The major result was that the mother-reared chimpanzees almost never succeeded in reproducing both the end and means of the novel actions (i.e., they did not imitatively learn them). In contrast, the enculturated chimpanzees and the human children imitatively learned the novel actions much more frequently, and they did not differ from one another in this learning. Relatedly, some human-raised chimpanzees sometimes learn to communicatively point for humans, and even to use something resembling human linguistic symbols, through rich social interactions with humans but without any systematic training per se (Savage-Rumbaugh et al., 1986).

These studies show that apes raised by human beings in a human-like cultural environment—sometimes with and sometimes without explicit training—can develop some human-like skills that they do not develop in their natural habitats or under more typical captive conditions. What exactly are the effective factors that produce these outcomes is not known at this time, but one plausible hypothesis is that in human-like cultural environments apes receive a kind of "socialization of attention." That is, apes in their natural habitats do not have anyone who points for them, shows them things, teaches them, or in general expresses intentions toward their attention (or other intentional states). In a human-like cultural environment, in contrast, they are constantly interacting with humans who show them things, point to things, encourage (even reinforce) imitation, and teach them special skills—all of which involve a referential triangle between human, ape, and some third entity. Perhaps it is this socialization into the referential triangle—of a type that most human children receive—that accounts for the special cognitive achievements of these special apes.

But it is important to recognize that apes raised in human cultural environments do not thereby turn into human beings. Although scientists have not probed to any great extent the limitations of human-raised apes' cognitive skills, some differences from human children are readily apparent. For example, it seems that it is still a rare event for an enculturated ape to simply show something to a human or ape companion declaratively, or to point to something just for the sake of sharing attention to it. They do not participate in extended joint attentional interactions in the same way as human children (Carpenter, Tomasello, and Savage-Rumbaugh, 1995), and when compared with the skills of human children their skills with human language are limited in a number of important ways (Tomasello, 1994). In tasks in which they must cooperate with conspecifics, without specific human training, ape skills of collaborative learning are curiously limited, and there is still very little, if any, behavior of enculturated apes that one would want to call intentional teaching (see Call and Tomasello, 1996, for a review).

The most plausible conclusion is thus that the learning skills that chimpanzees develop in the wild in the absence of human interaction (i.e., skills involving individual learning supplemented by emulation learning and ritualization) are sufficient to create and maintain their species-typical cultural activities, but they are not sufficient to create and maintain human-like cultural activities displaying the ratchet effect and cumulative cultural evolution. And it is perhaps worth noting that in their natural habitat chimpanzees' sister species, bonobos (*Pan paniscus*), have not so far been observed to show anything resembling the population-specific behavioral traditions of chimpanzees—which may suggest that the common ancestor to humans and these two sister species did not have well-developed cultural learning skills either. The fact that chimpanzees and bonobos raised from an early age and for many years in human-like cultural environments may develop some aspects of human social cognition and cultural learning demonstrates the power of cultural processes in ontogeny in a particularly dramatic way, and the fact that other animal species do not respond in this manner demonstrates the impressive social learning skills of the great apes. But responding to a culture and creating a culture *de novo* are two different things.

Human Cultural Evolution

We may conclude, then, that whereas chimpanzees clearly create and maintain cultural traditions broadly defined, these very likely rest on different processes of social cognition and social learning than the cultural traditions of human beings. In some cases this difference of process may not lead to any concrete differences of outcome in social organization, information transmission, or cognition. But in other cases a crucial difference emerges, and this manifests itself in processes of cultural evolution, that is, processes by which a cultural tradition accumulates modifications over time.

Cumulative Cultural Evolution and the Ratchet Effect

Some cultural traditions accumulate the modifications made by different individuals over time so that they become more complex, and a wider range of adaptive functions is encompassed—what may be called cumulative cultural evolution or the "ratchet effect" (see Figure 2.2). For example, the way human beings have used objects as hammers has evolved significantly over human history. This is evidenced in the artifactual record by various hammer-like tools that gradually widened their functional sphere as they were modified again and again to meet novel exigencies, going from simple stones, to composite tools composed of a stone tied to a stick, to various types of modern metal hammers and even mechanical hammers (some with nail-removing functions as well; Basalla, 1988). Although we do not have such a detailed artifactual record, it is presumably the case that some cultural conventions and rituals (e.g., human languages and religious rituals) have become more complex over time as well, as they were modified to meet novel communicative and social needs. This process may be more characteristic of some human cultures than others, or of some types of activities than others, but all cultures would seem to have at least some artifacts produced by the ratchet effect. There do not seem to be any behaviors of other animal species, including chimpanzees, that show cumulative cultural evolution (Boesch and Tomasello, 1998).

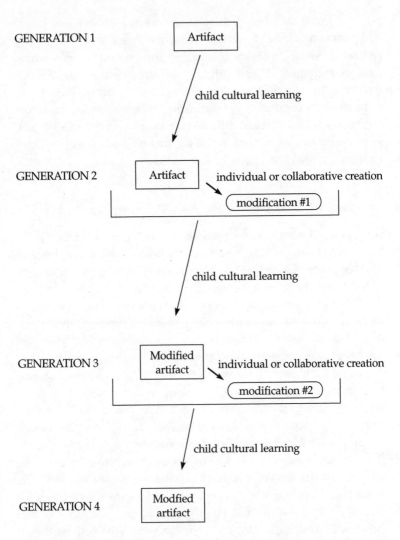

Figure 2.2 A simplified depiction of the ratchet effect working to produce an artifact with accumulating modifications.

Tomasello and colleagues (1993) argued that cumulative cultural evolution depends on imitative learning, and perhaps active instruction on the part of adults, and cannot be brought about by means of "weaker" forms of social learning such as local enhancement, emulation learning, ontogenetic ritualization, or any form of individual learning. The argument is that cumulative cultural evolution depends on two processes, innovation and imitation (possibly supplemented by instruction), that must take place in a dialectical process over time such that one step in the process enables the next. Thus, if one individual chimpanzee invented a more efficient way of fishing for termites by using a stick in a novel way that induced more termites to crawl onto it, youngsters who learned to fish via emulation of this individual would not reproduce this precise variant because they would not be focused on the innovator's behavioral techniques. They would use their own method of fishing to induce more termites onto the stick, and any other individuals watching them would use their own methods also, and so the novel strategy would simply die out with the inventor. (This is precisely the hypothesis of Kummer and Goodall, 1985, who believe that many acts of creative intelligence on the part of nonhuman primates go unobserved by humans because they are not faithfully preserved in the group.) On the other hand, if observers were capable of imitative learning they might adopt the innovator's new strategic variant for termite fishing more or less faithfully. This new behavior would then put them into a new cognitive space, so to speak, in which they could think about the task and how to solve it in something like the manner of the innovator (standing in her "cognitive shoes"). All of the individuals who had done this would then be in a position, possibly, to invent other variants that built on the initial one—which then others might adopt faithfully, or even build on, as well. The metaphor of the ratchet in this context is meant to capture the fact that imitative learning (with or without active instruction) enables the kind of faithful transmission that is necessary to hold the novel variant in place in the group so as to provide a platform for further innovations—with the innovations themselves varying in the degree to which they are individual or social/cooperative.

In general, then, human cultural traditions may be most readily distinguished from chimpanzee cultural traditions—as well as the few other instances of culture observed in other primate species—precisely by the fact that they accumulate modifications over time, that is to say, they have cultural "histories." They accumulate modifications and have histories because the cultural learning processes that support them are especially powerful. These cultural learning processes are especially powerful because they are supported by the uniquely human cognitive adaptation for understanding others as intentional beings like the self—which creates forms of social learning that act as a ratchet by faithfully preserving newly innovated strategies in the social group until there is another innovation to replace them.

I should acknowledge that things may not be quite as black and white as I have made them out to be. In a very interesting paper entitled "Why culture is common, but cultural evolution is rare," Boyd and Richerson (1996) hypothesize that humans and other primates both engage in the same kinds of social and imitative learning, but there may be a quantitative difference. Thus, chimpanzees may have some imitative learning abilities, but they may display them less consistently than humans or in a narrower range of contexts than humans—or it may even be that only some chimpanzee individuals have these skills. Boyd and Richerson argue that a rarity of key social learning processes could make cultural evolution of the cumulative type impossible. The basic problem would be that there is too much slippage in the ratchet, as, for example, one individual might imitatively learn another's innovation but then no other individuals could imitate her, or the individuals who did attempt to imitate her would do so only very poorly. The argument is thus that there is a quantitative difference in social learning skills that leads to a qualitative difference in the historical trajectories of the resulting cultural traditions. In either case, however—whether the difference between human and ape social learning skills is more qualitative and absolute or more quantitative and relative—the effect is that human beings currently have the social-cognitive and cultural learning skills to create, as a species, unique cognitive products based on cumulative cultural evolution.

The Sociogenesis of Language and Mathematics

The process of cumulative cultural evolution may be seen as an especially powerful form of collaborative inventiveness or sociogenesis. In human societies there are two basic forms of sociogenesis in which something new is created through the social interaction of two or more individuals in cooperative interaction, and indeed in many cases the new product could not have been invented by any of the individuals acting alone. The first form of sociogenesis is simply the form implied by the ratchet effect as described above for such things as hammers and linguistic symbols. An individual confronts an artifact or cultural practice that she has inherited from others, along with a novel situation for which the artifact does not seem fully suited. She then assesses the way the artifact is intended to work (the intentionality of the inventor), relates this to the current situation, and then makes a modification to the artifact. In this case the collaboration is not actual, in the sense that two or more individuals are simultaneously present and collaborating, but rather virtual in the sense that it takes place across historical time as the current individual imagines the function the artifact was intended to fulfill by previous users, and how it must be modified to meet the current problem situation.

The second kind of sociogenesis is the simultaneous collaboration of two or more individuals as they work on a problem together. Simultaneity is not absolute in such cases, as what typically happens is that the individuals engage in some kind of dialogic interaction in which one's inventive suggestions are responded to by the other, and so on in a manner that leads to a product that neither individual could have invented on its own. The collaboration is thus not virtual but actual, and it therefore has some special qualities, for example, in terms of the kind of immediate feedback that an individual may receive for his or her creative suggestions. The two forms of collaboration may occur together, of course, as when a small group of people attempt collaboratively to modify an artifact or practice they have inherited from others in order to meet new exigencies, and indeed this is probably the typical situation. It is also the case that many important cultural changes on a large scale involving such things as religions or governments or economic systems result from many people "cooperating" both simultaneously and successively over generations in a way that no one person or group of people intended or could have foreseen (this may be a third kind of "collaboration"). For example, market economies, although based on individual intentional acts, are not a cultural outcome that any one person envisioned or intended at the outset. These group-level processes are not well understood from a psychological point of view, but they clearly interact with the intentional level in interesting and important ways (see Hutchins, 1995).

The process of sociogenesis may be clearly seen in two very important cognitive domains: language and mathematics. I begin with language. Although on a general level all languages share some features, in concrete terms each of the thousands of languages of the world has its own inventory of linguistic symbols, including complex linguistic constructions, that allow its users to share experience with one another symbolically. This inventory of symbols and constructions is grounded in universal structures of human cognition, human communication, and the mechanics of the vocal-auditory apparatus. The particularities of particular languages come from differences among the various peoples of the world in the kinds of things they think it important to talk about and the ways they think it useful to talk about them—along with various historical "accidents," of course. The crucial point for current purposes is that all of the symbols and constructions of a given language are not invented at once, and once invented they often do not stay the same for very long. Rather, linguistic symbols and constructions evolve and change and accumulate modifications over historical time as humans use them with one another, that is, through processes of sociogenesis. The most important dimension of the historical process in the current context is grammaticization or syntacticization, which involves such things as freestanding words evolving into grammatical markers and loose and redundantly organized discourse structures congealing into tight and less redundantly organized syntactic constructions (see Traugott and Heine, 1991a, 1991b; Hopper and Traugott, 1993). Some examples will help to clarify:

- The future tense marker in virtually all languages is grammaticized from freestanding words for such things as volition or movement to a goal. So in English the original verb was *will*, as in *I will it to happen*, and this became grammaticized into *It will happen* (with the volitional component "bleached" out). Similarly, the original use of *go* was for movement, as in *I'm going to the store*, and this was grammaticized into *I'm going to send it tomorrow* (with the movement bleached out—see also *come*, as in *Come Thursday, I will be 46*).

- The English past perfective, using *have*, is very likely derived from sentences such as *I have a broken finger* or *I have the prisoners bound* (in which *have* is a verb of possession) into something like *I have broken a finger* (in which the possession meaning of *have* is bleached out and it now only indicates perfective aspect).

- English phrases such as *on the top of* and *in the side of* evolved into *on top of* and *inside of* and eventually into *atop* and *inside.* In some languages (although not in English) relator words such as these spatial prepositions may also become attached to nouns as case markers—in this instance as possible locative markers.

- Loose discourse sequences such as *He pulled the door and it opened* may become syntacticized into *He pulled the door open* (a resultative construction).

- Loose discourse sequences such as *My boyfriend . . . He plays piano . . . He plays in a band* may become *My boyfriend plays piano in a band.* Or, similarly, *My boyfriend . . . He rides horses . . . He bets on them* may become *My boyfriend, who rides horses, bets on them.*

- Similarly, if someone expresses the belief that Mary will wed John, another person may respond with an assent, *I believe that*, followed by a repetition of the expressed belief that *Mary will wed John*—which become syntacticized into the single statement *I believe that Mary will wed John.*

- Complex sentences may also derive from discourse sequences of initially separate utterances, as in *I want it . . . I buy it* evolving into *I want to buy it.*

Systematic investigation into processes of grammaticization and syntacticization is in its infancy (see Givón, 1979, 1995), and indeed the suggestion that languages may have evolved from structurally simpler to structurally more complex forms by means of processes of grammaticization and syntacticization is somewhat novel in this context—these processes are most often thought of by linguists as sources of change only. But grammaticization and syntacticization are able to effect serious changes of linguistic structure in relatively short periods of time—for example, the main diversification of the Romance languages took place during some hundreds of years— and so I see no reason why they could not also work to make a simpler language more complex syntactically in some thousands of years. Exactly how grammaticization and syntacticization happen in the concrete interactions of individual human beings and groups of human beings, and how these processes might relate to the other processes of sociogenesis by means of which human social interaction changes cultural artifacts, is a question for future linguistic research.

One possible implication of this view is that the earliest modern humans, originating in Africa some 200,000 years ago, were the individuals who first began to communicate symbolically—perhaps using some simple symbolic forms analogous to those used by human children. They then dispersed throughout the world, so that all current languages derive ultimately from that single proto-language—although if that proto-language was very simple each culture may have syntacticized and grammaticized discourse sequences in some fundamentally different ways from very early in the process. For those theorists who think this hypothesis is far-fetched, we need look no further than alphabetic writing to see a cultural invention that happened only once and that has retained some of its essential characteristics while at the same time taking on different forms in different cultures—and this has happened in only a few millennia instead of several scores of millennia as would have been the case for natural languages.

The case of the other intellectual pillar of Western civilization, mathematics, is interestingly different from the case of language (and indeed it bears some similarities, but also some differences, to writing). Like language, mathematics clearly rests on universally human ways of experiencing the world (many of which are shared with other primates) and also on some processes of cultural creation and sociogenesis. But in this case the divergences among cultures are much greater than in the case of spoken languages. All cultures have complex forms of linguistic communication, with variations of complexity basically negligible, whereas some cultures have highly complex systems of mathematics (practiced by only some of their members) as compared with other cultures that have fairly simple systems of numbers and counting (Saxe, 1981). This great variation means that no one has proposed that the structure of modern complex mathematics is an innate module, as they have in the case of language (although it would be logically possible to propose a theory along the lines of Chomsky's principles and parameters in which certain environmental variables that are not present in some cultures may in other cultures trigger certain innate mathematical structures).

In general, the reasons for the great cultural differences in mathematical practices are not difficult to discern. First, different cultures and persons have different needs for mathematics. Most cultures and persons have the need to keep track of goods, for which a few number words expressed in natural language will suffice. When a culture or a person needs to count objects or measure things more precisely—for example, in complex building projects or the like—the need for a more complex mathematics arises. Modern science as an enterprise, practiced by only some people in some cultures, presents a whole host of new problems that require complex mathematical techniques for their solution. But—and this is the analogy to writing—complex mathematics as we know it today can only be accomplished through the use of certain forms of graphic symbols. In particular, the Arabic system of enumeration is much superior to older Western systems for purposes of complex mathematics (e.g., Roman numerals), and the use of Arabic numerals, including zero and the place system for indicating different-sized units, opened up for Western scientists and other persons whole new vistas of mathematical operations (Danzig, 1954).

The history of mathematics is an area of study in which detailed examination has revealed myriad complex ways in which individuals, and groups of individuals, take what is passed on to them by previous generations and then make modifications as needed to deal with new practical and scientific problems more efficiently (Eves, 1961). Some historians of mathematics have detailed some of the specific processes by means of which specific mathematical symbols and techniques were invented, used, and modified (e.g., Danzig, 1954; Eves, 1961; Damerow, 1998). As just one well-known example, Descartes invented the Cartesian coordinate system in which he combined in a creative way some of the spatially based techniques used in geometry with some of the more arithmetically based techniques in other areas of the mathematics of his time—with the infinitesimal calculus being a variation on this theme. The adoption of this technique by other scientists and mathematicians ratcheted up the mathematical universe almost immediately, and thereby changed Western mathematics forever. And so, in general, the sociogenesis of modern Western mathematics, as practiced by only a minority of the people in these cultures, may be seen as a function of both the mathematical needs of the particular people involved and the cultural resources available to them. This assumes at least the primate understanding of small quantities as foundational, but modern mathematics very likely requires more than this. My hypothesis, to be elaborated in Chapter 6, is that building on the basic primate sense of quantity, human beings also use their formidable skills of perspective-taking and alternative construals of concrete objects and collections of objects (which have a social basis in skills of perspective-taking and linguistic communication) to construct complex mathematics. In some cultures the recruitment of these skills for mathematical ends is needed more than in others.

In both the cases of language and mathematics, then, the structure of the domain as it now exists has a cultural history (actually, many different cultural histories), and there are processes of sociogenesis that historical linguists and historians of mathematics have the opportunity to study (although most of these scholars are not directly interested in questions of psychology). The differences between the two cases are instructive. Although complexity takes many different forms in modern languages, complex language is a universal among all the peoples of the world. This is either because the original invention of many of the spoken symbols that makes language possible took place before modern humans diverged into different populations, or because the ability to create spoken symbols comes so naturally to humans that the different groups all invented them in similar though not identical ways after they diverged. Complex mathematics is not universal among cultures, or even among people in the cultures that have it. This is presumably because the cultural needs for complex mathematics and/or the invention of the required cultural resources came only after modern people had begun living in different populations, and apparently these needs and/or resources are not universally present for all peoples of the world today. And so one of the central facts about language that has led some linguists to hypothesize that some modern linguistic structures are innate—the fact that they are species unique and species universal whereas many mathematical and other cognitive skills are not (e.g., Pinker, 1994)—may just be the result of the vagaries of human cultural history in the sense that, for whatever reason, skills of linguistic communication evolved before modern humans diverged into separate populations.

The place where intellectual needs meet cultural resources most directly is of course in human ontogeny. Indeed, sociogenesis and cultural history may be seen as a series of ontogenies in which both immature and mature members of a culture learn to act effectively as they are exposed to problems and provided with resources, including social interactions with skilled problem solvers. The most basic cognitive skills required for the acquisition of language and the learning of complex mathematics, as two especially interesting examples, are universally available to human beings. But the many and various structures of these two cultural artifacts as manifest in the many different human societies of the world are not, indeed cannot be, directly encoded in the genes ahead of time. The overall model is thus that human beings have cognitive skills that result from biological inheritance working in phylogenetic time; they use these skills to exploit cultural resources that have evolved over historical time; and they do this during ontogenetic time.

Human Ontogeny

Following Vygotsky and many other cultural psychologists, I contend that many of the most interesting and important human cognitive achievements, such as language and mathematics, require historical time and processes for their realization—even if most cognitive scientists largely ignore these historical processes. In addition, I would claim, along with other developmental psychologists, that many of the most interesting and important human cognitive competencies require significant ontogenetic time and processes for their realization—even though these processes are also ignored by many cognitive scientists. Cognitive scientists' underappreciation of ontogeny and its formative role in the creation of mature forms of human cognition is due in large part to their overappreciation for a hoary philosophical debate that has outlived its usefulness, if indeed it was ever useful (Elman et al., 1997). And so, before proceeding to a detailed account of human cognitive ontogeny, I should at least briefly address this debate.

Philosophical Nativism and Development

Modern discussions of nature versus nurture and innate versus learned take their structure from the debates in eighteenth-century Europe between rationalist and empiricist philosophers arguing about the human mind and human moral qualities. These framing debates took place before Charles Darwin gave the scientific community new ways of thinking about biological processes. The introduction of Darwinian ways of thinking about phylogeny, and about the role of ontogeny in phylogeny, should have rendered the debate obsolete. But it did not, and indeed the rise of modern genetics has given it a new and concretized life in the form of genes versus environment. The reason the debate has not died out is that it is the natural way to answer the question: What determines trait X in adult human beings? Asking the question in this manner even allows for attempts to quantify the relative contributions of genes and environment for a given adult trait, such as "intelligence" (Scarr and McCarthy, 1983). Asking and answering the question in this way is analogous to asking what determined the outbreak of the French Revolution, and then quantifying the relative contributions of economics, politics, religion, and so forth. But Darwinian thinking is process thinking in which we do not think of categories of factors in some static atemporal "now." Although there are invariant processes such as genetic variation and natural selection, if we ask how a given species came to be what it is now (or how the French Revolution came about), the answer is a narrative that unfolds in time with different processes working in different ways at different points along the way.

This Darwinian way of thinking is the way we should think if we wish to understand the phylogeny and ontogeny of human beings. In phylogeny, Nature selects for ontogenetic pathways that lead to certain results in the sexually mature phenotype. I repeat, Nature selects for ontogenetic pathways that lead to certain phenotypic results. These pathways may rely either more or less on the exploitation of exogenous materials and information for their realization, and mammals in general, and primates and humans in particular, have evolved many ontogenetic pathways that simply could not develop without such exogenous materials and information. But regardless of the degree of exogenous material involved, under any ontogenetic scenario our goal as developmentalists, whether biological or psychological, is to understand the entire pathway for a given phenomenon and how it works.

It is very telling that there are essentially no people who call themselves biologists who also call themselves nativists. When developmental biologists look at the developing embryo, they have no use for the concept of innateness. This is not because they underestimate the influence of genes—the essential role of the genome is assumed as a matter of course—but rather because the categorical judgment that a characteristic is innate simply does not help in understanding the process. It would not be helpful to biologists, for example, to say that the emergence of limb buds in the tenth week of human embryological development is innate. If we are interested in the entire process by which limbs are formed in embryological development, we want first to map out steps in the development of limbs, and then to determine how processes of protein synthesis, cell differentiation, the interaction of the organism with intrauterine enzymes, and so on, participate at various points in the progression. If we would like to label as "innate" processes that share a certain set of characteristics—for example, that they depend very little on the existence of intrauterine enzymes for their operation—we may certainly do that and it may be useful for some purposes. But for the most part such labeling is simply not helpful in understanding the ontogenetic processes involved (see Wittgenstein's, 1953, argument that ill-formed philosophical problems are not solved—we simply cure ourselves of them).

But in cognitive science there has always been a strain of nativism that poses the question in essentially the same terms as the eighteenth-century European philosophers, with very little indication that Darwinian-style process thinking has had an impact (e.g., Chomsky, 1980; Fodor, 1983). Since these theorists mostly do not study directly the genetic processes involved but rather seek to infer them from logical considerations only, this theoretical perspective is perhaps best called philosophical nativism. This is not to say that the search for innate aspects of human cognition has not led to some very important insights. As just one example, this search has established that the ontogenetic process that Piaget hypothesized as crucial for infants' understanding of objects in space—namely, the manual manipulation of objects—cannot be a crucial ingredient since infants understand objects in space before they have manipulated them manually (Spelke, 1990; Baillargeon, 1995). This ruling out of one potential developmental process is a significant scientific discovery. But this discovery should not stop the process of inquiry—we should not simply say that X is innate and so our job is done—but rather it should lead us to ask other questions, for example, the role of visual experience by itself in the absence of manual manipulations in the development of a concept of object. This procedure is the one that developmental biologists follow, although of course they have more powerful methods at their disposal as they are able to intervene in the ontogeny of animal embryos in a way that cannot be done with human children. But through whatever means (e.g., studying the object concept in blind children), the goal is not to decide whether some structure is or is not "innate," but rather to determine the processes involved in its development. The search for the innate aspects of human cognition is scientifically fruitful to the extent, and only to the extent, that it helps us to understand the developmental processes at work during human ontogeny, including all of the factors that play a role, at what time they play their role, and precisely how they play their role.

The Individual and Cultural Lines of Development

Instead of innate versus learned, I prefer another dichotomy that some may consider just as troublesome: the Vygotskian dichotomy between the individual and the cultural lines of development. This distinction is essentially that between biological inheritance and cultural inheritance, although it concerns ontogeny instead of phylogeny. In my interpretation of this distinction, the individual line of cognitive development (what Vygotsky calls the "natural" line) concerns those things the organism knows and learns on its own without the direct influence of other persons or their artifacts, whereas the cultural line of cognitive development concerns those things the organism knows and learns that are derived from acts in which it attempts to see the world through the perspective of other persons (including perspectives embodied in artifacts). I must emphasize that this is a somewhat idiosyncratic way of conceptualizing cultural inheritance and development, much narrower than the conceptualizations of most cultural psychologists. I am not counting as cultural inheritance those things that the organism knows and learns on its own from its particular cultural setting or "habitus," for example, the child individually learning about the ways houses are laid out in her local environment (Kruger and Tomasello, 1996). My narrower definition of cultural inheritance—and therefore cultural learning and the cultural line of development—is focused on intentional phenomena in which one organism adopts another's behavior or perspective on some third entity.

The problem, of course, is that these two lines of development become inextricably intertwined very early in human development, and virtually every cognitive act of children after a certain age incorporates elements of both. For example, in later chapters I will document that in many ways children between the ages of one and three are "imitation machines" in that their natural response to many situations is to do what those around them are doing, and indeed they are very limited in what they individually create for themselves in most situations. However, some of the most interesting aspects of development during this period concern precisely the interactions between the individual and cultural lines of development, as the child takes the cultural conventions she has learned via imitation or some other form of cultural learning and then makes some creative leap that goes beyond them by discerning, all on her own, some categorical or analogical relationship—based on general primate skills of categorization. It is true that these creative leaps themselves sometimes rely more or less directly on some cultural tool such as language or mathematical symbols or conventional iconic images that help children to see categorical or analogical relationships. Nevertheless, all evidence points to the fact that by four to five years of age the balance between children's tendency to imitate others and their tendency to use their own creative cognitive strategies has shifted, since by this age they have internalized many different points of view, mostly through linguistic discourse, enabling them to reflect and plan for themselves in a more self-regulated manner—although again the tools with which they do this are sometimes cultural in origin.

Many cultural psychologists believe that trying to make this distinction is futile because the individual and the cultural are part of the same developmental process, and at any given age the child possesses knowledge and skills that are the result of a long dialectical process involving both sets of factors. I agree with this critique to some extent, but I still believe that attempting to isolate and assess the effects of the uniquely human adaptation for culture during human ontogeny is a useful enterprise. It is useful, first of all, because it helps us to answer the comparative-evolutionary question of how and why human beings differ cognitively from their nearest primate relatives—who develop in their own species-typical way without anything like the human version of the cultural line of development in which historically constituted artifacts and social practices are internalized by the developing young. Moreover, it is useful as well because it helps to capture what is perhaps the fundamental dialectical tension in human cognitive development: the tension between doing things conventionally, which has many obvious advantages, and doing things creatively, which has its own advantages as well.

The Dual Inheritance Model

Because the human mode of cultural organization is so distinctive when compared with those of other animal species, because raising nonhuman animals within a cultural context does not magically transform them into human-like cultural beings, and because there are some humans with biological deficits who do not participate fully in their cultures, the ineluctable conclusion is that individual human beings possess a biologically inherited capacity for living culturally. This capacity—which I have characterized as the capacity to understand conspecifics as intentional/mental agents like the self—begins to become a reality at around nine months of age, as we shall see in Chapter 3. In making a systematic comparison between humans and their nearest primate relatives, I have attempted to demonstrate that this capacity is readily identifiable, highly distinctive, and species unique—although it is very likely built upon the adaptation for relational thinking that distinguishes the cognition of primates from that of other mammals in general. The adaptive conditions under which this species-unique social-cognitive ability evolved are at present unknown, but one hypothesis is that it evolved only with modern *Homo sapiens* and that it is in fact the major cognitive characteristic distinguishing modern from premodern human beings.

This very small biological difference between humans and their closest primate relatives had, and continues to have, very great cognitive consequences. In addition to enabling humans to interact more flexibly and effectively with various kinds of entities and events in their environments, it also opens the way for the uniquely human form of cultural inheritance. Human cultural inheritance as a process rests on the twin pillars of sociogenesis, by means of which most cultural artifacts and practices are created, and cultural learning, by means of which these creations and the human intentions and perspectives that lie behind them are internalized by developing youngsters—as we shall see in later chapters. Together, sociogenesis and cultural learning enable human beings to produce material and symbolic artifacts that build upon one another, and so accumulate modifications through historical time (the ratchet effect), so that human children's cognitive development takes place in the context of something resembling the entire cultural history of their social group.

This is not to say that social-cultural processes can create new cultural products and cognitive skills out of nothing. Chimpanzees are very sophisticated creatures cognitively, and the common ancestors of humans and chimpanzees some 6 million years ago undoubtedly were as well. Processes of sociogenesis and cultural learning have as their foundation basic cognitive skills concerning space, objects, categories, quantities, social relationships, communication, and various other skills possessed by all primates. It is just that human cultural processes take these foundational cognitive skills in some new and surprising directions—and they do so very quickly from an evolutionary point of view. The alternative to this theoretical perspective is to attempt to account for each species-unique aspect of human cognition by invoking, one by one, genetic bases for each specific cognitive skill. For example, in attempting to account for the evolution of language, one could hypothesize that there was a genetic event, or multiple genetic events, in recent human history that gave modern languages their structures, and that this genetic event was basically unrelated to other such events for other uniquely human "innate modules" involving mathematics and the like (e.g., Tooby and Cosmides, 1989; Pinker, 1994, 1997). Although there can always be debate in individual cases, this explanatory strategy is not an unreasonable one if our only concern is one uniquely human cognitive module. But as the number of innate modules multiplies, the time problem becomes acute. We have at most only 6 million years, but much more likely only one-quarter of a million years, to create uniquely human cognition, and this is simply not sufficient, under any plausible evolutionary scenario, for genetic variation and natural selection to have created many different and independent uniquely human cognitive modules. A major advantage of the account presented here is thus that there is only one major biological adaptation—which could have happened at any time in human evolution including quite recently—and so the evolutionary time crunch that plagues more genetically based approaches simply does not arise.

3

JOINT ATTENTION AND CULTURAL LEARNING

He who considers things in their first growth
and origin . . . will obtain the clearest view of them.

—Aristotle

The conclusion from our comparison of human and nonhuman primates is that the understanding of conspecifics as intentional beings like the self is a uniquely human cognitive competency that accounts, either directly on its own or indirectly through cultural processes, for many of the unique features of human cognition. But this cognitive competency does not just emerge all at once in human ontogeny and then function in the same way throughout. To the contrary, the human understanding of others as intentional beings makes its initial appearance at around nine months of age, but its real power becomes apparent only gradually as children actively employ the cultural tools that this understanding enables them to master, most importantly language. To fully understand the human adaptation for culture, then, we need to follow out its developmental course for some time—and so that is what I intend to do in Chapters 4–6. In this chapter I describe and attempt to explain what happens at nine months of age.

Early Infant Cognition

By all appearances human neonates are extremely fragile and almost totally helpless creatures. They are unable to feed themselves, to sit or locomote independently, or to reach and grasp objects. Their visual acuity is very poor, and of course they know virtually nothing of the cultural and linguistic activities going on around them. It was thus reasonable for William James (1890) at the turn of the century to suppose that the infant's experiential world is "a blooming, buzzing confusion." But in the past two decades developmental psychologists have discovered that newborn and very young infants possess a number of cognitive competencies that are not readily apparent in their overt behavior. This is true for the understanding of objects, for the understanding of other persons, and for the understanding of self.

Understanding Objects

In his classic works on human infancy, Piaget (1952, 1954) provided a theory of infant cognition that is the starting point for all subsequent accounts. Piaget noted that at around four months of age infants begin reaching for and grasping objects; at around eight months of age they begin looking for objects that have disappeared, even removing obstacles in their attempts to grasp them; and at around twelve to eighteen months they begin to follow the spatial displacements of objects, both visible and invisible, to new locations, and to understand something of the spatial, temporal, and causal relations among objects. Piaget hypothesized that all of these developmental changes in sensory-motor behavior were a result of infants' active manipulations and explorations of objects, as they constructed reality through converging lines of sensory and motor information.

A major challenge to the Piagetian view has come from researchers who have found that human infants have some understanding of an independently existing physical world at an age that coincides with their earliest manipulations of objects—before they could have had time to use those manipulations to "construct" that world. For example, Baillargeon and associates (see 1995 for a review) have found that if infants are not required by researchers to manipulate objects—but only to view scenes and look longer when their expectations are violated—they display an understanding of objects as independent entities, existing when they are not being observed, by three or four months of age (at around the time of their very first deliberate manual manipulations). Using this same methodology, Spelke and colleagues (1992) have shown further that infants at this same early age understand a number of other principles that govern the behavior of objects including such things as that objects cannot be in two places at one time, that objects cannot pass through one another, and so forth. And again, infants seem to understand these principles before they have had much experience with manipulating objects. Human infants go on later in their first year of life to display other types of understanding of objects in space; for example, before their first birthdays they can categorize objects perceptually, estimate small quantities and keep track of them despite perceptual occlusion, mentally rotate objects, and navigate in space in ways suggesting something like a cognitive map (see Haith and Benson, 1997, for a review).

There are methodological issues surrounding this new way of assessing infant cognition in terms of looking behavior (see Haith and Benson, 1997), but the important point for current purposes is that these are all cognitive skills possessed by nonhuman primates. As detailed in Chapter 2, nonhuman primates are skillful at object permanence, cognitive mapping, perceptual categorization, estimating small quantities, and mentally rotating objects—presumably because they have a representational understanding of objects in space of the same general type as that of humans. Thus, human infants are simply playing out their primate heritage; it is just that, because they are born in such an altricial state perceptually and motorically, it takes them some time to do so.

Understanding Other Persons

There is not nearly as much research on young infants' understanding of other persons. It is clear that human infants are very social creatures from the moment they are born, if not before. From just a few hours after birth human infants look selectively at schematic drawings of human faces over other perceptual patterns (Fantz, 1963); while still *in utero* they seem to be in the process of habituating to their mothers' voices (Decasper and Fifer, 1980); and from fairly early in development infants clearly recognize other persons as animate beings that are different from physical objects (Legerstee, 1991)—all in the general primate pattern. However, there are two social behaviors that might suggest that human infants are not just social like other primates, but rather are "ultra-social."

First, as outlined by Trevarthen (1979) and others, from soon after birth human infants engage in "protoconversations" with their care-givers. Protoconversations are social interactions in which the parent and infant focus their attention on one another—often in a face-to-face manner involving looking, touching, and vocalizing—in ways that serve to express and share basic emotions. Moreover, these protoconversations have a clear turn-taking structure. Al-though there are differences in the way these interactions take place in different cultures—especially in the nature and amount of face-to-face visual engagement—in one form or another they seem to be a universal feature of adult-infant interaction in the human species (Trevarthen, 1993a, 1993b; Keller, Schölmerich, and Eibl-Eibesfeldt, 1988). Some researchers, especially Trevarthen, believe that these early interactions are "intersubjective," but in my view they cannot be intersubjective until infants understand others as subjects of ex-perience—which they will not do until nine months of age (see the next section). Nevertheless, these early interactions are deeply social in that they have emotional content and turn-taking structure.

Second, in the context of these early social interactions, human neonates mimic some body movements of adults, especially some movements of the mouth and head. Meltzoff and Moore (e.g., 1977, 1989) found that from very soon after birth human infants reproduce such things as tongue protrusions, mouth openings, and head move-ments. Although these actions are behaviors infants already know how to perform and so they are just increasing their frequency in the presence of a matching stimulus (as some bird species mimic the vocal productions of adults early in their development), Meltzoff and Moore (1994) found that six-week-old infants could modify one of their natural behaviors (tongue protrusions) to match the behav-ior of an adult as she moved it from one side of the mouth to the

other in an effortful manner. It is thus possible that neonatal imitation reflects a tendency of infants not just to mimic known movements but in some sense to "identify" with conspecifics (Meltzoff
and Gopnik, 1993). If true, this would be in line with Stern's (1985)
view that infants' matching of adult emotional states via "affect attunement" reflects a very deep identification process as well.

It is unclear whether nonhuman primates engage in protoconversations or neonatal mimicking in the same way as humans. For the
most part nonhuman primate mothers and infants do not engage in
the kinds of intense face-to-face engagement characteristic of Western middle-class mothers and infants, but they do stay in constant
physical contact and so their interactions may, like the interactions
of some non-Western mothers and infants, reflect protoconversations of a different sort. There is one study of a single, human-raised
chimpanzee infant mimicking tongue protrusion in much the same
way as human infants (Myowa, 1996), but there are no studies of
chimpanzee mimicking of other kinds of actions or the making of
adjustments to reproduce novel movements. Whether very young
human infants are social in ways unique to the species—or whether
human social uniqueness awaits further developments at nine
months of age or beyond—is thus an open question at this point. It is
in any case not an unreasonable hypothesis that human infants display an especially powerful social attunement with their caregivers
from soon after birth, as reflected in their tendency to interact both
in reciprocally sensitive ways in protoconversations and in ways
that require matching operations as they attempt to reproduce adult
behaviors.

Understanding Self

As infants interact with their physical and social environments, they
also experience themselves in certain ways. Of special importance,
in directing behaviors at external entities infants experience their
own behavioral goals as well as the outcome of their actions on the
environment as external entities accede to or resist their goal-
directed activities—the so-called "ecological self" (Neisser, 1988,

1995; Russell, 1997). In this way, infants come to know something of their own behavioral capabilities and limitations in certain situations, for example, as they refrain from reaching for objects that are too far away or that would require a destabilizing postural adjustment (Rochat and Barry, 1998). Also, when infants explore their own bodies they experience a correspondence of behavioral plan and perceptual feedback unlike anything else in their experience (Rochat and Morgan, 1995). Although very little research of this type has been done with nonhuman primates, there are studies showing that some species know enough about their own skills to "bail out" of tasks that exceed their capabilities (Smith and Washburn, 1997), and it would seem to be a common observation that nonhuman primates know something about their own motoric capabilities and limitations as they navigate through space in somewhat novel environments (Povinelli and Cant, 1996). It is thus very likely that human infants' sense of an ecological self is something they share with their primate relatives. There is very little research directed specifically at young infants' understanding of themselves as social agents, at least partly because it is unclear what a sense of social self means at this early age.

The Nine-Month Revolution

At around nine to twelve months of age human infants begin to engage in a host of new behaviors that would seem to indicate something of a revolution in the way they understand their worlds, especially their social worlds. If there is some question about whether infants' social cognition is different from that of other primates in the months before this revolution, after it there can be no doubt. At nine months of age human infants begin engaging in a number of so-called joint attentional behaviors that seem to indicate an emerging understanding of other persons as intentional agents like the self whose relations to outside entities may be followed into, directed, or shared (Tomasello, 1995a). In this section I describe this new set of behaviors, in the next section I attempt to explain their ontogenetic origins, and in the final section of the chapter I show how they lead

quite naturally into the processes of cultural learning that serve to launch infants into the world of culture.

The Emergence of Joint Attention

Six-month-old infants interact dyadically with objects, grasping and manipulating them, and they interact dyadically with other people, expressing emotions back and forth in a turn-taking sequence. If people are around when they are manipulating objects, they mostly ignore them. If objects are around when they are interacting with people, they mostly ignore them. But at around nine to twelve months of age a new set of behaviors begins to emerge that are not dyadic, like these early behaviors, but are triadic in the sense that they involve a coordination of their interactions with objects and people, resulting in a referential triangle of child, adult, and the object or event to which they share attention. Most often the term *joint attention* has been used to characterize this whole complex of social skills and interactions (see Moore and Dunham, eds., 1995). Most prototypically, it is at this age that infants for the first time begin to flexibly and reliably look where adults are looking (gaze following), to engage with them in relatively extended bouts of social interaction mediated by an object (joint engagement), to use adults as social reference points (social referencing), and to act on objects in the way adults are acting on them (imitative learning). In short, it is at this age that infants for the first time begin to "tune in" to the attention and behavior of adults toward outside entities.

Not unrelatedly, at around this same age infants also begin to actively direct adult attention and behavior to outside entities using deictic gestures such as pointing or holding up an object to show it to someone. These communicative behaviors represent infants' attempts to get adults to tune in to *their* attention to some outside entity. Moving beyond their dyadic ritualizations such as "arms-over-head" as a request to be picked up—which resemble in many ways chimpanzees' dyadic ritualizations (as described in Chapter 2)—these deictic gestures are clearly triadic in that they indicate for an adult some external entity. Also important is the fact that among these early deictic gestures are both imperatives, attempts to get the adult to do something with respect to an object or event, and declaratives, attempts to get adults simply to attend to some object or event. Declaratives are of special importance because they indicate especially clearly that the child does not just want some result to happen, but really desires to share attention with an adult. It is thus the contention of some theorists, including me, that the simple act of pointing to an object for someone else for the sole purpose of sharing attention to it is a uniquely human communicative behavior (e.g., Gómez, Sarriá, and Tamarit, 1993), the lack of which is also a major diagnostic for the syndrome of childhood autism (e.g., Baron-Cohen, 1993).

Based on the relatively consistent findings of many studies, it has been known for some time that all of these different behaviors—both those in which infants tune in to adults and those in which they try to get adults to tune in to them—typically emerge at nine to twelve months of age. Recently, however, Carpenter, Nagell, and Tomasello (1998) investigated this issue specifically by following the social-cognitive development of twenty-four children from nine to fifteen months of age. At monthly intervals these infants were assessed on nine different measures of joint attention: joint engagement, gaze following, point following, imitation of instrumental acts, imitation of arbitrary acts, reaction to social obstacles, use of imperative gestures, and use of declarative gestures (including proximal gestures such as "show" and distal gestures such as "point"). In each case, very stringent criteria were used to ensure that infants were attempting either to follow into or to direct the adult's attention or behavior (e.g., alternating attention between goal and adult)—not just reacting to a discriminative stimulus. The findings of most importance in the current context were these:

- Considered individually, each of the nine joint attentional skills emerged for most children between nine and twelve months of age.
- All of these skills emerged in close developmental synchrony for individual children, with nearly 80 percent of the infants mastering all nine tasks within a four-month window.

- Age of emergence was intercorrelated for all the skills (although only moderately since near simultaneous emergence of the skills led to low individual variability).

Importantly, the decalage that was observed within individual children's development had a clear explanation since there was a very consistent ordering of tasks across children. Twenty of the twenty-four children first passed tasks that required sharing/checking of adult attention in close proximity (e.g., simply looking up to the adult during joint engagement), then tasks that required following into adult attention to more distal external entities (e.g., gaze following), and finally tasks that required directing adult attention to external entities (e.g., pointing for an adult to a distal entity). Figure 3.1 depicts these three situations. The explanation for this ordering is that the tasks of sharing/checking simply required the child to look to the adult's face; in this case the children only had to know "that" the adult was present and attending. In contrast, the tasks in which infants either followed or directed adult attention required them to zero in on precisely "what" the adult was attending to—with comprehension (following adult attention or behavior) preceding production (directing adult attention or behavior). Quite clearly knowing "what" external entity an adult is focused on requires more precise joint attentional skills than simply knowing "that" an adult is attending to the interaction as a whole. The conclusion is thus that for virtually all infants the whole panoply of joint attentional skills emerge in fairly close developmental synchrony, in moderately correlated fashion, with a highly consistent ordering pattern across children reflecting the different levels of specificity in joint attention required.

The findings of this study are thus generally consistent with a whole host of studies in which one or more of these early social-cognitive skills are investigated individually (reviewed in detail by Carpenter, Nagell, and Tomasello, 1998). What this study demonstrates with special clarity is that the emergence of joint attentional skills at nine to twelve months of age is a coherent developmental phenomenon that requires a coherent developmental explanation.

This view is reinforced by the very different set of studies by Gergely and colleagues (Gergely et al., 1995; Csibra et al., in press). These researchers showed nine-month-old infants a dot on a screen moving in what to adult eyes was a clearly goal-directed manner toward a specific location on that same screen, detouring around an obstacle to do so. Infants clearly demonstrated that they viewed the movements of the dot as goal directed: they dishabituated if it made identical movements when the obstacle was removed (thus making the phantom detour unnecessary), but they remained habituated to the dot's behavior, however variable its trajectories might be, so long as it was directed to the same goal. Importantly, six-month-old infants did not show this same sensitivity to the goals of the actors. Rochat, Morgan, and Carpenter (1997) found similar evidence for nine-month-olds' but not six-month-olds' understanding of intentional action in a situation in which infants viewed one moving ball "chasing" another in a goal-directed manner. These findings using infant habituation and preferential looking techniques thus provide strong converging evidence for the importance of nine months of age in infants' social-cognitive development—using as a measure of

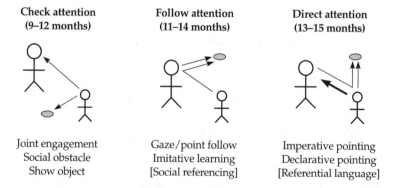

Check attention (9–12 months)	Follow attention (11–14 months)	Direct attention (13–15 months)
Joint engagement Social obstacle Show object	Gaze/point follow Imitative learning [Social referencing]	Imperative pointing Declarative pointing [Referential language]

Figure 3.1 Three main types of joint attentional interaction and their ages of emergence in the study by Carpenter, Nagell, and Tomasello (1998). (Approximately 80 percent of subjects in designated age ranges.)

infant cognition behavioral responses of a very different type from children's naturally occurring joint attentional behaviors.

Joint Attention and Social Cognition

There is currently much controversy over the nature of the infant social cognition that underlies these emerging triadic behaviors. Some theorists believe that human infants have adult-like social cognition from birth, and that the emergence of joint attentional behaviors at nine to twelve months of age simply reflects the development of behavioral performance skills for manifesting this cognition in overt behavior. For example, Trevarthen (1979, 1993a) has claimed that infants are born with a dialogic mind, with an innate sense of "the virtual other," and only need to acquire the motoric skills necessary to express this knowledge behaviorally. Trevarthen's evidence for this view is infants' complex dyadic social interactions in the early months, what he has dubbed "primary intersubjectivity." Most impressively, in the study of Murray and Trevarthen (1985), two-month-olds seemed to display an exquisite sensitivity to the contingencies of social interactions with others, which he interprets as evidence that the infant understands the subjectivity of the other. However, a number of researchers who have recently attempted to replicate these results have had mixed success in doing so, and more importantly none of them interprets infants' interactive behaviors as anything other than social contingency analysis (Rochat and Striano, 1999; Nadel and Tremblay-Leveau, 1999; Muir and Hains, 1999). In addition, it seems clear that five-month-old infants have all of the motoric skills necessary to follow the gaze of others (they visually track moving objects) and to point for them (they both reach for objects and extend their index fingers quite often), and so motoric limitations alone cannot explain why young infants, if they are so socially sophisticated, do not engage in triadic joint attentional behaviors—nor do motoric limitations explain infants' failures in looking-time studies involving intentional actions whose behavioral demands are minimal (e.g., those of Gergely et al., 1995).

Some other nativist theorists (e.g., Baron-Cohen, 1995) believe that infants are preprogrammed with several independent social-cognitive modules, including an Eye Direction Detector, an Intention Detector, and a Shared Attention Mechanism. In Baron-Cohen's view, each of these modules has its own predetermined developmental timetable that is affected neither by the ontogeny of the other modules nor by the organism's interactions with the social environment. Infants are not born knowing about other persons, but they do not have to learn about them either; the appropriate cognitive modules simply mature on their ineluctable timetables during the first months of life. The problem in this case is that the data simply are not consistent with this view. Evidence from the Carpenter, Nagell, and Tomasello (1998) study, and indirect evidence from other studies, shows that the key skills in this account (gaze following, understanding intentional action, and joint engagement) emerge in close developmental synchrony and in a correlated fashion at nine to twelve months of age. These facts are dissonant with an account in terms of several independent modules, nor is there any empirical support for the view that the emergence of these skills does not require some kind of social interaction with others (see also the critique of Baldwin and Moses, 1994).

Other theorists believe that infants' triadic interactions at nine to twelve months of age represent learned behavioral sequences. In particular, Moore (1996; Barresi and Moore, 1996) believes that the behaviors that emerge at nine to twelve months of age are independent behavioral skills, each of which has its own critical stimuli, environmental contingencies, and learning history that does not depend on sophisticated social-cognitive skills. For example, infants learn to follow gaze by turning (perhaps initially accidentally) in the direction of adults and then finding some interesting sight there. They look to the face of the adult in these and similar interactions because adult smiles and encouragement are rewarding as well. To explain the developmental synchrony and interrelatedness of the different social-cognitive skills, Moore invokes the emergence of a new information-processing ability to focus attention on two things simultaneously. The problem is that, to my knowledge, this information-processing ability has never been independently measured and related to early social cognition. Indeed, in the Carpenter, Nagell, and Tomasello (1998) study, there were several object-related tasks that might be expected to depend to some degree on this same hypothesized information-processing skill, but they did not fit into the observed developmental sequence of skills or correlate consistently with the social-cognitive measures.

In my view, then, the data force us to look for an explanation of joint attention that is more coherent than any of these alternatives, whether nativistic or learning-based, in the sense that it explains why all of the different joint attentional behaviors emerge as they do and when they do. That is, we need a theoretical account that answers both of these questions:

- Why do all of the joint attentional skills emerge together in correlated fashion?
- Why is nine months the age at which this happens?

My own candidate, not surprisingly, is the view that infants begin to engage in joint attentional interactions when they begin to understand other persons as intentional agents like the self (Tomasello, 1995a). Intentional agents are animate beings who have goals and who make active choices among behavioral means for attaining those goals, including active choices about what to pay attention to in pursuing those goals. Not all behavior is intentional in this sense, of course; for example, eye blinks and other reflexes may have biological functions that are analogous to goals, but goals are things that individuals have, and these individuals make voluntary choices about how to meet those goals based on their assessment of the current situation. Gergely et al. (1995) speak of these kinds of things as "rational" action—an organism's behavior makes sense to us if we understand how it is making behavioral choices that help it to achieve its goals.

In addition, I have argued that we should think of attention as a kind of intentional perception (Tomasello, 1995a). Individuals intentionally choose to attend to some things and not to others in ways that are directly related to the pursuit of their goals. Gibson and Rader (1979) give the example of a painter and a mountain climber staring at the same mountain in preparations for their respective activities; they see the same thing but they attend to very different aspects of it. The almost simultaneous ontogenetic emergence of the many different joint attentional behaviors, all of which rely in one way or another on the understanding of other persons as perceiving, behaving, goal-directed beings—supplemented by experimental findings such as those of Gergely and colleagues—strongly suggests that these joint attentional behaviors are not just isolated cognitive modules or independently learned behavioral sequences. They are all reflections of infants' dawning understanding of other persons as intentional agents. Perhaps no joint attentional behavior by itself provides unequivocal evidence for this understanding, but together they are convincing—perhaps especially those joint attentional behaviors that require the infant to determine precisely "what" the adult is focused on or doing, since they show a clear understanding of the adult's attention. But infants still have much to learn about other persons and how they work. In particular, we will see in later chapters that in acquiring their skills of linguistic communication young children learn much about how to follow into and direct adult attention very precisely. And, of course, one-year-old children do not know enough about the connection between perception and action to intervene effectively in the process, for example, by producing deceptive perceptual cues to trick the adult into acceding to their wishes—a skill that awaits some two or three years of further practice in interacting with others. What we are witnessing here is the very beginnings of the process.

The question thus arises: If the emergence of joint attention is indeed a revolution in infants' understanding of other persons, where does it come from? I have provided some evidence that from very early in development human infants may be social in some ways that other primates are not—as evidenced by their engaging in proto-conversations and neonatal mimicking—but these do not involve joint attention or any other form of the understanding of others as intentional agents. So the question that arises is how these earlier and later social-cognitive developments are related, if indeed they are related, and why they culminate in the understanding of others as intentional agents at precisely nine months of age.

A Simulation Explanation of the Nine-Month Revolution

Social theorists from Vico and Dilthey to Cooley and Mead have stressed that our understanding of other persons rests on a special source of knowledge that is not available when we attempt to understand the workings of inanimate objects, namely the analogy to the self. The key theoretical point is that we have sources of information about the self and its workings that are not available for any external entity of any type. As I act I have available the internal experience of a goal and of striving for a goal, as well as various forms of proprioception (correlated with exteroception) of my behavior as I act toward the goal—which serve to relate goal and behavioral means. To the extent that I understand an external entity as "like me," and can therefore attribute to it the same kinds of internal workings as my own, to that extent can I gain extra knowledge of a special type about how it works. Presumably, the analogy is closest and most natural when it is applied to other persons.

My theoretical attempt here is to use this general insight about the relation of self understanding and the understanding of others to explain the nine-month social-cognitive revolution. In general, the argument is that in attempting to understand other persons human infants apply what they already experience of themselves—and this experience of the self changes in early development, especially with regard to self-agency. The hypothesis is that as this new experience of self-agency emerges, a new understanding of others emerges as a direct result. The current approach may thus be thought of as one version of a simulation model in which individuals understand other persons in some sense by analogy with the self—since others are "like me"—in a way that they do not do, at least not in the same way, with inanimate objects—since they are much less "like me."

The Link between Self and Other

Relying mainly on findings from research on neonatal imitation, Meltzoff and Gopnik (1993) propose that infants understand that other persons are "like me" from birth—with much learning of specifics still to come (see also Gopnik and Meltzoff, 1997). But they do not give any account in which this "like me" stance plays an integral role in subsequent social-cognitive developments, and in particular they do not link it specifically to the emergence of joint attentional behaviors at nine to twelve months of age. Indeed, as adherents of one version of the "theory theory," Meltzoff and Gopnik believe that infants come to understand other persons by using the same kind of protoscientific theorizing they use in all other domains of cognition. The "like me" stance plays no real role in this process, but rather the new developments at nine months of age are just a result of direct observation of and inferences about the behavior of other people (and indeed Gopnik, 1993, argues that we know others' intentional states as well as we know our own, and in some cases better).

In agreement with Meltzoff and Gopnik, my own view is that infants' early understanding of other persons as "like me" is indeed the result of a uniquely human biological adaptation—although the precise age at which it emerges in ontogeny and the amount and types of personal experience necessary in the species-typical developmental pathway remain unclear (see Baressi and Moore, 1996). This understanding—which in any case is present within the first few months of life—is then a key element in infants' coming to understand others as intentional agents at nine months of age. That is, it becomes a key element when the other indispensable factor enters the picture—and this other factor explains why nine months is a special age. This other factor is infants' new understanding of their own intentional actions. Since other persons are "like me," any new understanding of my own functioning leads immediately to a new understanding of their functioning; I more or less simulate other persons' psychological functioning by analogy to my own, which is most directly and intimately known to me. Consequently, the specific hypothesis is that when infants come to a new understanding of their own intentional actions, they then use their "like me" stance to understand the behavior of other persons in this same way. And there is evidence that eight to nine months of age is indeed a special age in infants' understanding of their own intentional actions.

Self Becomes Intentional

In the first months of life infants understand that their behavioral actions achieve results in the external environment, but they do not seem to know how or why they do this. Piaget (1952, 1954) devised a number of clever experiments in which infants produced interesting effects on mobiles, toys, and household objects, and then were given the opportunity to reproduce those effects—sometimes in slightly modified circumstances that called for an accommodation on the infant's part. For the first six to eight months of life, Piaget's infants basically repeated behaviors that reproduced interesting results, but they made very few accommodations for the exigencies of particular situations. For example, if the infant managed to shake a rattle and produce an interesting sight and sound because her hand was tethered via a string to the suspended rattle, removal of the string did not lead to any changes of behavior; the infant made the same arm movements. Piaget observed many other instances of this "magical" thinking about how actions produce results in the external world.

But at around eight months of age, Piaget's infants seemed to display a new understanding of action-outcome relations. The new behaviors that evidenced this new understanding were (a) the use of multiple behavioral means to the same goal, and (b) the recognition and use of behavioral intermediaries in the pursuit of goals. For example, when the infants wanted to reach a toy, and Piaget placed a pillow as an obstacle in the way, prior to eight months of age the infants either would start interacting with the pillow, forgetting the original toy, or else would stay focused on the toy and simply become frustrated; but at eight months of age the infants reacted to the intervention of the pillow by pausing, then removing the pillow or smashing it down, then proceeding deliberately to grasp the toy.

The converse of the removal of obstacles was the use of intermediaries, mostly human intermediaries, to achieve goals. For example, when the infants wanted to operate some toy and could not, they would push the adult's hand toward it and wait for a result (in a very few cases they attempted to use inanimate intermediaries as tools, but these were mostly used a few months later).

Although it is fair to say that prior to eight months of age infants are acting intentionally in the general sense that they are acting toward a goal, the use of multiple means to the same end and the use of intermediaries indicates a new level of intentional functioning (Frye, 1991). A means that was useful toward a goal in one circumstance may be replaced by another in another circumstance; the infant must choose. And it may even happen that a behavior that on one occasion was an end in itself, for example, smashing down a pillow, is now only a means to a greater end (grasping the toy). The implication is thus that infants now have a new understanding of the different roles of ends and means in the behavioral act. They have come to differentiate the goal they are pursuing from the behavioral means they use to pursue that goal much more clearly than in their previous sensory-motor actions. When the infant removes an obstacle and proceeds without hesitation to the goal, it is plausible to assume that she had a distinct goal in mind ahead of time (presumably in the form of an imagined state of affairs in the world), kept this goal in mind throughout the time in which she was removing the obstacle, and clearly differentiated this goal from the various behavioral means among which she had to choose in order to attain the goal.

Simulating the Intentional Actions of Others

Piaget (1954) hypothesized that infants' initial attribution of causal powers to entities other than the self occurs with other persons: "People . . . are very probably the first objectified sources of causality because, through imitating someone else, the subject rapidly succeeds in attributing to his model's action an efficacy analogous to his own" (p. 360). This general approach is the essence of my account as well, although in his very cursory treatment of the subject Piaget does not make the critical distinction between the understanding of others as sources of self-movement and power, that is, as animate beings, and the understanding of others as beings that make behavioral and perceptual choices, that is, as intentional beings. Indeed, in my view, human infants very likely understand others as animate beings with powers of self-movement much before eight to nine months of age—in a manner similar to all primates—because this understanding does not rely on any kind of identification with the self or attribution of intentionality; self-generated movement can be directly perceived and distinguished from movement that is forced by outside agents. But understanding others as intentional beings— with goals, attention, and decision-making powers—is another thing again.

The distinction is critical. Consider the findings of Leslie (1984) and Woodward (1998). Infants five to six months of age show surprise when they observe other people's hands doing things that they normally do not do. Infants at this age thus seem to know that others are animate beings with powers of self-movement that behave in certain ways. This corresponds precisely to the way infants understand their own actions at this age, that is, as procedures that make things happen (see above). But understanding others as animate beings—that is, as beings that make things happen—is not the same thing as understanding others as intentional agents with an interrelated functioning of goal, attention, and behavioral strategy. In the current simulation theory, that awaits developments in which the infant differentiates goals from behavioral means in her own sensory-motor actions. This differentiation will then open up the possibility of understanding others not just as sources of animate power but as individuals who have goals and make choices among various behavioral and perceptual strategies that lead toward those goals. This provides for something of the directedness, or even "aboutness," dimension of intentionality that is missing when infants only understand that others have the power to make things happen in some global way.

The theory is thus that human infants identify with other human beings from very early in ontogeny, and that this is based on uniquely human biological inheritance (which may or may not require extended interactions with the social environment). As long as infants understand themselves only as animate beings with the ability to make things happen in some generalized way, for the first seven to eight months or so, that is how they also understand other persons. When they begin understanding themselves as intentional agents in the sense that they recognize that they have goals that are clearly separated from behavioral means, at eight to nine months of age, that is how they understand other persons as well. This understanding also paves the way for understanding the perceptual choices that others make—their attention as distinct from their perception—though we currently have little detailed understanding of this process. Although at this point we should not push the argument too far, it is also possible that infants make some of these same kinds of simulations, perhaps somewhat inappropriately, to inanimate objects and that this is the source of their understandings of how some physical events "force" others to happen: the first billiard ball is pushing the second with the same kind of force that I feel when I push it (Piaget, 1954). Perhaps this kind of simulation is weaker for infants than the simulation of other persons because the analogy between themselves and inanimate objects is weaker.

I should say at this point that there have been many objections to the simulation view based on what for me at least is a misunderstanding. The simulation view is often understood to mean that children must first be able to conceptualize their own intentional states before they can use them to simulate the perspective of others. This does not seem to be the case empirically: children do not conceptualize their own mental states before they conceptualize the mental states of others (Gopnik, 1993), nor do they talk about them earlier (Bartsch and Wellman, 1995). But this need not be a problem if simulation is not viewed as an explicit process in which the child conceptualizes some mental content, while still aware that it is her own mental content, and then attributes it to another person in a specific situation. My hypothesis is simply that children make the categorical judgment that others are "like me" and so they should work like me as well. There is no claim that in specific situations children can gain conscious access to their own mental states more easily than they can discern what another person's specific mental states might be; they simply perceive the other's general manner of functioning via an analogy to the self, with their ability to determine specific mental states in specific circumstances depending on many factors. In the most straightforward case, the child simply sees or imagines the goal-state the other person is intending to achieve in much the same way that she would imagine it for herself, and she then just sees the other person's behavior as directed toward that goal in much the same way that she sees her own.

Chimpanzees and Children with Autism

If we now return to a consideration of our nearest primate relatives, we may conclude the following. Chimpanzees and some other nonhuman primates clearly understand something of the efficacy of their own actions on the environment, and indeed they even engage in many kinds of intentional sensory-motor actions in which they use different means toward the same end, remove obstacles, and use intermediaries such as tools. If they do not understand others as intentional agents, as I believe they do not, then it cannot be because of this factor. Instead, the reason they do not understand others in this way, in my opinion, is the other factor: they do not identify with conspecifics in the same way as human beings do. Although it is pure speculation, one hypothesis is that this may also be the source of their difficulty with physical problems in which they must attempt to understand the causal relations among the actions of inanimate objects; they do not attempt to identify, however imperfectly, with the objects involved. An interesting twist to this story is provided by enculturated apes who seem to acquire some human-like joint attentional skills such as imperative pointing for humans and imitatively learning some instrumental skills (see Chapter 2). But these individual apes still do not point or use their other communicative signals for others declaratively—that is, just in order to share attention—and they do not engage in various other activities involving cooperation and teaching. The current hypothesis is that although these individuals may learn something about how humans are effective animate agents in their environments—who must be contacted to fulfill virtually every need and desire—no amount of training can provide them with the uniquely human biological predisposition for identifying with others in a human-like manner.

If we posit that human beings biologically inherit a special ability to identify with conspecifics, it is natural to look for individuals who have some kind of biological deficit in this ability, and these are, of course, children with autism. It is well known that children with autism have significant problems with joint attention and perspective-taking. For example, they show a number of deficits in the ability to jointly attend to objects with others (Loveland and Landry, 1986; Mundy, Sigman, and Kasari, 1990), they produce very few declarative gestures (Baron-Cohen, 1993), and they engage very little in symbolic or pretend play, which in many cases involves adopting the role of another. Some high-functioning children with autism can follow the gaze of another, but lower-functioning children with autism are very poor at accommodating to another's perceptual perspective (Loveland et al., 1991). Langdell's overall conclusion (cited in Baron-Cohen, 1988) is that children with autism as a group have "difficulty in taking another person's point of view," and Loveland (1993) characterizes them as basically "acultural." Currently there is no way to know the source of children with autism's problems—there are many competing theories—but one hypothesis is that they have difficulty in identifying with other persons, and this difficulty can take many different forms depending on such things as the developmental timing and severity of the insult and the other cognitive skills that an individual might or might not have to compensate.

Early Cultural Learning

The human understanding of conspecifics as intentional agents is thus a cognitive ability that emanates both from humans' identification with conspecifics, emerging very early in infancy and unique to the species, and from the intentional organization of their own sensory-motor actions, shared with other primates and emerging at around eight to nine months of age. Both of these skills are biologically inherited in the sense that their normal developmental pathways occur in a variety of different environments within the normal range (all of which include, of course, conspecifics).

This uniquely human form of social understanding has many profound effects on the way human children interact with adults and one another. In the current context the most important of these effects is that it opens the child to the uniquely human forms of cultural inheritance. Children who understand that other persons have intentional relations to the world, similar to their own intentional relations to the world, may attempt to take advantage of the ways other individuals have devised for meeting their goals. Children are also at this point able to tune into the intentional dimension of artifacts that people have created to mediate their behavioral and attentional strategies in specific goal-directed situations. The claim is thus that despite the rich cultural environment into which children may be born, if they do not understand others as intentional agents—as typically developing human infants before nine months of age, nonhuman primates, and most persons with autism do not—then they will not be able to take advantage of the cognitive skills and knowledge of conspecifics that is manifest in this cultural milieu. Once infants do begin to culturally learn from others, this process has some surprising consequences for how they learn to interact with objects and artifacts, for how they learn to communicate with other persons gesturally, and for how they learn to think about themselves.

Culture as Ontogenetic Niche

Organisms inherit their environments as much as they inherit their genomes—this cannot be stressed too much. Fish are designed to function in water, ants are designed to function in anthills. Human beings are designed to work in a certain kind of social environment, and without it developing youngsters (assuming some way to keep them alive) would not develop normally either socially or cognitively. That certain kind of social environment is what we call culture, and it is simply the species-typical and species-unique "ontogenetic niche" for human development (Gauvain, 1995). I will distinguish two ways in which the human cultural environment sets the context for the cognitive development of children: as cognitive "habitus" and as a source of active instruction from adults. Then I will consider how children learn in, from, and through this environment.

First, the people of a given social group live in a certain way— they prepare and eat foods in certain ways, they have a certain set of living arrangements, they go certain places and do certain things. Because human infants and young children are totally dependent on adults, they eat in these ways, live in these arrangements, and accompany adults as they go and do these things. Broadly speaking, we may call this the "habitus" of children's development (Bourdieu, 1977). Engaging in the normal practices of the people with whom she grows up—at whatever level of involvement and skill—means that the child has certain experiences and not others. The particular habitus into which a child is born determines the kinds of social interactions she will have, the kinds of physical objects she will have available, the kinds of learning experiences and opportunities she will encounter, and the kinds of inferences she will draw about the way of life of those around her. The habitus thus has direct effects on cognitive development in terms of the "raw material" with which the child has to work, and we can certainly imagine, if only in our nightmares, the havoc that would be wreaked on children's cognitive development if they were deprived of certain sets of those raw materials.

Although the habitus of groups of human beings and the habitus of groups of chimpanzees are clearly not the same, it is very likely that the processes of individual learning and inference by which the cognitive development of the two species is affected by their lifeways are in many ways similar. Developing chimpanzee youngsters also eat what their mothers eat and go where their mothers go and sleep where their mothers sleep. However, in addition, human adults universally take a more active, interventionist role in their children's development than do other primates and animals. While for many cultural skills adults take a laissez-faire attitude—and the extent of this differs significantly among different cultures—in all human societies there are some things that adults feel they need to help children to learn. In some cases they provide simple assistance, which may be called, after Wood, Bruner, and Ross (1976), scaffolding. Adults witness children struggling with a certain skill and they do various things to make the task simpler or to draw the child's attention to certain key aspects of the task, or they do a part of the task themselves so that the child will not be overwhelmed with too many variables. In some cultures this kind of instructional format simply takes the form of the adult requiring the child to sit and watch as she weaves a rug or prepares dinner or works in a garden (Greenfield and Lave, 1982). But in all human societies there are some tasks or pieces of knowledge that are thought to be so important that adults feel they must directly instruct youngsters in them (Kruger and Tomasello, 1996). These vary from highly important sustenance activities to the memorizing of family ancestors or religious rituals. The main point is that in both scaffolding and direct instruction the adult takes an interest in the child's acquisition of a skill or piece of knowledge and, in many cases, stays involved in the process until the child learns the material or reaches a certain proficiency level. Bullock (1987) in particular has stressed that such intentional instruction is a very powerful force in cultural transmission as it ensures, to a certain degree of likelihood, that a specific skill or piece of knowledge will indeed be passed along.

King (1991) has reviewed a wealth of evidence concerning the social learning of nonhuman primates and also possible instances of teaching by adult primates—what she calls "information donation." Regardless of the interpretation of a few interesting anecdotes, the picture is quite clear: developing youngsters in all primate species except humans are mostly left to themselves to acquire the information they need to survive and procreate; the adults do little to donate information to them. One of the most significant dimensions of human culture is therefore the way in which adults actively instruct youngsters. In combination with the general effects of living in a particular habitus, it is clear that the ontogenetic niche for developing human beings is a richly cultural one.

Imitative Learning

At around nine months of age human children are ready to participate in this cultural world in some profoundly new ways. The first and most important of these is that the nine-month-old's new understanding of other persons as intentional agents enables what I have called cultural learning, the ontogenetically first form of which is imitative learning. That is, whereas in early infancy there was some face-to-face dyadic mimicking of behavior, at nine months the infant begins to reproduce the adult's intentional actions on outside objects. This of course opens up the possibility of acquiring the conventional use of tools and artifacts of various types, and thus represents the first truly cultural learning in my fairly narrow definition of the term. Although there are few systematic data on the question, there are some suggestions that, contrary to popular beliefs, very young children do not often imitate behaviors that adults perform while ignoring the child, but much more often imitate behaviors that adults demonstrate "for" them (Killen and Uzgiris, 1981). If true, this would provide an interesting and fairly direct connecting link between adults' active instruction of children and the earliest forms of cultural learning.

Becoming a member of a culture means learning some new things from other people. But there are many ways to learn new things socially, as we saw in the review of primate social learning in Chapter 2. With respect to objects, including tools and artifacts, there are processes of (a) stimulus enhancement in which an adult picks up an object and does something with it, which makes infants more interested in touching and manipulating that object as well (which then facilitates their own individual learning); (b) emulation learning in which infants see an adult manipulate an object and so learn new things about the dynamic affordance of that object which they might not have discovered on their own; and (c) imitative learning in which the child is learning something about human intentional actions. Many of the classic studies of children's imitative learning have not included the kinds of control conditions needed to make sure that children are indeed imitating adults' intentional behavior, not simply reproducing the effects adults produce on objects. But there are several recent studies that have included these controls and so are especially convincing demonstrations of infant imitative learning.

Meltzoff (1988) had fourteen-month-old children observe an adult bend at the waist and touch his head to a panel, thus turning on a light. Most infants then performed more or less this same behavior—even though it was an unusual and awkward behavior and even though it would have been easier and more natural for them simply to push the panel with their hand. One interpretation of this behavior is that infants understood (a) that the adult had the goal of illuminating the light; (b) that he chose one means for doing so, from among other possible means; and (c) that if they had the same goal they could choose the same means—an act in which the child imagines herself in the place of the other. Imitative learning of this type thus relies fundamentally on infants' tendency to identify with adults, present from an early age, and on their ability to distinguish in the actions of others the underlying goal and the different means that might be chosen to achieve it, present from nine months. Otherwise, the infants might have engaged in emulation learning in which they simply turned on the light with their hands (which they did not), or else they would have just mimicked the action, like a parrot, without any regard for its goal-directed nature. This last interpretation is a possibility in Meltzoff's study, but it was essentially ruled out in the imitation tasks of Carpenter, Nagell, and Tomasello, (1998). They also gave young infants novel and unusual actions that produced interesting results, but they looked very carefully at the infants' accompanying behaviors as they reproduced the act. They found that between eleven and fourteen months of age the majority of infants both reproduced the unusual action and looked to the interesting result in anticipation—thus demonstrating that they were not just mimicking but rather were imitating a goal-directed action.

Two other recent studies have tested more directly what infants understand about others' intentional actions in the context of imitative learning. In the first, Meltzoff (1995) presented eighteen-month-old infants with two types of demonstrations (along with some control conditions). Infants in one group saw the adult perform actions on objects, much as in previous studies. Infants in the other group, however, saw the adult try but fail to achieve the end results of the target actions; for example, the adult tried to pull two parts of an object apart but never succeeded in separating them. Infants in this group thus never saw the target actions actually performed. Meltzoff found that infants in both groups reproduced the target actions equally well; that is, they appeared to understand what the adult intended to do and performed that action instead of mimicking the adult's actual surface behavior. (And they were much better in both of these conditions than in the control conditions in which the adult just manipulated the objects randomly and the like.) In the second study, Carpenter, Akhtar, and Tomasello (1998) studied infants' imitation of accidental versus intentional actions. In this study, fourteen- to eighteen-month-old infants watched an adult perform some two-action sequences on objects that made interesting results occur. One action of the modeled sequences was marked vocally as intentional ("There!") and one action was marked vocally as accidental ("Woops!")—with order systematically manipulated across sequences. Infants were then given a chance to make the result occur themselves. Overall, infants imitated almost twice as many of the adult's intentional actions as her accidental ones regardless of the order in which they saw them, indicating that they differentiated between the two types of actions and that they were able to reproduce, again, what the adult meant to do and not just her surface behavior.

Imitative learning thus represents infants' initial entry into the cultural world around them in the sense that they can now begin to learn from adults, or, more accurately, through adults, in cognitively significant ways. It is important that a number of studies have established that this learning is not just about the affordance of objects that are revealed when others manipulate them, or just about surface behavior in the sense of precise motor movements. Instead, from around their first birthdays, human infants begin to tune in to and attempt to reproduce both the adult's goal and the behavioral means with which she has chosen to pursue that goal. Because infants before this age do not perceive the behavior of others as intentional, they can only emulate the external results the behavior produces or mimic its sensory-motor form. After this age, they cannot but perceive Daddy as "cleaning the table" or "trying to open the drawer"—not simply as making specific bodily motions or producing salient changes of state in the environment—and these intentional actions are what they attempt to reproduce.

Learning the Intentional Affordances of Artifacts

Imitative learning plays an especially important role in children's interactions with certain types of objects, especially cultural artifacts. Early in development, as young infants grasp, suck, and manipulate objects, they learn something of the objects' affordances for action (Gibson, 1979). This is direct individual learning, and it may sometimes be supplemented by emulation learning in which the child discovers new affordances of objects by seeing them do things she did not know they could do. But the tools and artifacts of a culture have another dimension—what Cole (1996) calls the "ideal" dimension—that produce another set of affordances for anyone with the appropriate kinds of social-cognitive and social learning skills. As human children observe other people using cultural tools and artifacts, they often engage in the process of imitative learning in which they attempt to place themselves in the "intentional space" of the user—discerning the user's goal, what she is using the artifact "for." By engaging in this imitative learning, the child joins the other person in affirming what "we" use this object "for": we use hammers for hammering and pencils for writing. After she has engaged in such a process the child comes to see some cultural objects and artifacts as having, in addition to their natural sensory-motor affordances, another set of what we might call intentional affordances based on her understanding of the intentional relations that other persons have with that object or artifact—that is, the intentional relations that other persons have to the world through the artifact (Tomasello, 1999a).

The distinction between natural and intentional affordances is especially clear in children's early symbolic play because in symbolic play children basically extract the intentional affordances of different objects and play with them. Thus, a two-year-old may pick up a pencil and pretend it is a hammer. But as Hobson (1993) has pointed out, the child is doing more than simply manipulating the pencil in an unusual way. In early symbolic play the infant also looks to an adult with a playful expression—because she knows that this is not the intentional/conventional use of this object and that her unconventional use is something that may be considered "funny." One interpretation of this behavior is that symbolic play involves two crucial steps. First, the infant must be able to understand and adopt the intentions of adults as they use objects and artifacts; that is, the child first understands how we humans use pencils—their intentional affordances. The second step involves the child "decoupling" intentional affordances from their associated objects and artifacts so that they may be interchanged and used with "inappropriate" objects playfully. Thus, the child comes to use a pencil as one would conventionally use a hammer, smiling at the adult in the process to signal that this is not stupidity but playfulness. This ability to detach the intentional affordances of objects and artifacts and to interchange them relatively freely in symbolic play is, for me, very convincing evidence that the child has learned the intentional affordances embodied in many cultural artifacts in a way that is semi-independent of their materiality.

The process is illustrated especially clearly in a recent study by Tomasello, Striano, and Rochat (in press). They had children from eighteen to thirty-five months of age play a game in which the adult signaled which of several objects she wanted and the child pushed that object down a slide to her. In a warm-up task, children of all ages performed almost perfectly when the adult asked for an object by name. In the real task, the adult asked for the object by holding up a toy replica of the target object (e.g., asking for a real hammer by holding up a small plastic hammer). In this case, however, the younger children were very poor at interpreting the speaker's communicative intentions with the replica—a surprising finding since from the adult perspective the iconicity of the toy hammer should make it especially easy for the child to interpret. One possible reason for this difficulty is that the younger children engaged with the toy object as a sensory-motor object that afforded grasping, manipulating, and the like—which made it difficult to engage with purely as a symbol (and indeed the young children quite often reached for the toy object as the adult held it up). Interestingly, by the time they were twenty-six months old the children were good at using objects as symbols in this game, but not in one special case. They had great difficulties when the object being used as a symbol had another intentional use, for example, when the adult used a cup as a hat. It seems that this added another competing construal of the cup; that is, the cup was simultaneously:

- a sensory-motor object for grasping and sucking;
- an intentional artifact with a conventional use for drinking; and
- a symbol for a hat in this situation.

These results thus show quite clearly that children's understanding of the intentional affordances of objects—deriving ultimately from their observations of and interactions with other persons in the cultural line of development—are something different from, and indeed may compete with, their previously established understanding of the sensory-motor affordances of objects established in the individual line of development.

The hypothesis is thus that when children begin to understand other persons as intentional agents, and so to imitatively learn the conventional use of artifacts through them, the world of cultural artifacts becomes imbued with intentional affordances to complement their sensory-motor affordances—with children's very strong tendency to imitate adult interactions with objects clearly apparent (see Striano, Tomasello, and Rochat, 1999, and Chapter 4). In the domain of objects, this understanding opens up the possibility of symbolic play with the intentional affordances of various objects and artifacts.

Despite the interesting behaviors of some human-raised apes in manipulating human artifacts, this is all uniquely human behavior (Call and Tomasello, 1996). It should also be pointed out that something similar operates in the domain of social conventions that do not use objects, for example, language and other symbolic artifacts comprising communicative conventions, but because the process of learning is somewhat different in this case, I will save this discussion for the next chapter.

Learning to Communicate Gesturally

Another major domain in which imitative learning makes itself felt is the domain of gestural communication. The earliest gestures of human infants are typically dyadic ritualizations that are essentially the same as chimpanzee gestures (see Chapter 2). For example, many children the world over hold their hands over their heads when they want to be picked up (Lock, 1978). Like chimpanzee gestures, early gestures of this type are:

- dyadic, in the sense that there is no outside object involved;
- imperative, in the sense that they are about what the child wants; and
- ritualized, not imitated, so that they are signals (procedures for getting things done) not symbols (conventions for sharing experience).

Then at eleven to twelve months of age children also begin to produce triadic declarative gestures such as some forms of pointing. How children learn to point for other persons is not known at this time, but the two possibilities are ritualization and imitative learning.

Many infants use arm and index finger extension to orient their own attention to things, and, if the adult reacts appropriately, this kind of pointing may become ritualized. In this scenario it would be possible for an infant to point for others while still not understanding their pointing gestures for her—that is, she would understand pointing from her own perspective only—and indeed a number of empirical studies have found just such a dissociation between comprehension and production in many infants (Franco and Butterworth, 1996). Infants who have learned to point via ritualization will understand it only as an effective procedure for getting others to do things (a signal, just as chimpanzees understand their gestures), not as a shared symbol.

The alternative is that the infant observes an adult point for her and comprehends that the adult is attempting to induce her to share attention to something; that is, she comprehends the communicative goal of the gesture. The child then imitatively learns the gesture by seeing that when she has the same goal she can use the same means, thus creating an intersubjective gestural act for sharing attention. It is crucial that in this learning process the infant is not just mimicking adults sticking out their fingers; she is truly understanding and attempting to reproduce the adult's intentionally communicative act, including both means and end. It is crucial because an intersubjectively understood communicative device can only be created when the child first understands the adult's communicative intention, and then identifies with that communicative intention herself as she produces the "same" means for the "same" end. The intersubjectivity of the resulting communicative symbol—as we should call it in such cases—thus derives from the nature of the learning process. When imitative learning is involved the infant comes to understand that she is using the same communicative behavior as others; we "share" the symbol. I will return to this process in more detail in Chapter 4 when I detail something of the way children use so-called symbolic gestures and language.

Empirically we do not know whether infants learn to point via ontogenetic ritualization or imitative learning or whether, as I suspect, some infants learn in one way (especially prior to their first birthdays) and some learn in the other. And it may even happen that an infant who learns to point via ritualization at some later time comes to comprehend adult pointing in a new way, and so comes to a new understanding of her own pointing and its equivalence to the adult version. Thus, Franco and Butterworth (1996) found that when many infants first begin to point they do not seem to monitor the adult's reaction at all, but some months later they look to the adult after they have pointed to observe her reaction, and some months after that they look to the adult first, to secure her attention on themselves, before they engage in the pointing act. The hypothesis is thus that sometime soon after their first birthdays human infants begin to imitatively learn to point for others (whether or not they engaged in ritualized pointing prior to this), and it is at this moment that they learn the cultural convention or artifact of pointing in the sense that they understand its intentional and attentional significance.

Learning about Me

No one really knows how infants understand themselves, but Tomasello (1993, 1995b) proposed an account that derives directly from the current account in terms of the understanding of others as intentional agents. The idea is this. As infants begin to follow into and direct the attention of others to outside entities at nine to twelve months of age, it happens on occasion that the other person whose attention an infant is monitoring focuses on the infant herself. The infant then monitors that person's attention to *her* in a way that was not possible previously, that is, previous to the nine-month social-cognitive revolution. From this point on the infant's face-to-face interactions with others—which appear on the surface to be continuous with her face-to-face interactions from early infancy—are radically transformed. She now knows she is interacting with an intentional agent who perceives her and intends things toward her. When the infant did not understand that others perceive and intend things toward an outside world, there could be no question of how they perceived and intended things toward *me*. After coming to this understanding, the infant can monitor the adult's intentional relation to the world including herself (the "me" of William James and George Herbert Mead). By something like this same process infants at this age also become able to monitor adults' emotional attitudes toward them as well—a kind of social referencing of others' attitudes to the self. This new understanding of how others *feel* about me opens up the possibility for the development of shyness, self-consciousness, and a sense of self-esteem (Harter, 1983). Evidence for this is the fact that within a few months after the social-cognitive revolution, at the first birthday, infants begin showing the first signs of shyness and coyness in front of other persons and mirrors (Lewis et al., 1989).

It is important to emphasize that what happens at the first birthday is not the sudden emergence of a full-blown self-concept, but just the opening up of a possibility. That is, what infants' new-found social-cognitive skills do is to open up the possibility that they may now learn about the world from the point of view of others, and one of the things they may learn about in this way is themselves. Because in cultural learning the infant employs all of the basic learning and categorization processes that she employs in learning about the world directly, her simulations of others' perceptions of her are used to categorize herself relative to other people in various ways. This categorical component is an important dimension of self-concept as well, especially during the preschool period as children understand themselves in terms of concrete categories such as child, male, good at tree climbing, bad at bike riding, and so forth (Lewis and Brooks-Gunn, 1979).

The Ontogenetic Origins of Culture

I have hypothesized that the fundamental social-cognitive ability that underlies human culture is the individual human being's ability to and tendency to identify with other human beings. This capacity is a part of the unique biological inheritance of the species *Homo sapiens*. It may be a part of children's cognitive capacities by the time they are born, or perhaps a few months later. Which kinds of experiential factors, if any, play a role in the ontogeny of this capacity are unknown, and will continue to be unknown to some extent because human development is not something with which scientists can experiment at will. But for children to become significantly different from other primates cognitively, this unique ability must interact during ontogeny with other developing cognitive skills—most importantly, it must interact with the child's own developing intentionality as manifest in the differentiation between goals and behavioral means in her sensory-motor actions on the environment. Given infants' identification with others, experiencing their own intentionality in this new way leads nine-month-olds to the understanding that other persons are intentional agents, like me. This then opens up the possibility that infants may engage in cultural learning through these other persons.

This is nothing other than the ontogenetic origins of Vygotsky's cultural line of cognitive development. It is not that six-month-olds are not cultural beings in the sense that they are enmeshed in the habitus of their cultures. They are, and throughout the first nine months of life they are in the process of becoming members of their cultures in more and more active and participatory ways. But before they understand others as intentional beings with whom they can share attention to outside entities, they are only learning individually about the world into which they were born. After they understand others as intentional agents like themselves, a whole new world of intersubjectively shared reality begins to open up. It is a world populated by material and symbolic artifacts and social practices that members of their culture, both past and present, have created for the use of others. To be able to use these artifacts as they were meant to be used, and to participate in these social practices as they were meant to be participated in, children have to be able to imagine themselves in the position of the adult users and participants as they observe them. Children now come to comprehend how "we" use the artifacts and practices of our culture—what they are "for."

Monitoring the intentional relations of others to the outside world also means that the infant—almost by accident, as it were—monitors the attention of other persons as they attend to her. This then starts the process of self-concept formation, in the sense of the child understanding how others are regarding "me" both conceptually and emotionally. To presage a theme from Chapter 4, this ability to see the self as one participant among others in an interaction is the social-cognitive basis for the infant's ability to comprehend the

kinds of socially shared events that constitute the basic joint attentional formats for the acquisition of language and other types of
communicative conventions.

It is significant that children with autism have biological deficits in
precisely the complex of skills we have been focused on here (Baron-
Cohen, 1995; Hobson, 1993; Happé, 1995; Loveland, 1993; Sigman
and Capps, 1997). They have problems in a variety of joint attentional skills, they have problems in imitative learning, they do not
engage in symbolic play normally, they do not seem to have self-
understanding of the same type as typically developing children,
and they have difficulties in learning and using linguistic symbols in
communicatively appropriate ways (as we shall see in Chapter 4).
There is great variability in all of these things in children with
autism, fading over into allied disorders such as Asperger's Syndrome, and so it is dangerous to make any general claims. For now, I
would simply like to point out that if we think of the ontogeny of the
uniquely human social-cognitive ability to participate in culture not
as a direct causal connection from genes to adults, but rather as a
process that takes many months and years to unfold as children at
various stages of development interact with their physical and social
environments, we can certainly imagine that different kinds of problems at different developmental steps along the way can lead to radically different outcomes in the cognitive development of these unfortunate children.

Overall, virtually everyone agrees that something dramatic happens in human infants' social cognition at around nine months of
age. Whereas the social cognition of human infants before this age
shares much with that of nonhuman primates, with perhaps some
special features, by nine months of age there can be no doubt that
we are dealing with processes of social cognition that are unique to
the species. There is still a long way to go before children will understand such things as false beliefs, but in the current context the understanding of others as intentional agents is the crucial step in the
ontogeny of human social cognition because it enables infants to
begin their lifelong voyage down the cultural line of development.
By empowering them to engage in various processes of cultural

learning and the internalization of the perspectives of other persons, this new understanding enables infants to culturally mediate their understanding of the world through that of other persons, including the perspectives and understanding of other persons that are embodied in the material and symbolic artifacts created by other persons far removed in space and time.

4

LINGUISTIC
COMMUNICATION
AND SYMBOLIC
REPRESENTATION

Every particular notation stresses some particular point of view.

—Ludwig Wittgenstein

In discussions of human cognition from a phylogenetic point of view, language is often invoked as a reason for human cognitive uniqueness. But invoking language as an evolutionary cause of human cognition is like invoking money as an evolutionary cause of human economic activity. There is no question that acquiring and using a natural language contributes to, even transforms, the nature of human cognition—just as money transforms the nature of human economic activity. But language did not come out of nowhere. It did not descend on earth from outer space like some stray asteroid nor, despite the views of some contemporary scholars such as Chomsky (1980), did it arise as some bizarre genetic mutation unrelated to other aspects of human cognition and social life. Just as money is a symbolically embodied social institution that arose historically from previously existing economic activities, natural language is a symbolically embodied social institution that arose historically from previously existing social-communicative activities.

For children to learn to use linguistic or monetary symbols in the manner conventional for their societies, some ontogenetic analogue of those historically primary communicative and economic activities must first be present. In the case of language the ontogenetic analogue is, of course, the various joint attentional and nonlinguistic communicative activities in which prelinguistic children and adults participate—as just reviewed. But to learn a piece of language, additional joint attentional work is still needed. Determining the specific communicative intention of an adult when she uses an unknown piece of language in the context of a joint attentional activity is very far from straightforward. It requires that the child be able to understand the different roles that speaker and hearer are playing in the joint attentional activity as well as the adult's specific communicative intention within that activity—and then she must be able to express toward other persons the same communicative intention that was previously expressed toward her (see Hobson, 1993). Quite often she must do this not as adults stop what they are doing and attempt to teach her a word, but rather within the flow of naturally occurring social interactions in which both adult and child are attempting to get things done in the world.

The consequences of learning to use linguistic symbols and other symbolic artifacts are multifarious. Obviously they allow children to do things they would not otherwise be able to do in some particular situations, since these symbolic artifacts were created for the purpose of enabling or facilitating certain kinds of cognitive and social interactions. But more importantly, they lead to a radically new form of cognitive representation that transforms the way children view the world. Whereas nonhuman primates and human neonates cognitively represent their environments by preserving past perceptions and proprioceptions from their own experience (basically sensory-motor representations), once children begin the process of symbolically communicating with other intentional agents they go beyond these straightforward, individually based representations. The symbolic representations that children learn in their social interactions with other persons are special because they are (a) intersubjective, in the sense that a symbol is socially "shared" with other persons; and (b) perspectival, in the sense that each symbol picks out a particular way of viewing some phenomenon (categorization being a special case of this process). The central theoretical point is that linguistic symbols embody the myriad ways of construing the world intersubjectively that have accumulated in a culture over historical time, and the process of acquiring the conventional use of these symbolic artifacts, and so internalizing these construals, fundamentally transforms the nature of children's cognitive representations.

Social-Cognitive Bases of Language Acquisition

The account of the human adaptation for culture in Chapter 3 rested on children's emerging ability at nine to twelve months of age to understand other persons as intentional agents. This ability does not emerge in a vacuum, of course, but emerges *in situ* as the child is in the process of encountering other persons and interacting with them in various ways. In one of these ways other persons make funny noises and hand movements at the child and seemingly expect some response in return. To come to see these noises and hand movements as something with communicative significance that might be learned and used, the child has to understand that they are motivated by a special kind of intention, namely, a communicative intention. But understanding a communicative intention can only take place within some kind of joint attentional scene, which provides its social-cognitive ground; moreover, learning to express the same communicative intention (using the same communicative means) as other persons requires an understanding that the participant roles in this communicative event can potentially be reversed: I can do for her what she just did for me. The current account thus focuses on, in turn: (a) joint attentional scenes as the social-cognitive grounding of early language acquisition; (b) understanding communicative intentions as the main social-cognitive process by means of which children comprehend adult use of linguistic symbols; and (c) role-reversal imitation as the main cultural learning process by means of which children acquire the active use of linguistic symbols.

Joint Attentional Scenes

Many theorists, stretching back many centuries in the Western intellectual tradition, describe acts of linguistic reference in terms of just two items: the symbol and its referent in the perceptual world. But this view turns out to be quite inadequate. It is theoretically inadequate, as demonstrated by the philosophers Wittgenstein (1953) and Quine (1960), and it is empirically inadequate in many ways, perhaps especially its inability to account for the acquisition and use of linguistic symbols whose connections to the perceptual world are tenuous at best, that is to say, most linguistic symbols that are not proper names or basic-level nouns (e.g., verbs, prepositions, articles, conjunctions; see Tomasello and Merriman, eds., 1995). We must therefore explicitly acknowledge the theoretical point that linguistic reference is a *social* act in which one person attempts to get another person to focus her attention on something in the world. And we must also acknowledge the empirical fact that linguistic reference can only be understood within the context of certain kinds of social interactions that I will call joint attentional scenes (Bruner, 1983; Clark, 1996; Tomasello, 1988, 1992a).

Joint attentional scenes are social interactions in which the child and the adult are jointly attending to some third thing, and to one another's attention to that third thing, for some reasonably extended length of time. Terms that have been used in past discussions are such things as *joint attentional interaction, joint attentional episode, joint attentional engagement,* and *joint attentional format.* I am introducing a novel, though related, term to make sure that I am able to highlight with enough emphasis two essential features that have not always been highlighted in previous discussions of this general phenomenon.

The first essential feature concerns what is included in joint attentional scenes. On the one hand, joint attentional scenes are not perceptual events; they include only a subset of things in the child's perceptual world. On the other hand, joint attentional scenes are also not linguistic events; they contain more things than those explicitly indicated in any set of linguistic symbols. Joint attentional scenes thus occupy a kind of middle ground—an essential middle ground of socially shared reality—between the larger perceptual world and smaller linguistic world. The second essential feature needing emphasis is the fact that the child's understanding of a joint attentional scene includes as an integral element the child herself and her own role in the interaction conceptualized from the same "outside" perspective as the other person and the object so that they are all in a common representational format—which turns out to be of crucial importance for the process of acquiring a linguistic symbol.

I may illustrate these two essential features of joint attentional scenes with an example. Suppose that a child is on the floor playing with a toy, but also is perceiving many other things in the room. An adult enters the room and proceeds to join the child in her play with the toy. The joint attentional scene becomes those objects and activities that the child knows are part of the attentional focus of both herself and the adult, and they both know that this is their focus (it is not joint attention if, by accident, they are both focused on the same thing but unaware of the partner; Tomasello, 1995a). In this case, such things as the rug and the sofa and the child's diaper are not part of the joint attentional scene, even though the child as an individual may be perceiving them basically continuously, because they are not part of "what we are doing." On the other hand, if the adult enters the room with a new diaper and readies the child for a diaper change on the rug, then the joint attentional scene is something totally different. In this case, the focal items include the diapers, the pins, and perhaps the rug—but not the toys because "we" have no goals with respect to the toys. The point is that joint attentional scenes are defined intentionally; that is, they gain their identity and coherence from the child's and the adult's understandings of "what we are doing" in terms of the goal-directed activities in which we are engaged. In one case we are playing with a toy, which means that certain objects and activities are part of what we are doing, and in another case we are changing a diaper, which brings into existence, from the point of view of our joint attention, a whole different set of objects and activities. In any given joint attentional scene, then, we are mutually concerned with only a subset of all the things we might be perceiving in the situation.

But the joint attentional scene is not the same thing as the referential scene symbolized explicitly in a piece of language; the joint attentional scene simply provides the intersubjective context within which the symbolization process occurs. For example, using adults to highlight the general principles involved, let us suppose that an

American is in a Hungarian train station when a native speaker approaches and starts talking to her in Hungarian—out of nowhere, so to speak. It is very unlikely that in this situation the American visitor will acquire the conventional use of any Hungarian word or phrase. But suppose now that the American goes to the window where train tickets are sold, manned by another Hungarian speaker, and begins trying to obtain a ticket. In this situation it is possible that the visitor may learn some Hungarian words and phrases because the two interactants share an understanding of each other's interactive goals in this context in terms of gaining information about train schedules, obtaining a ticket, exchanging money, and so forth—goals expressed directly through the execution of meaningful and already understood actions such as the actual giving and exchanging of ticket and money. The key for language learning in such a situation would be for the native speaker to use some novel word or phrase in a way that suggested her reason for making that utterance at that time—for example, in reaching for the bills in the visitor's hand or in offering her ticket or some change. In such cases the learner makes an inference of the following type: if that unknown expression meant X, then it would be *relevant* to the ticketseller's goal in this joint attentional scene (Sperber and Wilson, 1986; Nelson, 1996). The referential scene as symbolized in language thus concerns only a subset of things that are going on in the intentional interactions in the joint attentional scene.

The second key fact about joint attentional scenes is that, from the child's point of view, they include on an equal conceptual plane all three participating elements: the entity of joint attention, the adult, and the child herself. The inclusion of the child herself is not something that I, or anyone else to my knowledge, have emphasized previously, and indeed joint attention is sometimes characterized as the child coordinating attention between just two things: the object and the adult. But as outlined in Chapter 3, as the child begins to monitor adults' attention to outside entities, that outside entity sometimes turns out to be the child herself—and so she begins to monitor adults' attention to her and thus to see herself from the outside, as it were. She also comprehends the role of the adult from this same outside vantage point, and so, overall, it is as if she were viewing the whole scene from above, with herself as just one player in it. This is as opposed to the way other primate species and six-month-old human infants view the social interaction from an "inside" perspective, in which the other participants appear in one format (third-person exteroception) and "I" appears in another different format (first-person proprioception; see Barresi and Moore, 1996). The distinction I am highlighting here is the same one made by imagery theorists when they distinguish mental images from the ego view (e.g., I see a ball speeding away from my foot) and images from an external view (e.g., I see myself [my whole body] kicking the ball—from an external perspective, in much the same way I see other people kicking balls).

The importance of this way of understanding joint attentional scenes cannot be overstated. To work as a "format" for language acquisition, the joint attentional scene must be understood by the child as having participant roles that are, in some sense, interchangeable (Bruner, 1983). This allows the child, as we shall see in a moment, to take the adult's role and use a novel word to direct the adult's attention in the same way the adult just used it to direct hers: what I will call role-reversal imitation. For now, let me simply depict a hypothetical joint attentional scene, taken from the child's point of view, as in Figure 4.1. The key points are that (a) out of the perceptual scene the joint attentional scene focuses on a subset of objects and activities for mutual consideration, and out of the joint attentional scene the referential scene focuses on a subset of objects and activities for mutual consideration; and (b) the child is viewing herself as a participant in the scene on a par with the adult and the entity of joint attention.

Understanding Communicative Intentions

Let us imagine now that an adult addresses a novel piece of language to an infant too young to comprehend or participate in a joint attentional scene, much less to understand language. For infants this young the adult is just making noises. Infants this young may on occasion, of course, learn to associate one of these noises with a perceptual event in much the same way a household pet may understand that the sound *dinner* heralds the arrival of food. But this is not language. Sounds become language for young children when and only when they understand that the adult is making that sound with the intention that they attend to something. This understanding is not a foregone conclusion, but a developmental achievement. It requires the understanding of other persons as intentional agents, as outlined in Chapter 3; it requires participation in a joint attentional scene, as just elaborated; and it also requires the understanding of a particular kind of intentional act within a joint attentional scene, namely, a communicative act expressing a communicative intention.

One way to make the point is to look at the behavior of apes and human two-year-olds as experimenters try to communicate with

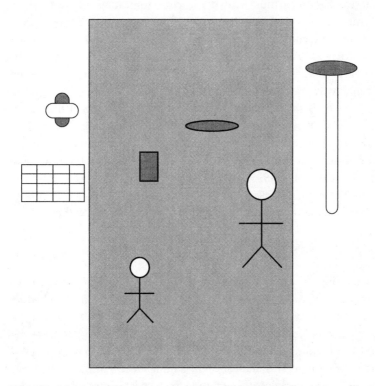

Figure 4.1 A joint attentional scene containing child (self), adult, and two objects of joint attention, with three perceived objects not in the joint attentional scene.

them using communicative signs that are totally novel for them. Tomasello, Call, and Gluckman (1997) did just this, indicating for both chimpanzees and two- to three-year-old human children which of three distinct containers contained a reward by (a) pointing to the correct container; (b) placing a small wooden marker on top of the correct container; or (c) holding up an exact replica of the correct container. Children already knew about pointing, but they did not know about using markers and replicas as communicative signs. They nevertheless used these novel signs very effectively to find the reward. In contrast, no ape was able to do this for any of the communicative signs that it did not know before the experiment. One explanation of these results is that the apes were not able to understand that the human being had intentions toward their own attentional states. The apes thus treated the communicative attempts of the human as discriminative cues on a par with all other types of discriminative cues that have to be laboriously learned over repeated experiences. The children, in contrast, treated each communicative attempt as an expression of the adult's intention to direct their attention in ways relevant to the current situation.

That is to say, the children understood something of the experimenter's communicative intentions. The conceptualization and explanation of communicative intentions has a rich philosophical history (see Levinson, 1983, for a useful review), but I will follow along the lines of Clark (1996), who gives a more psychologically based account of some of these same issues. In the current analysis, to understand your communicative intention I must understand that:

You intend for [me to share attention to (X)].

According to all analysts from Grice (1975) forward, the understanding of a communicative intention must have this embedded structure. Thus, if you come and push me down into a chair I will recognize your intention that I sit down, but if you tell me "Sit down" I will recognize your intention that I attend to your proposal that I sit down. This analysis makes quite clear that the understanding of a communicative intention is a special case of the understanding of an intention; it is understanding another person's intention toward my attentional state. Understanding this is clearly more complex than understanding another person's intention *simpliciter.* To understand that another person's intention is to kick a ball, I must simply determine her goal with respect to the ball. But to understand what another person intends when she makes the sound "Ball!" in my direction, I must determine her goal with respect to my intentional/attentional states toward some third entity.

The current account thus derives in a fairly straightforward way from my previous analysis of children's understanding of others as intentional agents, and their understanding and viewing of the self as an intentional agent who participates in joint attentional scenes like other intentional agents. In this formulation, only a child who can monitor the intentional states of others toward herself—indeed toward her own intentional states—can understand a communicative intention. If we attempt to display this diagrammatically, and differentiate it from the case of chimpanzees who do not understand communicative intentions, we get something like Figure 4.2. Figure 4.2a depicts the experience of the chimpanzee as it sees another individual "arm-raise." The chimpanzee first sees the "arm-raise"; this is followed by its expectation of what is going to happen next (given its experience in similar situations in the past). Figure 4.2b depicts the experience of the child as she successfully comprehends the adult's linguistic attempt to get her to attend to an outside entity. The first panel depicts the child viewing herself externally as a participant in the interaction in which the adult is trying to get her to attend to X, and the second panel depicts the child actually responding appropriately to the adult's proposal and coming to share attention to X with her (both participants attend to the object and to one another's attention to the object).

Role-Reversal Imitation and Intersubjectivity

Now that the child is equipped to comprehend the communicative intentions of other persons, she must be able to use this comprehension to learn to produce the piece of language she has compre-

Figure 4.2a What chimpanzees conceptualize when they perceive and interpret a gestural signal: first they see the partner gesture, and then they imagine what the partner will do next. Self is not conceptualized.

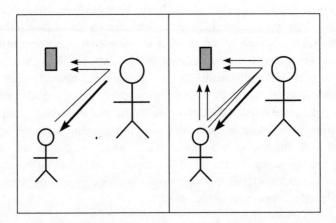

Figure 4.2b What human infants conceptualize when they perceive and interpret a linguistic symbol: first they understand that the partner intends for them to share attention, and then they imagine what the sharing would be like. Sharing means that both partners attend both to the referent and to one another's attention to the referent. Self is conceptualized in the same way as the partner.

hended. This of course brings us back to cultural learning, that is, imitative learning. But in learning to produce a communicative symbol the process of imitative learning is different from the imitative learning of other types of intentional actions. For example, if the child sees an adult operate a novel toy in a particular way and then imitatively learns to do the same thing, there is a parallel in the way the adult and child treat the toy—the child just substitutes herself for the adult. However, when an adult addresses the child with a novel communicative symbol intended to refer her attention to that toy, and the child wants to imitatively learn this communicative behavior, the situation changes. The reason is that, as just elaborated, the adult's goal in using the communicative symbol involves the child herself—specifically, the adult intends things toward the child's attentional state. Consequently, if the child simply substitutes herself for the adult she will end up directing the symbol to herself—which is not what is needed.

To learn to use a communicative symbol in a conventionally appropriate manner, the child must engage in what I have called role-reversal imitation (Tomasello, in press). That is, the child must learn to use a symbol toward the adult in the same way the adult used it toward her. This is clearly a process of imitative learning in which the child aligns herself with the adult in terms of both the goal and the means for attaining that goal; it is just that in this case the child must not only substitute herself for the adult as actor (which occurs in all types of cultural learning) but also substitute the adult for herself as the target of the intentional act (i.e., she must substitute the adult's attentional state as goal for her own attentional state as goal). If we look back at the second panel of Figure 4.2b, we see that the role reversal involved in this kind of imitative learning derives in a straightforward way from the external view inherent in the joint attentional scene. The child's role and the adult's role in the joint attentional scene are both understood from an "external" point of view, and so they may be interchanged freely when the need arises. (An interesting twist on this story is that some children at an early age, and all children at later ages, learn new pieces of language from observing third parties talking to one another (e.g., Brown, in press). The process of substituting participants for one another is still the basic process; it is just that in this case the child is not one of the original participants in the linguistic interchange. Learning language in this way has not been studied in enough detail for us to know how children accomplish this feat, or if it creates special difficulties for them early in development.

The result of this process of role-reversal imitation is a linguistic symbol: a communicative device understood intersubjectively from both sides of the interaction. That is to say, this learning process ensures that the child understands that she has acquired a symbol that is socially "shared" in the sense that she can assume in most circumstances that the listener both comprehends and can produce that same symbol—and the listener also knows that they can both comprehend and produce the symbol. The process of understanding communicative signals—as in chimpanzee and some prelinguistic infant gestural communication—is very different in that each participant understands its own role only, from its own inside perspective. But even in the case of nonlinguistic gestures, if the learning process involves the understanding of communicative intentions and the execution of role-reversal imitation inside a joint attentional scene, the product will be a communicative symbol. Thus, if a child learns to point for others by imitatively learning the pointing gesture from adults pointing for her, then her pointing thereby becomes symbolic (see also infants' early "symbolic gestures," from waving "bye-bye" to flapping the arms for a bird, as studied by Acredolo and Goodwyn, 1988). It is interesting to note also that the intersubjectivity inherent in socially shared symbols, but not in one-way signals, sets up many kinds of pragmatic "implicatures" of the type investigated by Grice (1975) concerning expectations that other persons will use the conventional means of expression—that we both know they know—and not others that are more cumbersome or indirect. This happens, for example, when a child comprehends that a novel symbol is being used to indicate some novel aspect of a situation because if the adult had intended some previously-communicated-about aspect of the situation she would have used a known symbol (so-called fast mapping; Carey, 1978).

Overall, then, acquiring the conventional use of intersubjectively understood linguistic symbols requires a child to:

- understand others as intentional agents;
- participate in joint attentional scenes that set the social-cognitive ground for acts of symbolic, including linguistic, communication;
- understand not just intentions but communicative intentions in which someone intends for her to attend to something in the joint attentional scene; and
- reverse roles with adults in the cultural learning process and thereby use toward them what they have used toward her—which actually creates the intersubjectively understood communicative convention or symbol.

Learning linguistic symbols in this way puts young children in a position to begin taking advantage of all kinds of social skills and knowledge preexisting in their local communities and cultures as a whole. But it does more than that. What makes linguistic symbols truly unique from a cognitive point of view is the fact that each symbol embodies a particular perspective on some entity or event: this object is simultaneously a rose, a flower, and a gift. The perspectival nature of linguistic symbols multiplies indefinitely the specificity with which they may be used to manipulate the attention of others, and this fact has profound implications for the nature of cognitive representation, which we will explore later. But in the current context—in which we are concerned with how young children learn new linguistic symbols—it creates a problem. The problem is that this great specificity requires the child not just to determine that the adult has intentions toward her attention, but to identify the specific target the adult intends for her to identify in a specific joint attentional scene.

Social-Interactive Bases of Language Acquisition

We have now equipped the child with several kinds of social-cognitive skills (and we have assumed general primate skills of perception, memory, categorization, and so forth), but there is still the issue of how these skills are used in practice to learn linguistic symbols. The problem—first articulated by Wittgenstein (1953) and then elaborated by Quine (1960)—derives from the perspectival nature of linguistic symbols (although this is not the way these philosophers formulated the issue). Because of the perspectival nature of linguistic symbols, there are no algorithmic procedures for determining a person's specific communicative intention in a specific instance. When an adult holds up a ball and says *dax*, how does the child know whether the adult is referring to just that entity, or to its color, or to some larger class of entities (such as toys), or to the act of holding things up, or to any of an infinite number of other things? Some researchers have attempted to solve this problem by proposing that by the time language acquisition begins children are equipped with certain word-learning "constraints" that automatically orient them to the speaker's intended reference in useful ways (e.g., Markman, 1989, 1992; Gleitman, 1990).

I am skeptical of solutions involving "preestablished harmony" of this type, and have opted instead for an approach based on children's social-pragmatic understanding of adults' communicative intentions in context (Tomasello, 1992a, 1995c, in press). Thus, at least part of my solution to Wittgenstein's problem lies in the child's understanding of adult communicative intentions as grounded inside a meaningful joint attentional scene—what Wittgenstein called a "form of life"—with this understanding being independent of any understanding of the to-be-learned language (although it may, of course, depend on the child's understanding of other language in the situation). How this works in practice is often quite subtle and complex, as children must identify adult communicative intentions in the flow of ongoing social interaction and discourse. Another part of the solution derives from the same place as the problem. The perspectival nature of linguistic symbols means that in many cases these symbols contrast in meaning with one another—they are in a sense defined with respect to one another, as in *buy, sell, loan, borrow*—and this helps children to learn subtly different meanings, especially after they have learned some basic words.

Joint Attention and Early Language

Bruner (1975, 1983) was the first researcher of children's language acquisition to appreciate Wittgenstein's problem and to propose an answer. Following Wittgenstein's general approach, Bruner claimed that the child acquires the conventional use of a linguistic symbol by learning to participate in an interactive format (form of life, joint attentional scene) that she understands first nonlinguistically, so that the adult's language can be grounded in shared experiences whose social significance she already appreciates. One key component of this process is obviously a child who can understand adults as intentional beings so that she can share attention with them in specific contexts. But another component is the preexisting and external social world in which the child lives. To acquire language the child must live in a world that has structured social activities she can understand, as our hypothetical visitor to Hungary understood the process of buying tickets and going places on trains. For children, this often involves the recurrence of the same general activity on a regular or routine basis so that they can come to discern how the activity works and how the various social roles in it function. And of course if we are interested in language acquisition it must be the case that the adult uses a novel linguistic symbol in a way that the child can comprehend as relevant to that shared activity (in a way that the first Hungarian speaker at the train station did not). In general, if a child were born into a world in which the same event never recurred, the same object never appeared twice, and adults never used the same language in the same context, it is difficult to see how that child—whatever her cognitive capabilities—could acquire a natural language.

A variety of studies have shown that after children have begun progressing in language acquisition they learn new words best in joint attentional scenes that are socially shared with others, often ones that are recurrent in their daily experience such as bathing, feeding, diaper changing, book reading, and traveling in the car. These activities are in many ways analogous to the buying-tickets-in-a-train-station scenario in that the child understands her own and the adult's goals in the situation, which enables her to infer the relevance of the adult's language to those goals, which leads to inferences about her precise focus of attention. Thus, Tomasello and Todd (1983) documented that children who spent more time in joint attentional activities with their mothers between the ages of twelve and eighteen months had larger vocabularies at eighteen months of age (see also Smith et al., 1988; Tomasello, Mannle, and Kruger, 1986). With regard to the adult's use of language inside these joint attentional scenes, Tomasello and Farrar (1986) found both correlational and experimental support for the hypothesis that mothers who used their language in attempts to follow into their child's attention (i.e., to talk about an object that was already the focus of the child's interest and attention) had children with larger vocabularies than mothers who used their language in attempts to direct the child's attention to something new (see also Akhtar, Dunham, and Dunham, 1991; Dunham, Dunham, and Curwin, 1993).

Perhaps of special importance, Carpenter, Nagell, and Tomasello (1998) found some similar relationships at an even earlier age, indeed as children were just beginning to learn and use language. They found that infants who spent more time in joint attentional engagement with their mothers at twelve months of age comprehended and produced more language at that same early age and in the months immediately following. They also found that mothers who followed into their child's attentional focus with words at twelve months of age had children with larger comprehension vocabularies in the months immediately following (with relationships to language production showing up a bit later). When these two variables—the time the child spent in joint attentional engagement and the mother's tendency to "follow into" the child's attentional focus when she used referential language—were used together in regression equations, over half of the variance in children's language comprehension and production was predicted at several points during the period from twelve to fifteen months of age, with each variable accounting for significant amounts of unique variance. A number of measures of children's nonsocial cognitive development—mostly involving their knowledge of objects and space—emerged in an uncorrelated fashion with language and the other joint attentional activities, providing evidence that the correlation of joint attentional engagement and language was not just the result of some generalized developmental advance.

The clear finding of this study—which confirms the correlational and experimental findings of similar studies with slightly older children—is that children's emerging ability to engage in nonlinguistically mediated joint attentional activities with adults at around one year of age is integrally related to their newly emerging linguistic skills (see Rollins and Snow, 1999, for some similar findings for joint attention and early syntactic skills). This finding is important because it demonstrates that the well-known age correspondence between joint attentional skills and language—both emerge in the months on either side of the child's first birthday, with nonlinguistic joint attentional skills emerging a bit earlier—is not a coincidence. The problem that this finding presents for theories of early language acquisition that do not focus on the social dimensions of the process is immediate and serious. For theories that focus primarily on the cognitive dimensions of word learning (e.g., Markman, 1989) or on the associative learning processes involved (Smith, 1995), the question is why language acquisition begins when it does. Why does it begin directly on the heels of the emergence of joint attentional skills? And any answer that invokes non-social cognitive or learning processes—for example, that children at one year of age for the first time become able to conceptualize or learn new sorts of things in general—must then answer the question of why early language emerges in a correlated fashion with nonlinguistic social-cognitive and social-interactive skills. To my knowledge, the only existing theory of early word learning and language acquisition that can account for these findings is the social-pragmatic theory as espoused by Bruner (1983), Nelson (1985), and Tomasello (1992a, 1995c, in press).

Interestingly, in the Carpenter, Nagell, and Tomasello (1998) study the relationships with maternal "following in" language and the child's language learning became weaker as the child got older. This is an intriguing finding because it suggests the possibility that mothers using their language to follow into the child's attentional focus is a kind of scaffolding for early language acquisition in that it helps nascent language learners to discern the adult's communicative intentions, but that this kind of scaffolding is not necessary as the child gets older and becomes more skillful at determining those communicative intentions in less accommodating linguistic interactions. Indeed, from at least eighteen months of age, young children show truly astounding abilities to discern adult communicative intentions in a wide variety of interactive contexts that are not specifically adapted for them.

Learning Words in the Flow of Social Interaction

It happens with some frequency in Western middle-class culture that an adult holds up or points to an object while telling the child its name. The social dimensions of this process are manifest: the child must somehow determine which aspect of the situation the adult wants her to focus her attention on. Despite the complexities of this situation as analyzed by Wittgenstein and Quine, this case is nevertheless *relatively* simple because such things as visually following gaze direction and pointing gestures are so basic for infants. It turns out, however, that in many cultures of the world adults do not engage in this kind of naming game with young children (Brown, in press). Moreover, even in Western middle-class culture adults do not frequently use this naming game with words other than object labels. For example, they use verbs most often to regulate or anticipate children's behavior, not to name actions for them; indeed it would seem bizarre if an adult were to exclaim to the child: "Look, this is an instance of putting (or giving or taking)" (Tomasello and Kruger, 1992). Instead, children hear many verbs mostly as the adult directs their behavior in such utterances as "Put your toys away" while pointing to the toybox. It is clear that in such cases the social-pragmatic cues that might indicate the adult's intended referent for the child (i.e., the action of putting) are much more subtle, complex, and variegated than in the ostensive object-naming context, and indeed they change in fundamental ways from situation to situation: the adult requests the child to eat her peas by directing the spoon at the child's face, requests that the child give her something by holding out her hand, and requests that the toys be put away by pointing to the destination desired. There is thus no standardized "original naming game" for verbs as there is for object labels for some children (Tomasello, 1995c). The situation only gets more complex if we bring in other types of words such as prepositions (Tomasello, 1987).

A number of recent studies have demonstrated experimentally that young children can learn new words in a variety of complex social-interactive situations. They learn new words not just when adults stop and name objects for them but also in the ongoing flow of social interaction in which both they and the adult are trying to do things. In none of these cases can the child count on the adult following into her already established focus of attention; rather, she must adapt to the adult's focus of attention. For example, Baldwin (1991, 1993) taught nineteen-month-old infants new words in two new situations. In one situation the adult followed into the infant's focus of attention, and, as in other studies, the infants learned the new word quite well—better than in any other condition in fact. But the adult also successfully taught the infants new words in a situation in which the adult looked at and labeled an object the child was not looking at, thus requiring the child to look up and then determine the adult's attentional focus.

My collaborators and I have conducted a series of studies that demonstrate the same point but even more dramatically. In all of the studies we set up situations in which an adult talked to a child as they engaged together in various games, with novel words being introduced as naturally as possible into the flow of the game. In all cases there were multiple potential referents available; that is, there were multiple novel referents for which the child had no existing means of linguistic expression and the novel word was introduced in a single type of linguistic context. Various social-pragmatic cues to the adult's intended referent were provided in different studies to see if children were sensitive to them. The studies were designed so that none of the well-known word-learning constraints that various investigators have proposed (e.g., whole object, mutual exclusivity, syntactic bootstrapping; Markman, 1989, Gleitman, 1990) would be helpful to the child in distinguishing among possible referents. The studies were also designed so that eye-gaze direction was never diagnostic of the adult's referential intention. In all studies the children ranged from eighteen to twenty-four months of age, and in all cases the majority of children learned the novel words in either comprehension or production or both (and better than in various control conditions).

To give something of the feel for the kinds of situations in which children managed to read the adult's communicative intentions, and so learn the new word, I summarize here seven situations in which eighteen- to twenty-four-month-old children learned new words with some facility. In each case, the original study gives the details of control conditions and the like.

- In the context of a finding game, an adult announced her intention to "find the toma" and then searched in a row of buckets all containing novel objects. Sometimes she found it in the first bucket searched. Sometimes, however, she had to search longer, rejecting unwanted objects by scowling at them and replacing them in their buckets until she found the one she wanted. Children learned the new word for the object the adult intended to find (indicated by a smile and termination of search) *regardless of whether or how many objects were rejected during the search process.* (Tomasello and Barton, 1994; Tomasello, Strosberg, and Akhtar, 1996)

- Also in the context of a finding game, an adult had the child find four different objects in four different hiding places, one of which was a very distinctive toy barn. Once the child had learned which objects went with which places, the adult announced her intention to "find the gazzer." She then went to the toy barn, but it turned out to be "locked." She frowned at the barn and then proceeded to another hiding place, saying "Let's see what else we can find," and took out an object with a smile. Later, children demonstrated that they had learned "gazzer" for the object they knew the experimenter wanted in the barn *even though they had not seen the object after they heard the new word, and even though the adult had frowned at the barn and smiled at a distractor object.* (Akhtar and Tomasello, 1996; Tomasello et al., 1996)

· An adult set up a script with a child in which a novel action was performed always and only with a particular toy character (e.g., Big Bird on a swing, with other character-action pairings demonstrated as well). She then picked up Big Bird and announced "Let's meek Big Bird," but the swing was nowhere to be found—so the action was not performed. Later, using a different character, children demonstrated their understanding of the new verb *even though they had never seen the referent action performed after the novel verb was introduced.* (Akhtar and Tomasello, 1996)

· An adult announced her intention to "dax Mickey Mouse" and then proceeded to perform one action accidentally and another intentionally (or sometimes in reverse order). Children learned the word for the intentional not the accidental action *regardless of which came first in the sequence.* (Tomasello and Barton, 1994)

· A child, her mother, and an experimenter played together with three novel objects. The mother then left the room. A fourth object was brought out and the child and experimenter played with it, noting the mother's absence. When the mother returned to the room, she looked at the four objects together and exclaimed "Oh look! A modi! A modi!" Understanding that the mother would not be excited about the objects she had already played with previously, but that she very well might be excited about the object she was seeing for the first time, *children learned the new word for the object the mother had not seen previously.* (Akhtar, Carpenter, and Tomasello, 1996)

· An adult introduced a child to a curved pipe, down which objects could be thrown to great effect. In one condition she first threw one novel object down, and then another, and then announced "Now, modi" as she threw another novel object. In this condition children thought *modi* was the name of that object. In another condition the adult took out a novel object and first did one thing with it, and then another thing, and then announced "Now, modi" as she threw it down the pipe. In this condition children thought *modi* was the name of the action of throwing objects down a pipe. The common element is that in each case *the child assumed that the adult was talking about the entity, either object or action, that was new in the communicative situation.* (Tomasello and Akhtar, 1995)

- An adult played a merry-go-round game with a child several times. They then moved on to do something else. The adult then returned to the merry-go-round. As she did so, in one condition she readied the merry-go-round for play, then held out a novel object to the child while alternating gaze between child and merry-go-round, saying "Widgit, Jason." In this case, the children thought that *widgit* was a request for them to use the new toy with the merry-go-round. In the other condition the adult did not ready the merry-go-round for play and did not alternate gaze to the apparatus, but instead simply held out the novel object to the child and said "Jason, widget" while alternating gaze between object and child. In this case, children thought that *widgit* was the name of the object, not the action associated with the merry-go-round. (Tomasello and Akhtar, 1995)

Although any one of these studies might be explained in other ways (e.g., see Samuelson and Smith, 1998), in my view when they are considered as a group most plausible explanation is that by the time they are eighteen to twenty-four months of age children have developed a deep and flexible understanding of other persons as intentional beings, and so they are quite skillful at determining the adult's communicative intentions in a wide variety of relatively novel communicative situations—assuming that they can find some way to understand these situations as joint attentional scenes. The assumption that the adult's language is relevant to their social and instrumental activities is simply the natural expression of this intentional understanding. Thus, in several of these studies, the child had to first understand that she and the adult were playing a finding game. Given this intentional understanding (and a few details of the game itself), the child could then infer that when the adult frowned at an object it was not the one she was seeking—unless the frown came when the adult was trying unsuccessfully to open the toy barn containing the desired toy, in which case the frown meant frustration at not being able to obtain the intended toy. The point is that the adult's specific behaviors such as a smile or a frown are not sufficient by themselves to indicate for the child the adult's intended referent. But in a mutually understood joint attentional scene, they may be. It is also important to note that in the two last studies described, the event structure of the game and the adult's behavior and discourse were such powerful indicators of intentionality that the child was led to believe that the exact same utterance in one case indicated an object and in another case indicated an action.

The overall picture is this. To acquire the conventional use of a linguistic symbol, the child must be able to determine the adult's communicative intentions (the adult's intentions toward her attention), and then engage in a process of role-reversal imitation in which she uses the new symbol toward the adult in the same way and for the same communicative purpose that the adult used it toward her. Initially, at one year of age, children are able to accomplish this feat mostly in highly repetitive and predictable joint attentional scenes in which the adult follows into the child's attentional focus. But as children become more skillful at determining adult communicative intentions in a wider variety of joint attentional scenes, highly structured formats with highly sensitive adults become less crucial to the process; the child must establish joint attention in more active ways by determining the adult's attentional focus in a highly varied set of social-communicative contexts. Of possible relevance to this account is the finding that some children acquire their native language in cultures in which there is very little of the heavy scaffolding and attentional sensitivity that characterize many Western middle-class families (Schieffelin and Ochs, 1986). Although quantitative studies have yet to be done, by some accounts these children seldom acquire large numbers of words before their second birthdays (L. deLeon, personal communication), possibly implying that these children acquire the vast majority of their linguistic symbols only after they are able to be more active in establishing joint attentional scenes and determining adult communicative intentions within the flow of ongoing social interaction.

Perspective, Contrast, and Bootstrapping

All of these word-learning studies, as well as most other word-learning studies, have to do with how children determine, in a given situation, the specific object, event, or property to which the adult is referring. Learning what an adult *means* in using a particular word or linguistic expression in general is something else again. And so, for example, when the child in an experiment picks out a particular object for the *dax*, we still do not know what other things she might also be willing to call a *dax* (e.g., all things of a particular shape, all things that roll); that is, we do not know either the intension or the extension of her understanding of the word's conventional use. Since most words in natural languages are categorical, we may talk about the cognitive categories that underlie the use of these words. But I prefer to use the more general term *perspective*, which includes as a special case the possibility of placing the same entity into different conceptual categories for different communicative or other purposes. We may then say that linguistic symbols are social conventions for inducing others to construe, or take a perspective on, some experiential situation.

The perspectival nature of linguistic symbols is an integral part of the view of language known as Cognitive or Functional Linguistics. Langacker (1987a) posits three major types of perspective—what he calls construal operations—although he enumerates others as well:

- granularity-specificity (desk chair, chair, furniture, thing);
- perspective (chase-flee, buy-sell, come-go, borrow-lend); and
- function (father, lawyer, man, guest, American).

Fillmore (1985) stresses the role of the recurrent contextual frames within which individual linguistic terms take their meaning. The idea is that invoking a particular linguistic symbol quite often brings with it a perspective on the surrounding context, for example, calling the same piece of real estate *the coast, the shore,* or *the beach,* depending on the contextual frame within which the speech occurs— or calling the same event *selling* or *marketing* depending on the point of view taken on the event. Metaphorical construals point out the freedom and flexibility of this process, as we may say that *Life is a beach* or *The doe is marketing her wares.* In all cases, then, the use of a particular linguistic symbol implies the choice of a particular level of granularity in categorization, a particular perspective or point of view on the entity or event, and in many cases a function in a context. And there are many more specific perspectives that arise in grammatical combinations of various sorts (*He loaded the wagon with hay* versus *He loaded hay onto the wagon,* or *She smashed the vase* versus *The vase was smashed*). Although more will be said about this process in Chapter 5, I take it as obvious that the only reason languages are constructed in this way is that people need to communicate about many different things in many different communicative circumstances from many different points of view—otherwise each entity or event, or even each type of entity or type of event, would have its own one true label—and that would be the end of it.

The most important issue in the current context is what this fact about the nature of language implies about language acquisition (we will explore its ramifications for cognitive representation below). On the one hand the perspectival nature of language would seem to present the child with great difficulties involving referential indeterminacy and the like, but on the other hand perspectives contrast with one another—in effect constrain one another—and so make the problems a bit more manageable. Let us look very briefly at an example (see Clark, 1997, for many other examples for slightly older children). From eighteen to twenty-four months of age my daughter acquired a number of different ways of asking for objects (Tomasello, 1992b, 1998). The major ways were these:

- ask for it by name (and she had many object labels);
- ask for it with the pronoun *that* or *this;*
- ask to *hold* it (typically when you were doing so and she wanted to);
- ask to *have* it (generic);
- ask for it *back* (after you took it from her);
- ask to *get* it for her (typically when inaccessible to her);
- ask to *give* it to her (when you now have it);
- ask to *share* it (i.e., use it along with you);
- ask to *use* it (i.e., use it alone and then return it to you);
- ask to *buy* it for her (at a store);
- ask to *keep* it (if you were threatening to take it away).

Two aspects of these perfectly mundane examples are important to highlight. First is simply that during the early stages of language acquisition the child comes to see that there are many different ways of looking at the same situation; the child learns that the adult is choosing one way, as opposed to other possible ways, of symbolizing the referential scene—and she learns to do the same thing. Sometimes I may ask for an object with some generic request term, but sometimes a situation that takes into account more of the specifics of the particular situation is preferable; I can ask to *have* an object, but perhaps my request would be more effective if I just asked to *use* it; I can ask for the object by name, or I can simply ask for *that* or *it*. What the child is learning at this point is that a linguistic symbol embodies a particular way of construing things—a particular perspective—that is tailored to some communicative situations but not to others. That children do in some sense understand this aspect of the functioning of linguistic symbols is suggested by the fact that they can, from soon after they have started using language productively (eighteen to twenty-four months), refer to the exact same referent with different linguistic expressions in different communicative circumstances (Clark, 1997). It is also a common observation that in their language production children of this age can also hold up a single object and then attribute to it different properties such as *wet*, or *blue*, or *mine* (Bates, 1979). There are some types of linguistic symbols that may be used widely across situations with basically the same meaning, for example, basic-level object names like *cat* and *apple*, but there are always choices—and indeed even basic-level object names are quite often replaced with pronouns by young children in some situations. Linguistic symbols thus come to represent for children perspectives that have some freedom from the perceptual situation, in the sense that other linguistic symbols could have been chosen to indicate the same experience for different communicative purposes.

The second point is that this ability to contrast linguistic expressions with one another in the "same" communicative situation plays a key role in the learning of new words, especially those that have more closely specified meanings. For example, my daughter's learning of terms like *share* and *use* would have been almost impossible, in my view, if she had not already had more generic terms such as *give* and *have* for the basic situation of transfer of possession. The point is that the details of the use of these more specific terms are understood by the child as she first encounters them only in contrast with the generic terms that the adult might have used but did not (Clark, 1987). Why did Mother say I could not *have* it but I could *use* it? Why did she call this thing that looks to me like a dog a *cow*? Some theorists have characterized this process of contrast as an a priori constraint on language acquisition (Markman's, 1989, mutual exclusivity), but I prefer the characterization in terms of a learned pragmatic principle concerning how people use linguistic symbols. Thus, Clark's (1988) argument is that the principle that all words contrast with one another in meaning in some way is really a principle of rational human behavior along the lines of "If someone is using *this* word, rather than *that* word in the current situation, there must be some reason for it." The child then examines the current situation to see if she can discover what distinguishes, for example, the current situation, about which the adult said *share*, from the more common situation in which both she and the adult say *give* or *have*. Although the process has not been studied in much detail, being able to contrast word meanings with one another in this way almost certainly facilitates children's acquisition of new words, particularly those that are "spin-offs" of more conceptually basic situations (see Tomasello, Mannle, and Werdenschlag, 1988, for one example).

Another similar process should also be mentioned in this context, and that is the process of learning new linguistic expressions with help from the linguistic context within which they are embedded. Some versions of this process have been conceived of as so-called syntactic bootstrapping in which the child uses everything from the presence of grammatical markers such as *the* to whole syntactic constructions as hints to the meaning of a word (Brown, 1973; Gleitman, 1990). But there are other, more mundane versions of bootstrapping that are less syntactically based. That is, if the child hears *I'm tamming now* as the adult bangs her hand against the desk, the child can infer that the action being referred to by *tamming* is not one that changes the state of the object acted upon because the desk is not even mentioned (see Fisher, 1996). More subtle versions of this process may also occur if the child hears, for example, a verb with a particular locative preposition, as in *He is meeking it out of the box*, in which case she can assume that the "out of" meaning is not a part of the verb's meaning since it has its own expression in the prepositional phrase. This process may be thought of as a kind of contrast as well, in that the child must apportion the meaning of the adult's utterance as a whole into its component parts, each of which plays its role in the meaning as a whole; the novel word must then be assigned its portion of the whole—what Tomasello (1992b) called a functionally based distributional analysis (see also Goodman, McDonough, and Brown, 1998). In combination with the principle of contrast as traditionally conceived, then, the child who knows some language can hear a new word and contrast it with others that the speaker might have chosen in its stead (paradigms), as well as with the other words in the utterance that are doing their part to express the entire utterance meaning (syntagms). The inferences children make in such instances are in all cases pragmatic in the sense that they are grounded in children's understanding of why the adult has chosen to use this word in this way in the current utterance in the current joint attentional scene. The ability to make these inferences presumably increases as children learn more language.

We may thus characterize the essence of linguistic symbols as (a) intersubjective and (b) perspectival. A linguistic symbol is intersubjective in the sense that it is something the user produces, understands, and understands that others understand; but this intersubjectivity may also be characteristic of other types of communicative symbols, including everything from the symbolic gestures of eighteen-month-olds to the flags of nations. Therefore, intersubjectivity is of crucial importance for understanding the way linguistic symbols work—and how they are distinguished from the communicative signals of other animal species—but it does not single out linguistic symbols among other types of human symbols. What distinguishes linguistic symbols most clearly is their perspectival nature. This feature derives from the human ability to take different perspectives on the same thing for different communicative purposes and, conversely, to treat different entities as the same for some communicative purpose; as perspectives are embodied in symbols, they create contrasts. The intersubjectivity of linguistic symbols becomes apparent to young children very early in the process of language acquisition, but their perspectival nature emerges more gradually as the child sees that there are alternative ways to look at things and talk about them. This creates problems for acquisition—because now the possibilities for intended referents are multiplied indefinitely—but it also creates some constraints as the child learns things about why people choose one means of expression over another in particular communicative circumstances.

Sensory-Motor and Symbolic Representation

There is no question that the acquisition of language enables human children to communicate and interact with conspecifics in uniquely powerful ways. Language is a much more powerful medium of communication than the vocal and gestural communication of other primate species, if for no other reason than the greater specificity and flexibility of reference it enables. But in addition I would claim that the process of acquiring and using linguistic symbols fundamentally transforms the nature of human cognitive representation.

Although much has been written about language and cognitive representation, I believe that the importance of the intersubjective and perspectival nature of linguistic symbols has not been fully appreciated. Many researchers do not believe that acquiring a language has any great effect on the nature of cognitive representation because they view linguistic symbols as simply handy tags for already formulated concepts (e.g., Piaget, 1970). Other researchers characterize nonlinguistic cognition in terms of a kind of "language of thought," and thereby, in my opinion, miss the essential difference between nonsymbolic and symbolic forms of representation (e.g., Fodor, 1983). The researchers who are specifically concerned with the influence of language on cognition (e.g., Lucy, 1992; Levinson, 1983) have mostly focused on the effect of acquiring one or another particular natural language on processes of nonlinguistic cognition, not on the effect of acquiring a language as opposed to no language. The major exception to this general neglect is Premack's (1983) proposal, based on work with language-trained and non-language-trained apes, that nonlinguistic representation is imagistic whereas linguistic representation is propositional. However, the term *propositional* is not especially helpful in this context because, prototypically, a proposition can only be realized in some configuration of linguistic symbols. I believe we must go deeper than that.

Categories and Image Schemas

Remembering specific objects, conspecifics, events, and all other aspects of personal experience—and in some cases anticipating future experiences based on this recall—is the *sine qua non* of cognition, and many mammalian species have cognitive representations of this type. In addition, many mammalian species form categories of perceptual and motor experiences, in the sense that they treat as similar all phenomena that are identical for some perceptual or motor purpose (see Chapter 2). Perhaps not surprisingly, human infants also remember various kinds of learning experiences from the first few weeks of life, and they begin to form perceptual categories of objects and events from fairly early in development as well, from three to six months for some kinds of perceptual forms (see Haith and Benson, 1997, for a review). Prelinguistic infants also may be able to understand some very simple causal sequences in which one event "enables" another (Mandler, 1992; Bauer, Hestergaard, and Dow, 1994).

The ability of organisms to operate not only with perceptions of the environment but also with sensory-motor representations of the environment—especially object categories and image schemas of dynamic events—is one of the most remarkable phenomena of the natural world. Most importantly, it gives organisms the ability to profit from personal experience via memory and categorization and so to be less dependent on Nature's ability to foresee the future via specific, and often inflexible, biological adaptations. The kinds of sensory-motor representations that human infants work with, to my mind at least, seem to be of this same general type. However, adult human beings naturally create—and post-infancy children naturally learn and use—another form of representation. They create and use exogenous, socially constituted, publicly displayed symbols such as language, pictures, texts, and maps. The hypothesis is that working with these kinds of external, cultural representations in social interaction has important implications for the nature of internal, individual representations—in a way reminiscent of some of Vygotsky's (1978) proposals about internalization, but with some differences as well based on the greater knowledge we now have of processes of language acquisition and symbolic development.

The Internalization of Joint Attention into Symbolic Representation

One of the most interesting things about the process of language acquisition is that the adults from whom the child is learning went through the same process earlier in their lives, and across generations the symbolic artifacts that comprise English, Turkish, or whatever language, accumulate modifications as new linguistic forms are created by grammaticization, syntacticization, and other processes of language change—so that today's child is learning the whole historically derived conglomeration. Consequently, when the child learns the conventional use of these well-traveled symbols, what she is learning is the ways that her forebears in the culture have found it useful to manipulate the attention of others in the past. And because the people of a culture, as they move through historical time, evolve many and varied purposes for manipulating one another's attention (and because they need to do this in many different types of discourse situations), today's child is faced with a panoply of different linguistic symbols and constructions that embody many different attentional construals of any given situation. Consequently, as the child internalizes a linguistic symbol—as she learns the human perspectives embodied in a linguistic symbol—she cognitively represents not just the perceptual or motoric aspects of a situation but also one way, among other ways of which she is aware, that the current situation may be attentionally construed by "us," the users of that symbol. The way that human beings use linguistic symbols thus creates a clear break with straightforward perceptual or sensory-motor representations, and it is due entirely to the social nature of linguistic symbols.

It might be objected that nonhuman primates (and human infants) also have many different ways of cognitively construing or representing one and the same situation: one time a conspecific is a friend and the next time an enemy; one time a tree is for climbing to avoid predators and the next time it is a place for making nests. There is no question that in these different interactions with the same entity the individual is deploying its attention differentially depending on its goal at that moment; in Gibsonian terminology, the animal is attending to different affordances of the environment depending on its goal. But shifting attention sequentially in this manner as a function of goal is not the same thing as knowing simultaneously a number of different ways in which something might be construed—in effect, imagining at the same time a number of different possible goals and their implications for attention. An individual language user looks at a tree and, before drawing the attention of her interlocutor to that tree, must decide, based on her assessment of the listener's current knowledge and expectations, whether to use *That tree over there, It,*

The oak, That hundred-year-old oak, The tree, The bagswing tree, That thing in the front yard, The ornament, The embarrassment, or any number of other expressions. She must decide if the tree *is in/is standing in/is growing in/was placed in/is flourishing in* the front yard. And these decisions are not made on the basis of the speaker's direct goal with respect to the object or activity involved, but rather on the basis of her goal with respect to the listener's interest and attention to that object or activity. This means that the speaker knows that the listener shares with her these same choices for construal—again, all available simultaneously. Indeed, the fact that the speaker is, while she is speaking, monitoring the listener's attentional status (and vice versa) means that both participants in a conversation are always aware that there are at least their two actual perspectives on a situation, as well as the many more that are symbolized in unused symbols and constructions.

It seems significant also that linguistic symbols have a materiality to them, in the form of a reliable sound structure, because this is the only way in which they could be socially shared. These public symbols—which the speaker hears herself produce as she produces them—are thus available for perceptual inspection and categorization themselves (which is not true, at least not in the same way, for private sensory-motor representations). This external nature opens the possibility for an additional layer of cognitive representations as children perceive these linguistic symbols while they are being used and construct categories and schemas of them in the form of abstract linguistic categories and constructions—such as nouns and verbs or the transitive or ditransitive constructions in English—which lead to such immensely important abilities as the capacity to metaphorically construe objects as actions, actions as objects, and all kinds of entities in terms of other entities (a phenomenon to be explored more fully in the next chapter). It is difficult to see how a Barbary macaque going about its daily business would have the possibility of taking its own cognitive representations of the environment—in the form of sensory-motor categories and image schemas—and using them as things to be categorized, schematized, and otherwise cognitively manipulated. The public nature of linguistic symbols opens the way for children to treat their cognitive construals as objects of interest, attention, reflection, and mental manipulation in their own right.

The point is not just that linguistic symbols provide handy tags for human concepts or even that they influence or determine the shape of those concepts, though they do both of these things. The point is that the intersubjectivity of human linguistic symbols—and their perspectival nature as one offshoot of this intersubjectivity—means that linguistic symbols do not represent the world more or less directly, in the manner of perceptual or sensory-motor representations, but rather are used by people to induce others to construe certain perceptual/conceptual situations—to attend to them—in one way rather than in another. The users of linguistic symbols are thus implicitly aware that any given experiential scene may be construed from many different perspectives simultaneously, and this breaks these symbols away from the sensory-motor world of objects in space, and puts them instead into the realm of the human ability to view the world in whatever way is convenient for the communicative purpose at hand.

What I want to claim is that participation in these communicative exchanges is internalized by the child in something like the way Vygotsky envisioned it. Internalization is not a mystical process, as some envision it, but merely the normal process of imitative learning as it takes place in this special intersubjective situation: I learn to use the symbolic means that other persons have used to share attention with one another. In imitatively learning a linguistic symbol from other persons in this way, I internalize not only their communicative intention (their intention to get me to share their attention) but also the specific perspective they have taken. As I use this symbol with other persons, I monitor their attentional deployment as a function of the symbols I produce as well, and so I have at my disposal both (a) the two real foci of self and communicative partner and (b) the other possible foci symbolized in other linguistic symbols that might potentially be used in this situation.

Some of the effects of operating with symbols of this type are obvious, in terms of flexibility and relative freedom from perception. But some are more far-reaching and quite unexpected, I think, in the sense that they give children truly new ways of conceptualizing things such as treating objects as actions, treating actions as objects, and myriad types of metaphorical construals of things. These new ways of thinking result from the accumulated effects of engaging in linguistic communication with other persons for some years during early cognitive development. I deal with these more fully in Chapters 5 and 6.

Objects as Symbols

The distinction between sensory-motor representations, based mainly on perception, and linguistic representations, based mainly on conceptual construal and perspective, is not wholly confined to language. There is another phenomenon of early cognitive development that has some similarity to the acquisition and use of linguistic symbols, and that is symbolic play. Somewhere around two years of age young children begin to use objects in various ways that have been called symbolic—as discussed briefly in Chapter 3. For example, a twenty-four-month-old might push a block along the floor and make noises such as "Vroom!" It is almost certainly the case that many of these behaviors, especially when they are produced by children below two years of age, are not truly symbolic, but rather are simply imitations of adult actions with those objects. But at some point children do come to use objects as symbols, and it is no accident that it is in the same general time frame, with perhaps a bit of a lag, as the acquisition of linguistic symbols. My proposal is that children learn to use objects as symbols in much the same way they learn to use linguistic symbols. They begin by attempting to understand another person doing something symbolic "for" them (despite the claims of some researchers, I do not believe that twenty-two-month-olds invent symbols for themselves; see Striano, Tomasello, and Rochat, 1999, for evidence). They see, through whatever means, that Daddy wants me to construe the block as a car, and then they learn to do this "for" other persons in much the way that they reverse roles and produce linguistic symbols for other persons; the fact that the symbol is for the benefit of others is indicated by the way the child looks to other people (and sometimes smiles) when producing a play symbol. Early play symbols are thus both imitated from others and produced for others as attempts to get them to construe things in a certain way. As they get older, of course, children begin to produce play symbols solely for themselves, much as they begin to talk to themselves only after they have learned first to talk with others.

In a series of elegant experiments, DeLoache (1995) has shown that children have special difficulty in understanding an adult's intention that they use a physical object as a symbol—for example, a scale model of a room to be used as a complex symbol for the whole room. DeLoache claims that this difficulty emanates from the fact that they cannot easily see the scale model as both a real object, with sensory-motor affordances, and a symbolic object with the intentional/symbolic affordances given to it by the adult demonstrator—what she calls "the dual representation problem." It is noteworthy in this context that in the study by Tomasello, Striano, and Rochat (in press; described in Chapter 3) somewhat younger children displayed this difficulty in especially poignant form as they often physically reached for a toy replica that the adult wanted them to see as symbolic. Children had further difficulty when they tried to interpret the adult's communicative intention that they see an artifact with other intentional affordances as a symbol, for example, to see a cup as a hat. The problem would seem to be that a cup is not only a sensory-motor object, and not only a symbol for a hat, but also a cultural artifact with intentional affordances for drinking. Because in this situation there are actually three competing representational construals of the object—sensory-motor, intentional, and symbolic—the researchers dubbed this the "triune representational problem."

When combined with my analysis of linguistic symbols and gestures, then, the outcome is as follows. By twelve to eighteen months of age children comprehend and sometimes use linguistic symbols on the basis of their skills of social cognition and cultural learning, and at around this same age they begin to comprehend and use symbolic gestures as well. They may begin to comprehend and use objects as symbols in this same general time period, but construing one object as if it were another—in either comprehension or production—is difficult for children this young because they cannot inhibit their sensory-motor schemes that activate whenever a manipulable object enters prehensile space, and thus this skill emerges a bit later. Additional difficulties are created when children attempt to comprehend and use an object with a known intentional affordance to symbolically represent another object in an unconventional way (e.g., a cup is a hat)—clearly indicating the competing construals. At some point children do learn to deal effectively with objects used as symbols, including many kinds of graphic symbols, scale models, numerals, graphs, and the like. In doing so they internalize the communicative intentions behind the physical symbol—what the map maker is telling the map reader, so to speak—and these are another source of rich cognitive representations with a perspectival dimension that, like linguistic symbols, may be internalized and used as aids for thinking. For now the central point is simply that the cultural/intentional/symbolic dimension of children's cognitive representations in early childhood makes itself felt not only in language but also in other forms of symbolic activity, and these other forms provide additional support for the view of human symbols as inherently social, intersubjective, and perspectival—which makes them fundamentally different from the forms of sensory-motor representation common to all primates and other mammals.

Symbolic Representation as Attention Manipulation

In the current theoretical perspective, learning to use linguistic symbols means learning to manipulate (influence, affect) the interest and attention of another intentional agent with whom one is interacting intersubjectively. That is to say, linguistic communication is nothing other than a manifestation and extension, albeit a very special manifestation and extension, of children's already existing skills of joint attentional interaction and cultural learning. Deploying these social-cultural skills to acquire a linguistic symbol in the flow of social interaction—in which children and adults are doing things in the world and attempting to manipulate one another's attention at the same time—requires some special manifestations of these skills including the understanding of joint attentional scenes, the understanding of communicative intentions, and the ability to engage in role-reversal imitation.

The modes of cognitive representation that children develop in learning a language are unique in the animal kingdom and emerge directly from these uniquely human joint attentional activities. As children try to discern the adult's communicative intention in using a particular symbol inside a joint attentional scene, and so to learn the conventional use of the linguistic symbol for themselves, they come to see that these special communicative devices known as linguistic symbols are both intersubjective, in that all users know that they "share" the use of these symbols with others, and perspectival, in that they embody different ways a situation may be construed for different communicative purposes. The latter feature in particular removes linguistic symbols to a very large extent from the perceptual situation at hand—but not just because they can stand for physically absent objects and events and other "dumb" forms of displacement (Hockett, 1960). Rather, the intersubjective and perspectival nature of linguistic symbols actually undermines the whole concept of a perceptual situation by layering on top of it the multitudinous perspectives that are communicatively possible for those of us who share the symbol.

This inherently and indivisibly social nature of linguistic symbols is seen very clearly when we ask the question: Could a single individual, who had no language at all, invent a "private language" for herself (Wittgenstein, 1953)? While mature language users might invent new symbols solely for their own private use (I may disagree with Wittgenstein on that), it is my contention that it would be totally impossible for a single person, who had never experienced language as used by other persons, to invent for herself, with no social partner and no preexisting symbols at all, a "private language" consisting of linguistic symbols similar to those that make up modern languages. This is quite simply because (a) there would be no way to constitute their intersubjectivity, and (b) there would be no communicative motivation or opportunity for taking different perspectives on things.

Any account that relies so heavily on the role of language in children's cognitive development must address the issue of children whose skills of linguistic communication do not develop normally. Deaf children come immediately to mind, but of course practically all deaf children in the modern world learn either their own special natural language or something very close to it. And even the deaf children studied by Goldin-Meadow (1997)—who have not been exposed to a systematic sign language—grow up in situations in which people are continuously expressing communicative intentions toward them in various visually based ways. The degree to which these children learn different conceptual perspectives on things from these alternative forms of symbolic communication is an interesting question. Children with specific language impairment (SLI) also present an interesting case in that they have troubles both with language acquisition and also with a number of nonlinguistic cognitive skills, ranging from analogical reasoning to social cognition (for recent reviews see Leonard, 1998; Bishop, 1997). And, of course, in many ways the most interesting case is that of children with autism. Despite the popular image, which mainly focuses on high-functioning children with autism, about half of all these children learn no language at all—presumably because they do not understand the communicative intentions of others in the species-typical manner. But interestingly, it has been known for some time that children with autism also do not engage in symbolic play in a typical manner, and there are some indications that these two skills may be correlated: the children who are better at language are also more likely to engage in symbolic play with objects (Jarrold, Boucher, and Smith, 1993; Wolfberg and Schuler, 1993). Whether or not these deficits in symbolic abilities have implications for the cognitive representation of children with autism is unknown, but one characteristic of children with autism that is commented upon frequently is their tendency to approach things in the same way—from the same perspective—time after time. It thus may be that the difficulties of children with autism in understanding other persons as intentional agents leads to deficits in their symbolic skills, which then may create difficulties in representing situations perspectivally.

5

LINGUISTIC CONSTRUCTIONS AND EVENT COGNITION

*When words in our ordinary language have prima facie analogous
grammars we are inclined to interpret them analogously.*

—Ludwig Wittgenstein

My account of children's acquisition of linguistic symbols has so far focused on just one kind of linguistic symbol, the word. But at the same time that they are acquiring their first words children are also acquiring more complex linguistic constructions as kind of linguistic gestalts. The plausibility, even necessity, of this view becomes apparent as soon as we focus on word learning as something other than the learning of names for objects. Thus, for example, when children learn the word *give,* there is really no learning of the word apart from the participant roles that invariably accompany acts of giving: the giver, the thing given, and the person given to; in fact, we cannot even conceive of an act of giving in the absence of these participant roles. The same could be said of the words *out, from,* and *of,* which can only be learned as relationships between two other entities or locations. If we are interested in the role of language acquisition in cognitive development, therefore, we must investigate not only children's acquisition of words but also their acquisition of larger linguistic constructions as meaningful symbolic units, including whole sentence-level constructions (e.g., locative constructions or yes-no questions). Indeed, since children almost never hear individual words in isolation, outside of some larger and more complex utterance, we should probably conceptualize word learning as simply the isolation and extraction of a language's simplest linguistic constructions (Langacker, 1987a; Fillmore, 1985, 1988; Goldberg, 1995).

It must be emphasized at the outset that linguistic constructions may be either concrete—based on specific words and phrases—or abstract—based on word-general categories and schemas. For example, concrete constructions such as *She gave him a pony, He sent her a letter,* and *They e-mailed me an invitation,* instantiate the abstract English ditransitive construction described abstractly as Noun Phrase + Verb + Noun Phrase + Noun Phrase. Some linguists and psycholinguists believe that young children operate from the beginning with abstract, adult-like, linguistic constructions—because they are born with certain innate linguistic principles (e.g., Pinker, 1994). But this theory can work only if all languages work with the same basic linguistic principles, which they do not (for recent reviews documenting cross-linguistic variability much too great to be instantiated in an innate universal grammar, see Comrie, 1990; Givón, 1995; Dryer, 1997; Croft, 1998; van Valin and LaPolla, 1996; Slobin, 1997). The alternative is the view that early in ontogeny individual human beings learn to use their species-universal cognitive, social-cognitive, and cultural learning abilities to comprehend and acquire the linguistic constructions their particular cultures have created over historical time by processes of sociogenesis (Tomasello, 1995d, 1999b). In this view, complex linguistic constructions are just another type of symbolic artifact that human beings inherit from their forebears—although these artifacts are in some ways special as their systematic nature evokes from children attempts at categorization and schematization. That is to say, children hear only concrete utterances, but they attempt to construct abstract linguistic constructions out of these, and this process has important implications for their cognitive development, especially with regard to the conceptualization of complex events, states of affairs, and their interrelations.

I would like to deal with this very complex topic as simply as I can. Consequently, my procedure will be to focus on the three aspects of the language-acquisition process that are most relevant for current concerns. First is the developmental steps involved in the acquisition of relatively large-scale linguistic constructions; second is the process by which large-scale linguistic constructions are learned; and third is the role of large-scale linguistic constructions in children's cognitive development in general.

First Linguistic Constructions

Children talk about events and states of affairs in the world. Even when they use the name of an object as a one-word utterance, "Ball," they are almost always asking someone either to *get* them the ball or else to *attend* to the ball. Simply naming objects for no other purpose except to name them is a language game that some children play, but this is typically only some children in some Western middle-class homes and concerns only basic-level objects; no children anywhere simply name actions ("Look! Putting!") or relationships ("Look! Of!"). We should approach early language, therefore, with an eye to the entire events and states of affairs involved—complex scenes of experience with one or more participants in their spatio-temporal settings—because this is what children talk about. As they develop, they do this with holophrases, verb island constructions, abstract constructions, and narratives.

Holophrases

By the time children begin acquiring the linguistic conventions of their communities at around one year of age, they have already been communicating with others gesturally and vocally for some months—both imperatively to request things of others and declaratively to point things out to them (Bates, 1979). Children of all cultures thus learn and use their earliest linguistic symbols both declaratively and imperatively, and they soon learn to ask for things interrogatively as well—each being accomplished with a distinctive intonational pattern (Bruner, 1983). Across all the languages of the world the scenes of experience that children talk about most often are such things as (Brown, 1973):

- the presence-absence-recurrence of people, objects, and events (*hi, bye, gone, more, again, another, stop, away*);
- the exchange-possession of objects with other people (*give, have, share my, mine, Mommy's*);
- the movement-location of people and objects (*come, go, up, down, in, out, on, off, here, there, outside, bring, take, Where go?*);
- the states and changes of states of objects and people (*open, close, fall, break, fix, wet, pretty, little, big*);
- the physical and mental activities of people (*eat, kick, ride, draw, hug, kiss, throw, roll, want, need, look, do, make, see*).

It is important to note that virtually all of these events and states are either intentional or causal events themselves, or else the endpoints or results or movements of a causal or intentional act that the child is attempting to get the adult to pay attention to or bring about through intentional action (Slobin, 1985)—the point being that from the beginning children talk about scenes of experience structured by their species-unique understanding of the intentional-causal structure of events and states of affairs in the world.

The child's major symbolic vehicle at this early stage is what is often called a holophrase: a single-unit linguistic expression intended as an entire speech act (e.g., "More," used to mean "I want more juice"). The holophrases with which children begin to talk about events represent many different kinds of linguistic structures in different languages. Thus, in English, most beginning language learners use a number of so-called relational words such as *More, Gone, Up, Down, On,* and *Off,* presumably because adults use these words in salient ways to talk about salient events (Bloom, Tinker, and Margulis, 1993). In Korean and Mandarin Chinese, in contrast, young children learn fully adult verbs for these same events from the beginning—because this is what is most salient in adult speech to them (Gopnik and Choi, 1995). In both cases, to learn to talk about the event more fully, the child must fill in some missing linguistic elements such as the participants involved, for example, from simply "Off" to "Shirt off" or "Take shirt off" or "You take my shirt off." In addition, however, most children begin language acquisition by learning some unparsed adult expressions as holophrases—such things as "I-wanna-do-it," "Lemme-see," and "Where-the-bottle." In these cases, to have a full understanding of both the construction and its constituent parts, the child must at some point isolate or extract the linguistic elements from the whole expression (Peters, 1983; Pine and Lieven, 1993); and indeed this process is the predominant one for children acquiring those languages that have many internally complex "one-word sentences" in adult speech (i.e., so-called agglutinating languages such as many Eskimo languages). The general principle is that young children come equipped to move in either direction—part to whole or whole to parts—in learning to talk fully about the basic scenes of their experience.

Verb Island Constructions

As children begin to produce utterances that have more than one level of organization, that is, as they begin to produce utterances with multiple meaningful components, the most interesting question cognitively is how they use those component parts to linguistically partition the experiential scene as a whole into its constituent elements—including especially the event (or state of affairs) and participants involved. And ultimately children must also learn ways to symbolically indicate the different roles the participants are playing in the event, such things as agent, patient, instrument, and the like.

Children produce many of their early word combinations with a formula in which there is one event or state word that is constant and one participant word that is variable across enactments. This pattern is presumably acquired as children notice adults saying such things as *More juice, More milk, More cookies, More grapes,* leading to the schema *More* ___ (see Braine, 1976, for cross-linguistic documentation). These so-called pivot constructions have no symbolic indications of the different roles being played by different event participants. Children do learn fairly quickly to symbolically indicate participant roles in these schemas, however, the most common symbols cross-linguistically being word order (as in English) and the use of special case markers (as in Turkish or Russian). As they do this, however, they do not do it for whole classes of events—such as all transitive utterances—but they do it for individual verbs on a one-by-one basis. For example, in studying my daughter's language development, I found that during exactly the same developmental period in which she was using some of her verbs in only one type of schema and that schema was quite simple (e.g., *Cut ___*), she used other verbs in more complex schemas of several different types (e.g., *Draw ___, Draw ___ on ___, I draw with ___, Draw ___ for ___, ___ draw on ___*). In addition, the "same" participant was symbolically indicated inconsistently across verbs; for example, the instruments of some verbs were indicated by the preposition *by* or *with*, while the instruments of other verbs were not—demonstrating that she did not have a general linguistic category of "instrument" but rather possessed some more verb-specific categories such as "thing to draw with" and "thing to cut with." Her other categories were thus likewise verb-specific, for example, "kisser," "person kissed," "breaker," "thing broken" (Tomasello, 1992b).

The verb island hypothesis proposes that children's early linguistic competence is comprised totally of an inventory of linguistic constructions of this type: specific verbs with slots for participants whose roles are symbolically marked on an individual basis (see Figure 5.1). At this early stage children have made no generalizations about constructional patterns across verbs, and so they have no verb-general linguistic categories, schemas, or marking conventions (Lieven, Pine, and Baldwin, 1997; Berman and Armon-Lotem, 1995; Pizutto and Caselli, 1992; Rubino and Pine, 1998; for reviews see Tomasello, 1999b; Tomasello and Brooks, 1999). To repeat, the inventory of verb island constructions—in effect a simple list of constructions organized around individual verbs—makes up the totality of children's early linguistic competence; there are no other hidden principles, parameters, linguistic categories, or schemas that generate sentences.

This item-specific way of using language is not something that goes away quickly. Indeed, in the view of many linguists, more of adult language is item-specific than is generally realized, including idioms, clichés, habitual collocations, and many other "non-core" linguistic constructions (e.g., How ya doing, He put her up to it, She'll get over it; Bolinger, 1977; Fillmore, Kay, and O'Conner, 1988). But children keep this organization for some time for *all* of their language. Their sentence-level constructions are verb island constructions that are abstract with respect to the participants involved (they have open participant slots) but are totally concrete with respect to the relational structure as expressed by the verb and syntactic symbols (word order and grammatical case marking). It is interesting from a cognitive point of view that children find it so easy to freely substitute participants for one another in the slots of these constructions. One hypothesis is that this ability derives from children's foundational nonlinguistic ability to conceptualize all of the participants in a joint attentional scene from an external perspective so that they become, in effect, totally interchangeable (see Chapter 4). But not so for events and states of affairs; events and states are "what we

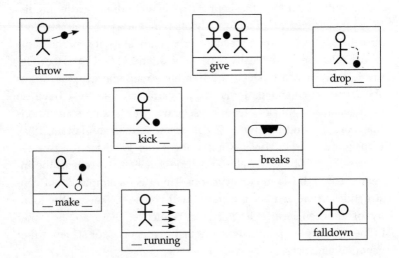

Figure 5.1 Simplified depictions of some verb island constructions. This depicts the totality of the child's earliest syntactic skills.

are doing" or "what is going on" intentionally, which makes them not interchangeable, and so children relate to them on an individual basis only.

Abstract Constructions

The mastery of verb island constructions is a major way station on the road to adult linguistic competence—a kind of base camp that is the goal of the early part of the journey but that, once reached, becomes only a means to the end of more abstract and productive linguistic constructions. These more abstract constructions are simply cognitive schemas that, like other cognitive categories and schemas, are built up slowly as patterns are extracted across individual verb island constructions—resulting in a prototype at the center of the construction and more peripheral exemplars that differ from it in various ways. Some of these more abstract constructions still have particular words as integral parts, whereas others are completely word general. Among the first constructions of English-speaking children that contain basically all of the elements contained in the corresponding adult constructions, and that have a certain degree of abstractness, are:

- imperatives *(Roll it! Smile! Push me!);*
- simple transitives *(Ernie kissed her; He kicked the ball);*
- simple intransitives *(She's smiling; It's rolling);*
- locatives *(I put it on the table; She took her book to school);*
- resultatives *(He wiped the table clean; She knocked him silly);*
- datives/ditransitives *(Ernie gave it to her; She threw him a kiss);*
- passives *(I got hurt; He got kicked by the elephant);*
- attributives and identificationals *(It's pretty; She's my mommy; It's a tape recorder).*

The main point is that at some developmental moment the construction, as an abstract structure, is itself a symbol, carrying meaning to some degree independently of any of the words involved.

Thus, most speakers of English attribute very different meanings to the nonce verb *floos* in the following utterances:

X floosed Y the Z.
X floosed Y.
X floosed Y on the Z.
X floosed.
X was floosed by Y.

In these examples we can see that the construction itself carries meaning (since the nonce verb *floos* carries none), and therefore that it is a symbolic entity with a meaning of its own—at least somewhat independent of the specific words involved (Goldberg, 1995).

Again it is important to emphasize that even adult language is not a wholly abstract affair. Recent psycholinguistic experiments have demonstrated that even adults operate much of the time with item-based, verb-centered linguistic structures; for example, when the verb *rob* is used they work with participant categories such as "robber," not with something more abstract such as "agent" or "subject" (see, e.g., Trueswell, Tanenhaus, and Kello, 1993; McCrae, Feretti, and Amyote, 1997). This is not surprising, since even when adults possess abstract categories and schemas in a cognitive domain they still rely in much of their cognitive processing on the concrete items and structures that, in some sense, constitute the substance of the abstract categories and schemas (Barsalou, 1992). And so the overall point is that young children begin with linguistic constructions based on particular linguistic items, and only gradually form more abstract constructions—which may then become symbolic entities that serve as an additional layer of linguistic competence.

Narratives

Children also routinely experience complex linguistic constructions in discourse in which multiple simple events or states of affairs are chained together into some kind of complex narrative—typically with one or more participants constant across events and causal or

intentional links giving the entire sequence the kind of rational coherence that distinguishes a "story" from a random chain of events.
How children learn to do this—how they learn to track the same
participants across multiple events and roles and to comprehend
and use the various "little words" that connect these events and
roles (*so, because, and, but, since, however, despite,* etc.) so as to make
them a story—is not a well-understood process (for interesting
analyses and discussions see Nelson, 1989, 1996; Berman and Slobin,
1995).

Learning Linguistic Constructions

Human children are biologically prepared in numerous ways to acquire a natural language, that is, with basic cognitive, social-cognitive,
and vocal-auditory skills. Nevertheless—and even if children possess
an innate universal grammar equally applicable to all the languages of
the world—individual children still need to learn the particular linguistic constructions, both concrete and abstract, of their particular
languages. Most important are three sets of processes: cultural learning, discourse and conversation, and abstraction and schematization.

Cultural Learning

Fundamentally, the way the child learns a concrete linguistic construction—composed of specific linguistic items—is the same way
she learns words: she must understand which aspects of the joint attentional scene the adult intends for her to attend to when using this
linguistic construction, and then culturally (imitatively) learn that
construction for that communicative function. There are, of course,
some differences as well, emanating from the internal complexities
of linguistic constructions and, at a later developmental period, from
the abstractness of constructions. But I will save these additional issues for the next two subsections, concentrating for the moment on
children's learning of verb island constructions as concrete symbolic
units.

It is important that initially what the child is learning is a construction composed of concrete words not abstract categories—that is, verb island constructions—and so general processes of cultural learning, specifically imitative learning, are sufficient to account for the acquisition process (with one exception; see below). This point is illustrated by a recent set of experiments in which my colleagues and I have taught young children novel verbs in carefully controlled ways. In each case we taught them a novel verb in one and only one linguistic construction and then tried to see if we could get them to use it in some other linguistic constructions. We tried to do this by asking leading questions. So, for example, the child might have seen Ernie doing something to a ball and heard us say "The ball is getting dacked by Ernie" (a passive construction). We then asked "What's Ernie doing?"—which would normally be answered by "He's dacking the ball" (an active, transitive construction). But we found that it is very difficult to get children younger than three to three and a half years to use these novel verbs in any ways other than the ways they have heard them being used (Ahktar and Tomasello, 1997; Tomasello and Brooks, 1998; Brooks and Tomasello, in press; for reviews see Tomasello and Brooks, 1999; Tomasello, 1999). And we have conducted many control procedures to rule out other explanations for children's conservatism involving difficulties with nonlinguistic "performance factors" and the like. Interestingly—and this is the one exception to imitative learning as the explanation for children's learning of linguistic constructions—these same children are not conservative in this same way with object labels; no matter which construction they hear it in, children who learn that an object is called a *wug* will use it in all kinds of productive ways in their existing verb island constructions (Tomasello, Akhtar, et al., 1997). This is simply another way of demonstrating that verb island constructions have relatively open slots for their participants (typically indicated with a name-of-object label).

Together these studies demonstrate that whereas young children are able to form a category of object names (corresponding to something like "noun") from very early in language development, when it comes to the central relational structure of an utterance—what it is about from an intentional point of view—they basically just imitatively learn to use the same words in the same way as the adult; that is to say, they learn a verb island construction composed of specific words indicating the relational structure of the utterance with some open slots for participants/nouns. Virtually all of the creativity that young children show in their early language—for example, Braine's (1963) famous "Allgone sticky"—derive from children putting new and different linguistic material in the participant/noun slots in verb island constructions. To repeat: although later children will be more creative in their language use, early on they learn to talk about the relational or event structure of the scenes of their life in exactly the same way they hear adults talking about them, using exactly the same words and linguistic constructions. This is cultural learning, that is to say, imitative learning, pure and simple.

Discourse and Functionally Based Distributional Analysis

Despite the fundamental similarity of the cultural learning process for words and verb island constructions, there is of course a major difference, and that has to do with the internal complexity of constructions. To fully comprehend a large-scale linguistic construction, the child must understand that the adult's utterance, in addition to expressing a communicative intention as a whole, also contains isolable symbolic elements, each of which plays a distinct role in that communicative intention. Said another way, the child must learn that the various linguistic symbols in a complex utterance partition the referential scene into isolable perceptual/conceptual elements, and that these two sets of elements—the symbolic and the referential—must be aligned appropriately. This seems very complex, but in reality the child must accomplish this to some imperfect degree even to learn a single word—because even in this case she must isolate both the to-be-learned word and the to-be-learned referent, each of which is embedded in its own set of complexities. For instance, in the word learning studies by Tomasello et al. described in Chapter 4, some children may have understood the adult's overall communicative intention in saying "Let's go find the toma" from the nonlinguistic context of the finding game alone—with the only symbolic element clearly isolated from the surrounding symbolic complexities being the word *toma* and with the only referential element clearly isolated from the surrounding perceptual complexities being the sought-for object. Understanding the whole utterance *Let's go find the toma*—that is, understanding the adult's overall communicative intention and how each linguistic element or complex of elements contributes to that communicative intention—is just an elaboration of this process.

This elaboration rests most importantly on children's interactive discourse with other persons in which different utterance elements are highlighted in different ways. Most important are the facts that (a) the child often knows some of the words in the utterance already and (b) the child can often build on the adult's previous discourse turn. For example, if an adult said to an American three-year-old "Ernie is dacking Bert" while the two of them were watching a novel activity unfold, the child very likely would know that *dacking* indicated the novel activity because she would know from previous experience that the adult was referring to the salient activity in front of them and that the words *Ernie* and *Bert* indicated the familiar participants in this activity (see Fisher, 1996). She would thus have a good chance of understanding the whole construction and the role of all the different elements in it.

In addition, the role of back-and-forth discourse with an adult is also very likely key in explicating for children the communicative function of different linguistic elements in larger linguistic constructions (K. E. Nelson, 1986). Thus, while participating in discourse with an adult the child can often see the different roles being played by different elements as the speakers go back and forth, sometimes repeating elements from their interlocutor's last utterance as they introduce new elements, as in:

CHILD: On the chair.
ADULT: OK, we'll meek it on the chair.

In this instance it is likely that the child knows the adult's overall communicative intention, and knows the communicative role of that portion of the adult's utterance that repeats hers—which should help her to isolate the role of the new word(s) she does not know. Similarly, adult and child sometimes create so-called vertical structures in which they build, across the discourse turns, one construction (Scollon, 1973), as in:

CHILD: I'll smash it.
ADULT: With the gazzer.

Again, these kinds of sequences should help children to parse utterances into their components and to determine what these components do communicatively.

The overall proposal is thus what Tomasello (1992b) called functionally based distributional analysis: to understand the communicative significance of a linguistic structure of any type the child must determine the contribution it is making to the adult's communicative intention as a whole. Figure 5.2 provides a highly oversimplified depiction of the process. Note that this process applies equally well to the learning of words and to the learning of larger linguistic constructions—or any other linguistic units, for that matter—although of course different aspects of the process are of special importance in different cases. And note that this process does not in any way conflict with or compete with processes of cultural learning; the only issue here is what units children are imitatively learning and how they manage to isolate these units so that they can imitatively learn their conventional use. Cultural learning in language acquisition always concerns learning to use a symbolic form for its conventional communicative function; it is just that understanding the surrounding discourse in which a linguistic form is embedded is virtually always an essential aspect of understanding its communicative function.

Abstraction and Schematization

Very little is known about how young children abstract or schematize across verb island constructions and create more abstract, productive, and adult-like constructions. One hypothesis is that they simply form a linguistic constructional schema the same way they form event schemas in nonlinguistic cognition (as studied, for example, by Nelson, 1986, 1996). Thus, recent research has shown that young children remember event sequences better if there is variability in the different enactments in the events in terms of who the participants are (Bauer and Fivush, 1992). This would correspond to the forming of verb island schemas on the basis of different instances of, for example, a kicking event, each of which had different participants. Perhaps children form more general schemas simply by schematizing in the same way across different types of events—so that many instances of X *kicks* Y and X *loves* Y and X *finds* Y and so forth come to be seen, on another level of organization, as instances of a more general schema still (see Gentner and Markman, 1997, on analogy and structure mapping). There is presumably some "critical mass" of different verb island schemas that need to be categorized in this way for the process to work (Marchman and Bates, 1994).

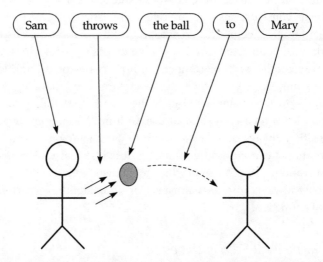

Figure 5.2 A highly simplified depiction of a referential scene and language that goes with it, after a functionally based distributional analysis in which the child understands the communicative function of each linguistic element.

Obviously, the age at which children master an abstract construction will be a function of both the social-cognitive skills involved in understanding the communicative function of the construction and the cognitive and vocal-auditory skills involved in mastering the construction's symbolic form (its length and complexity, the saliency and consistency of its syntactic symbols, etc.)—and also, possibly, the number and consistency of the verb island constructions that must be abstracted across. But once children have begun forming an abstract construction, there arises the problem, as in all categorization and schematization, of overgeneralization. To learn to use the adult construction in an adult-like way, children must make appropriate generalizations, not only about which verbs may occur in particular constructions, but also about which verbs may not (e.g., we don't say "She donated him the book"; Pinker, 1989). What the actual constraints on constructions are, and how children acquire them, is not well understood, but by all indications children are three years of age or more before they begin making overgeneralizations with their newly formed sentence-level constructions (e.g., "Don't giggle me" as an instance of using an intransitive verb nonconventionally in a transitive construction; Bowerman, 1982), and about four to four and a half before they begin to restrict their usage of these productive constructions in adult-like ways so as to avoid making overgeneralization errors of this type (see Tomasello, 1999b, for a review). The abstractness of whole sentence-level linguistic constructions may thus be seen as a U-shaped developmental pattern, in much the same way as the well-known English past tense: children learn item-based constructions; they generalize across these, sometimes to the point of overgeneralization; and then they cut back these generalizations to their conventional breadth by a variety of processes.

It is interesting and important to note that processes of categorization and schematization come from the individual line of cognitive development, as these are things the child does on her own. Of course what she is categorizing or schematizing comes straight from the cultural repository of linguistic symbols and constructions the culture has built up and saved over many generations. But the child does not experience abstract linguistic constructions directly; she hears only concrete utterances and must create the abstractions herself. Thus, language acquisition is a key arena in which we may see the complex interplay between the individual and cultural lines of cognitive development, as children individually create abstract linguistic constructions, but do so using the culturally conventional symbolic artifacts (constructions) that already exist in their social groups.

Linguistic Cognition

If we viewed language as something separate from cognition we could now ask the question of how the acquisition of language "affects," "is affected by," or "interacts" with cognition. My own view, however, is simply that language is a form of cognition; it is cognition packaged for purposes of interpersonal communication (Langacker, 1987a, 1991). Human beings wish to share experience with one another and so, over time, they have created symbolic conventions for doing that. The process of acquiring these symbolic conventions leads human beings to conceptualize things in some ways that they would not do otherwise—what Slobin (1991) calls "thinking for speaking"—because human symbolic communication requires some unique forms of conceptualization if it is to work effectively. I would thus prefer to speak simply of linguistic cognition, and in particular of three aspects of linguistic cognition: the partitioning of referential scenes into events (or states) and their participants, the taking of perspectives on referential scenes, and the categorization of referential scenes.

Events and Participants

Perhaps the most cognitively significant outcome of acquiring a natural language is that the language user partitions her world into discrete units of particular kinds. This partitioning process does not create new conceptual material, of course, but it serves to package existing conceptual material in special ways—often in ways that an individual would not need if she was not engaged in linguistic communication. Given that the major function of language is to manipulate the attention of other persons—that is, to induce them to take a certain perspective on a phenomenon—we can think of linguistic symbols and constructions as nothing other than symbolic artifacts that a child's forebears have bequeathed to her for this purpose. In learning to use these symbolic artifacts, and thus internalizing the perspectives behind them, the child comes to conceptualize the world in the way that the creators of the artifacts did.

The most fundamental cognitive distinction employed by natural languages is the distinction between events (or states of affairs) and the participants in them. This distinction is multiply determined and is manifest in different ways in different languages, the most important determinants being (a) the cognitive distinction between "thing-like" phenomena and "process-like" phenomena (Langacker, 1987b), and (b) the communicative distinction between "discourse topic"—what we are talking about—and "discourse focus"—what we are saying about it (Hopper and Thompson, 1984). Thus, some languages have two different types of words each of which is prototypically used for only one of these types of elements—mostly called nouns and verbs—whereas other languages have a stock of words each of which can be used for either type of element equally well depending on the linguistic context in which it is used—much like the English words *brush, kiss, call, drink, help, hammer, hug, walk*, etc.

As outlined above, young children begin their linguistic careers by using holophrases to express their communicative intentions, but they soon begin to do more complex things. Most importantly, across development they learn to:

- use word combinations in which they parse their communicative intention into some differentiated elements, mostly corresponding to a word for an event or state of affairs, on the one hand, and a participant, on the other (e.g., ___ *off, Throw* ___, *More* ___);

- use verb island constructions in which they symbolically indicate the participants for their roles in the events or states, mostly with word order or case marking—but they do this in a verb-specific manner only; and
- categorize, or schematize, verb island schemas into more abstract linguistic constructions that enable many productive linguistic generalizations.

What this entire progression means is that young children come to "slice and dice" the scenes of their experience in many and varied ways—based on their acquisition and use of the linguistic constructions that make up a natural language—and then to categorize or schematize their ways of doing that—based on their own individual cognitive skills for finding patterns in experience. A summary of this progression is given in Table 5.1.

Table 5.1 Young children's conceptual parsing and categorization of scenes of experience as occasioned by the acquisition of a natural language.

Approximate age	Experiential scene	Language
9 months	Joint attentional scenes (not symbolized)	—
14 months	Symbolized scenes (undifferentiated symbolization)	Holophrases
18 months	Partitioned scenes (differentiating of event and participant)	Pivot-like constructions
22 months	Syntactic scenes (symbolic marking of participants)	Verb island constructions
36 months	Categorized scenes (generalized symbolic marking of participant roles)	Verb-general constructions

Although it is presumably the case that other animal species perceive and deal with both objects and events, they have no occasion to conceptualize or communicate about an event and its participants (each with its role clearly indicated) as a coherent cognitive unit. Human beings do not do this either if they are interacting with the world directly, as when they are making and using tools to achieve some concrete instrumental aim. However, human beings do parse the world into events or states and their role-defined participants when they communicate with one another linguistically. They do this, first of all, because there are good cognitive and communicative reasons for doing so (see above; Langacker, 1987b; Hopper and Thompson, 1984), and, second of all, because this is the way their forebears have done it. Nevertheless, each language learner is exposed to the particular ways her particular forebears have made this distinction in myriad particular conceptual situations, and she must learn to do it in those same ways if she is to communicate effectively with her groupmates.

Perspective-taking

Every speech event is different, and so on each occasion of language use the speaker must find some way to "ground" the referential scene she is talking about in the current joint attentional scene that she shares with her interlocutor. Said another way, the speaker must choose symbolic means of expression that are adapted for the specific communicative context, including the knowledge, expectations, and perspective of her interlocutor on this particular occasion. This is true for the way speakers choose to designate for their interlocutor both the participants and the event involved, and it is true for the perspective speakers take on the scenes as a whole as well.

First, when people want to designate a particular object for someone they have a number of choices, including such things as proper names (*Bill Clinton*), common nouns (*the president*), and pronouns (*he*)—depending on their judgment of what information the listener needs on this particular occasion (i.e., on their assessment of exactly what is and is not shared in the current joint attentional scene).

Proper nouns use unique and individual designations, and are used when the speaker and listener both know that person by name. Common nouns are categorical in nature and so they must be used together with other linguistic symbols to identify the specific individual intended; for example, special symbols called determiners are used when the speaker can assume that the listener is able to identify the indicated individual with just a categorical hint (e.g., *the X, that Y, this Z*), and complex constructions such as modified noun phrases (*the blue car*) or relative clauses (*the cat you found yesterday*) are used when the speaker determines that the listener must do more work to identify the intended individual. Pronouns are used when both individuals know precisely what is being referred to in the joint attentional scene. In this same general manner, the speaker often needs to identify a particular event for the listener, isolating it from the continuous flow of events in experience. For example, without knowing anything else we know that *He kicked it* designates a different specific event from *He will kick it* (assuming the same speaker at the same time). Langacker's (1991) model is of the joint attentional scene (ongoing speech event) as the centering point from which any specific event may be located in time as past, current, or future—or in some cases in imagined time, such as an event that I hope will happen.

At the level of whole utterances, speakers ground their speech in the current joint attentional scene by adapting their talk about the referential scene for the listener's knowledge, expectations, and current focus of attention at this particular moment. An example will help to clarify. Let us imagine a scene in which a person named Fred throws a rock through a window, breaking it. We may use many different utterance-level constructions to highlight or background different aspects of the event and to take different perspectives on all of it. We could multiply the possibilities endlessly by using different verbs and nouns (*shattered, vandalized, the man, the burglar, my brother,* etc.), but in this case let us just focus on a straightforward description using as the main content words only *Fred, rock, window,* and *broke* (and restrict the speaker's communicative intention to a simple informative statement).

Fred broke the window.
The rock broke the window.
Fred broke the window with a rock.
The window broke.
The window got broken.
The window got broken by a rock.
The window got broken by Fred.
The window got broken by Fred with a rock.
It was Fred that broke the window.
It was the rock that broke the window.
It was the window that broke.
It was the window that got broken.

Even keeping the same basic words—and so holding constant the different perspectives embodied in different choice of words—there are still many different ways to describe a single scene using some very basic and common sentence-level constructions of the English language. In each case one of the participants is singled out as the "primary focal participant" (subject), and the other potential participants are either included as the "secondary focal participant" (direct object), included as an ancillary participant (marked by a preposition), or excluded altogether. The reason that a speaker may use one of these descriptions over another has to do with her assessment of which one fits best with her own communicative goals and with the communicative needs and expectations of the listener. For example, if the speaker surmises that the listener believes that Bill broke the window, she may shake her head and say "It was *Fred* that broke the window," or if she thinks that the listener only cares about the window and its fate, without regard for the cause, she may just say "The window got broken." Thus, Talmy (1996) describes the use of particular linguistic constructions as different ways of "windowing" and "gapping" attention, and Fisher, Gleitman, and Gleitman (1991) characterize constructions as a kind of "zoom lens" which the speaker uses to direct the listener's attention to a particular perspective on a scene.

Such linguistic esoterica are essential for answering a very simple, yet very profound, question, and that is: Why are human languages so inordinately complex? The answer involves primarily two sets of factors. Natural languages are complex, first of all, because human beings want to talk about complex events and states of affairs with multiple participants related to one another in complex ways; we need to deal with the breaking event and with Fred and with the rock and with the window, and we need to mark each of these for the role it plays in the event as a whole. But if that were all there was to it we could simply say *Fred break window rock* and be done with it. Much additional complexity results from the speaker's need to ground the referential scene in the joint attentional scene she is currently sharing with the listener; that is to say, much syntactic complexity results from the pragmatics of communication. This is true of grounding reference to particular participants and events in the current joint attentional scene (e.g., with determiners or tense markers), and it is also true of the process of taking different perspectives on events as the speaker windows and gaps different aspects of the event for the listener (e.g., by making the window or the rock or Fred the primary focus of the utterance).

The most common and recurrent utterance-level constructions in a language provide pre-set packages, conventionalized over historical time, for doing just these kinds of things, and so children just learn them. But they must still develop the pragmatic ability to choose among these different options effectively in different communicative circumstances. Indeed, it is not always easy to tell in a particular situation whether a child is just using the linguistic construction that first comes to mind, or whether she is actively choosing one linguistic construction over another for a principled communicative reason. But, in general, as in all cases in which the perspective of the child and that of her communicative partner diverge, adapting sensitively to another person's perspective is a significant developmental achievement for young children—and it very likely awaits the emergence of their ability to understand the other person as something like a mental agent with thoughts and beliefs of her own.

Derivations, Metaphors, and Stories

Abstract constructions form the basis for much of children's linguistic creativity, and each child must construct them individually as she discerns patterns in the utterances she hears from mature users of the language. This makes abstract linguistic constructions especially interesting cognitively since they are based both on the learning of culturally conventional linguistic structures and on children's individual cognitive skills of categorization and schema formation, which derive, in the final analysis, from their biological inheritance as individual primates. In addition, however, abstract linguistic constructions lead to some unique cognitive operations that have no parallel in the animal kingdom. The interaction between abstract linguistic constructions and concrete individual words creates powerful new possibilities for derivational, analogical, and even metaphorical construals of things. For example, in English, we may construe:

- properties and activities as if they were objects (*Blue is my favorite color; Skiing is fun; Discovering the treasure was lucky*);
- objects and activities as if they were properties (*His mousy voice shook me; His shaven head distracted her; His Nixonesque manner offended me*);
- objects and properties as if they were activities (*She chaired the meeting; He wet his pants; The paperboy porched the newspaper*);
- just about any particular events and objects as if they were others (*Love is a rose; Life is a journey; An atom is a solar system*).

Human beings create these kinds of analogies when the resources in their linguistic inventory are insufficient to meet the demands, including expressive demands, of a particular communicative situation. That is, it is difficult to imagine that human beings would conceptualize actions as objects or objects as actions—or engage in anything beyond the most rudimentary forms of metaphorical thinking—if it were not for the functional demands placed on them as they adapt conventional means of linguistic communication for particular communicative exigencies. The important point in the current context is that the abstract structures created as children go from more verb-specific to more verb-general linguistic constructions readily accommodate conceptual material of all types when the communicative need arises—even material that is explicitly contradictory, as in some modern poetry (and in sentences such as *Colorless green ideas sleep furiously*). And lest it be thought that this grammatical flexibility is simply a convenient communicative device with no enduring cognitive consequences, Wittgenstein (1953) exposed some of the many philosophical puzzles generated by the fact that people tend to look for things or substances for all entities that are described linguistically by nouns (e.g., a thought, an expectation, infinity, language).

The role of narratives in human cognition should also be recognized, if only briefly. Bruner (1986, 1990) in particular has argued that the stories told by a culture (or other social unit such as a family) are a major part of the way it views itself, and so come to shape the cognition of its individual members as well. For example, the canonical stories of a culture concerning its origins, its heroes and heroines, key events in its history, and even mythological events in its prehistory, all are the way they are for good reasons—presumably having to do with what kinds of things a culture thinks are important, what kinds of explanations it values, what kinds of narrative construals and genres it has created as conventional for whatever reason, and so forth and so on. Extended narratives too, then, serve to channel human linguistic cognition in directions it might not otherwise take.

Language and Cognition

Linguistic constructions are special types of linguistic symbols, and learning whole linguistic constructions—internally complex linguistic symbols that have been conventionalized historically to deal with complex but recurrent communicative functions—orients children to aspects of their experience to which they might not orient were it not for language. In particular, it leads them to:

- parse the world into events and participants;
- view complex events from various perspectives that connect either more or less well with the current joint attentional scene; and
- create abstract constructions with which they can view virtually any experiential phenomenon in terms of virtually any other (actions as objects, objects as actions, and all kinds of other conceptual metaphors).

Acquiring language thus leads children to conceptualize, categorize, and schematize events in much more complex ways than they would if they were not engaged in learning a conventional language, and these kinds of event representations and schematizations add great complexity and flexibility to human cognition.

It is also important that in children's acquisition of complex linguistic constructions they are initially so conservative, in the sense that they generally imitate exactly the relational structure of the constructions they are learning from mature language users (verb island constructions). The importance of this observation is simply that the human adaptation for cultural learning is a very strong tendency, even in a domain—the acquisition of complex linguistic constructions—where it has classically been thought to play a minor role. Importantly, this tendency is perfectly consistent with children's imitative tendencies in (a) tool use tasks—especially two-year-olds as in the study of Nagell et al., 1993 (see Chapter 2; see also Want and Harris, 1999); (b) word learning tasks—again especially two-year-olds (the Tomasello et al. studies reviewed in Chapter 4); and (c) object manipulation and symbolic play tasks—again especially two-year-olds (Tomasello, Striano, and Rochat, in press, and Striano, Tomasello, and Rochat, 1999, reviewed in Chapter 3). The overall conclusion is thus that during the period from one to three years old, young children are virtual "imitation machines" as they seek to appropriate the cultural skills and behaviors of the mature members of their social groups.

This imitative tendency is not all-pervasive, of course, as children do some creative things with cultural artifacts and linguistic conventions from early in development, and it is certainly a tendency that recedes in influence in later cognitive development as children do various kinds of novel things with the cultural tools they have mastered. But initially—in the period in which they first begin to acquire the artifacts and conventions of their culture between the ages of one and four years—human children have a very strong imitative tendency. Their initial reaction in many problem-solving situations is to imitate the behavior of those around them, just as adults in many situations quickly resort to imitation if they have not mastered all the skills involved or are otherwise unsure of what to do. One of the most interesting issues about linguistic symbols and constructions is thus that they create a palpable tension between the need to "do it the way adults do it," the imitative learning of linguistic symbols and constructions, and the need to be creative in adapting these culturally inherited artifacts to the communicative situation at hand—and in making generalizations about ways to do this. Young children's very strong tendency to imitate what others are doing thus shows up again and again in their early cognitive development, leading to the conclusion that the early childhood period is largely concerned with children's entry into the world of culture through their mastery of the artifacts and conventions that predate their arrival on the scene—which they may then adapt for creative uses as their mastery progresses.

The classic approach to questions of language and cognition is to compare the cognitive skills of people learning different languages. But my interest here is in learning a language, any language, versus learning no language at all. The various people in the modern world who do not learn language normally are of course all apposite to my claims, but, as elaborated in Chapter 4, none of them represents a very good case of a languageless, much less a cultureless, being. And it seems to be the case empirically that various substitutes and variations on linguistic symbols, such as manual sign languages, are all equally effective as language in directing attention and cognition if they are, like natural languages, based on intersubjectively shared and perspectivally based conventional symbols.

6

DISCOURSE AND REPRESENTATIONAL REDESCRIPTION

Any utterance is a link in a very complexly organized chain of utterances.

—Mikhail Bakhtin

In broad outline, virtually all of what I have discussed so far is universal among all the infants and young children of the world: they identify with other persons; perceive other persons as intentional agents like the self; engage with other persons in joint attentional activities; understand many of the causal relations that hold among physical objects and events in the world; understand the communicative intentions that other persons express in gestures, linguistic symbols, and linguistic constructions; learn through role-reversal imitation to produce for others those same gestures, symbols, and constructions; and construct linguistically based object categories and event schemas. These cognitive skills enable young children to begin to move down the cultural line of development in earnest, that is, to begin to culturally learn (appropriate, acquire) the skills, practices, and domains of knowledge unique to their social groups. Nevertheless, even as children move along these culturally specific developmental pathways during the early childhood period and beyond, there are still some developmental processes, and even some milestones along the way, that are universal. The challenge in looking at children during these later developmental periods is therefore to explain both the culturally specific and the culturally universal aspects of human cognitive ontogeny.

The culturally specific aspects of human cognition are explained by theorists of all persuasions in basically the same way: children learn what they are exposed to, and different cultures expose them to different things. Whether the theorists are cultural psychologists focused on processes of cultural interaction or more individualistic theorists focused on individual problem solving (e.g., neo-Piagetians or neo-nativists), to explain how children learn about dinosaurs, or Greek history, or ancestors, or rug weaving, there is really no alternative to the individual child acquiring knowledge within particular social and physical contexts. But when it comes to culturally universal skills and knowledge, theoretical difficulties arise. Debates about the universal aspects of human cognitive development are currently dominated by individualistic theorists, most of whom have a fundamental concern with the degree to which various cognitive skills and domains of knowledge are "innate" and/or "modular" (e.g., see Hirschfield and Gelman, eds., 1994; Wellman and Gelman, 1997). In none of the individualistic approaches is there any role for social and cultural processes in the development of basic and universal cognitive structures, beyond simply their role in exposing the child/scientist/machine to different kinds of "input" or "data" within different specific domains of knowledge. Cultural psychologists, in contrast, have been much concerned with social and cultural processes in childhood cognitive development—a focus on these processes defines the approach, after all—but for the most part they have been so concerned with the culturally specific aspects of cognitive development that they have virtually ignored the role of social and cultural processes in the ontogeny of the most basic and universal aspects of human cognition.

My own view is that social and cultural processes—of a type that is common across all cultures—are an integral and essential part of the normal ontogenetic pathways of many of the most fundamental and universal cognitive skills of humans, especially those that are unique to the species. Some of these social-cultural processes are so obvious that they are rarely commented upon by any theorist, for example, the "transmission" of knowledge and information from adults to children via language and other symbolic media. Some of these processes are a bit less obvious and are the concern of some neo-Vygotskian cultural psychologists only, for example, the role of cultural artifacts in mediating children's interactions with their environments. And some of these processes, I believe, are not at all obvious and have not been given the attention they deserve by any contemporary theorist. They have been neglected mainly because they involve processes of linguistic communication and discourse—processes in which children engage other minds dialogically—and these processes are either underappreciated or misunderstood by theorists of both persuasions. Individualistic theorists mostly accept the view that language is a domain-specific competence that does not interact in important ways with other cognitive competences, whereas cultural psychologists, despite some attention to the role of language in socializing behavior and forming simple categories, have mostly not attended at all to the role of linguistic communication in the development of complex cognitive skills.

The current hypothesis is that the perspectival nature of linguistic symbols, and the use of linguistic symbols in discourse interactions in which different perspectives are explicitly contrasted and shared, provide the raw material out of which the children of all cultures construct the flexible and multi-perspectival—perhaps even dialogical—cognitive representations that give human cognition much of its awesome and unique power. In this chapter, I attempt to spell out this view. First, I outline several ways in which processes of linguistic communication and discourse are constitutive of human cognitive development during the early childhood period—from simply exposing children to factual information to transforming the way they understand and cognitively represent the world by providing them with multiple, sometimes conflicting, perspectives on phenomena. Second, I examine in a more detailed way how these linguistic processes contribute to children's cognitive development in the two primary domains of knowledge elaborated from infancy: the understanding of social-psychological (intentional) agency and the understanding of physical (causal) events and relations. Third, I examine how some special types of linguistic interaction and discourse lead, at the end of the early childhood period, to the vitally important processes of self-regulation, metacognition, and representational redescription—which together lead to dialogical cognitive representations.

Linguistic Communication and Cognitive Development

At least since Sapir and Whorf, but really since Herder and Humboldt, the influence of linguistic communication on cognition has been a topic of singular interest to philosophers, psychologists, and linguists. The focus of virtually all theorists has been on how the acquisition of one particular natural language (e.g., Hopi) versus another (e.g., English) affects the way in which human beings conceptualize the world—the hypothesis of "linguistic determinism." Recent research suggests that this hypothesis is almost certainly true in one form or another, be it the "strong" form in which particular languages influence nonlinguistic cognition in particular ways (e.g., Lucy, 1992; Levinson, 1983) or the "weak" form in which learning and using a particular language draw attention to certain aspects of situations as opposed to others—so-called thinking for speaking (Slobin, 1991). However, there is an even more fundamental question, and that is the role of linguistic communication—using any natural language versus not using one at all—in cognitive development in general. We are back to *Gedanken* experiments here—infants on desert islands and the like— and not actual empirical research directly addressing the question. Nevertheless, I believe that on theoretical grounds, supplemented by some relevant empirical research and observations, we may come to some fairly firm conclusions about the role of linguistic communication in cognitive development. In particular, I wish to focus on three dimensions of the process: (1) the cultural "transmission" of knowledge to children via linguistic communication; (2) the ways in which the structure of linguistic communication influences children's construction of cognitive categories, relations, analogies, and metaphors; and (3) the ways in which linguistic interaction with others (discourse) induces children to take different—sometimes conflicting, sometimes complementary—conceptual perspectives on phenomena.

Knowledge Transmission and Instruction
via Linguistic Communication

It is a point so obvious that it is seldom, if ever, mentioned. If children did not have available to them adult instruction through language, pictures, and other symbolic media, they would know the same amount about dinosaurs as did Plato and Aristotle, namely, zero. Indeed, if human children wandered around all day on their own in solitary fashion—as do the individuals of some primate species—they would know not much more than zero about any of the topics in which their expertise is currently studied by developmental psychologists, from dinosaurs to biology to baseball to music to mathematics. Beyond fundamental skills of primate cognition, therefore, children's domain-specific knowledge and expertise depend almost totally on the accumulated knowledge of their cultures and its "transmission" to them via linguistic and other symbols, including both writing and pictures. The amount of knowledge that any individual organism can gain by simply observing the world on its own is extremely limited.

The process by which knowledge and skills are "transmitted" to children is different in different cultures, with children in modern Western cultures given much more verbal and literacy-based instruction than children in many nonliterate cultures—who are typically enjoined to simply watch adults and learn by observing their performance of some skilled practice. But even nonliterate cultures have important domains of knowledge that are almost exclusively in symbolic format, and so they can only be transmitted symbolically—most clearly knowledge concerning things removed in space and time such as characteristics of distant relatives and ancestors, myths and some religious rituals, some knowledge of local flora and fauna, and so forth. The adults of all human societies thus provide their children with fairly substantial amounts of direct instruction and explanation, at least some of it via language and other symbolic media, about one or another domain of knowledge valued by the culture (Kruger and Tomasello, 1996).

The Structuring Role of Language

Acquiring a natural language does more than expose children to culturally important information, however. Acquiring a natural language also serves to socialize, to structure culturally, the ways in which children habitually attend to and conceptualize different aspects of their worlds. As they attempt to comprehend acts of linguistic communication directed to them, children engage in certain very special processes of categorization and conceptual perspective-taking. Language does not create these fundamental cognitive abilities, of course, as many animal species create different conceptual categories for various instrumental purposes, and children can take the perspective of others without language. But language adds another set of conceptual categories and perspectives to the human repertoire—categories and perspectives constructed for purposes of linguistic communication.

Categorizing the world for purposes of linguistic communication in some cases has unique properties. Although some categories embodied in language may be straightforward reflections of nonlinguistic categories that could potentially be identical to those of other species (and may be formed by human infants prior to language), others reflect the peculiarities of human linguistic communication, and, most importantly, they reflect the whole system of options open in particular communicative situations. Thus, for example, each time a person wishes to make reference to an object for another person, she must choose whether to call it such things as *the dog, that animal over there, it, the cocker spaniel, Fido*, and so forth. As she depicts the event she must choose to say *The dog bit . . .* or *The man was bitten by . . .* The choices made are determined in large part by the speaker's evaluation of the listener's communicative needs and what would help to make the communicative point—what kind of description at what level of detail and from what perspective is needed for successful and effective communication, as outlined in Chapters 4 and 5. Given that languages work mainly categorically (they have not evolved as massive lists of proper names for individual objects and events), the categories and schemas immanent in language enable children, among other things, to take multiple perspectives on the same entity simultaneously: this object is both a rose and a flower at the same time (and many other things) depending on how I wish to construe it in this particular communicative situation. There is no good evidence that nonhuman animals or prelinguistic human infants categorize or perspectivize the world in this hierarchically flexible manner (Tomasello and Call, 1997). Other animals may be able to take different perspectives on things in different circumstances, but because they do not have available the many perspectives of others as embodied in language, they do not understand that there are a multitude of ways that a phenomenon may be construed simultaneously.

The categories children encounter in language involve both static entities such as objects and properties and dynamic entities such as events and relations. By far the most studied cognitive categories concern objects and their properties, and indeed many of the initial models of knowledge representation in Cognitive Psychology were composed of hierarchies of object categories exclusively, and most of the domains of knowledge that cognitive psychologists study are defined by the objects involved (e.g., types of animals, other "natural kinds," and artifacts). Event and relational categories are hierarchically organized to some degree as well, and some domains of expertise are defined almost exclusively by certain types of events (e.g., the domains of baseball or chess), so that similar studies of event cognition could also be done (Barsalou, 1992). But by far the most interesting and cognitively significant manifestation of relational categories in language concerns analogies and metaphors—which are interesting precisely because they are composed of events and relations that can be recognized as "similar" across different object domains. What makes analogies and metaphors so interesting is that they are different from object categories in one fundamental way. Objects are the same objects regardless of the context in which they are encountered: a *Tyrannosaurus rex* is a *Tyrannosaurus rex* whether it is studied in its natural context or in a museum, or if it walks through a Broadway play. But events and relations are more dependent on object context: photosynthesis can take place only within the context of plants—because it is a process that depends on the presence of certain specific objects and substances—so that if we wanted to talk about photosynthesis in the domain of automobiles we would have to invoke some kind of analogy or metaphor in which we substituted objects for one another (e.g., carburetors for mitochondria) so as to preserve the same relational structure in the different object domains (Gentner and Markman, 1997).

Recent work in cognitive and functional linguistics has shown that metaphors permeate even the most ordinary uses of natural language (e.g., Lakoff, 1987; Johnson, 1987; Gibbs, 1995). Adults tell children with regularity, for example, to "toe the line" or to "put that out of your mind" or not to "lose patience." Comprehending these figurative ways of talking takes children down the path of drawing analogies between the concrete domains they know from their sensory-motor experiences and the more abstract domains of adult interaction and social and mental life that they are in the process of learning about. After enough of certain kinds of metaphorical expressions, children should presumably be able to construct the kinds of broad and pervasive metaphorical understandings that lead to productivity—as in the famous "love is a journey" metaphor of Lakoff and Johnson (1980), in which our relationship is "off track" or "on track" or "going nowhere" or "moving fast," with the possibility that people who know this pattern can then come up with novel metaphors that cohere (e.g., "We set out for married life but we did not pack the right things for the trip"). It takes children some time to appreciate metaphorical language explicitly, presumably because relational mappings of this sort are quite complex (see Winner, 1988, for a review). But it is of crucial importance for the current argument that Gentner and Medina (1997) have recently reviewed a wealth of empirical evidence and concluded that children's appreciation of analogical/metaphorical thinking is strongly facilitated by, perhaps even enabled by, their encounters with relational language (see also Gentner et al., 1995).

Relatedly, it is interesting and important that as children become more proficient with the various abstract constructions of their native language, they are able to construe things they know to be of one type as if they were of another type—as discussed in Chapter 5. The point is so important that it bears repetition here. Over ontogenetic time children detect abstract patterns in the language they hear around them, leading them to construct myriad different linguistic generalizations, from categories of objects to schematized and abstract linguistic constructions. For various kinds of communicative and expressive purposes, people of all cultures have applied these abstract categories and schemas over historical time in ways that are novel, such that their comprehension requires the construing of aspects of reality in metaphorical, analogically based ways (Lakoff, 1987; Johnson, 1987; Gentner and Markman, 1997). This includes everything from the derivational process by means of which events are construed as objects *(Skiing is fun)* and objects as events *(They tabled the motion)* to explicit metaphors such as people "blowing their tops" or "boiling over with anger." Children encounter this aspect of the linguistic inventory of their culture and must deal with it, and eventually come to use it. The kind of flexibility of thinking that results is, in a word, unthinkable in animal species whose individual members do not communicate with one another symbolically and so do not store up a repertoire of abstract symbolic construals.

The point is not that language creates *ex nihilo* the ability to categorize, to perspectivize, or to make analogies or metaphors. That is impossible because language depends on these skills, and they may be present in basic form in either nonhuman primates or prelinguistic infants. But what has happened is that in collaboration over historical time human beings have created an incredible array of categorical perspectives and construals on all kinds of objects, events, and relations, and then they have embodied them in their systems of symbolic communication called natural languages. As children develop ontogenetically, they use their basic skills of categorization, perspective-taking, and relational thinking—in concert with their ability to comprehend the adult's communicative intentions—to learn the use of the relevant symbolic forms. This enables them to take advantage of a vast number of categories and analogies that other members of their culture have seen fit to create and symbolize, and that they very likely would never have thought to create on their own. In addition, of course, in some cases they also may generalize across these and create novel categories and analogies on their own—once again the individual line of development working on materials supplied by the cultural line of development—which other persons may then adopt.

Discourse and Conceptual Perspective-taking

An important aspect of the role that language acquisition plays in cognitive development is thus the categories, relations, and conceptual perspectives embodied in conventional linguistic structures—from words to syntactic constructions to conventional metaphors—with which young children must operate in normal discourse interactions. In addition, however, sometimes the semantic content of the discourse, what is being talked about over multiple discourse turns, expresses differing and sometimes conflicting construals of things. Thus, people sometimes disagree or express different knowledge about things in their conversations—which provides children with differing explicit perspectives about a phenomenon immediately at hand. Also, the adult sometimes fails to comprehend the child's utterance, or vice versa, and so asks for a clarification (discourse about the *form* of what the speaker has just said). Finally, sometimes the child expresses a view on something and then her interactive partner expresses a view about that view (discourse about the *content* of what the speaker has just said). Each of these three types of discourse—disagreements, clarification sequences, and didactic interactions—provides its own version of discourse perspective.

First, in extended discourse people express different knowledge and perspectives explicitly as they converse about a topic, including both disagreements and misunderstandings. For instance, the child may express the view that a sibling ought to share her toy, whereas the sibling may express the contrary view that she should not. Or the child may express the view that there is more water in a beaker that is taller, whereas a peer may express the contrary view that the other one has more water because it is wider. The key point in these cases is that there are two conflicting views that are in effect expressed simultaneously about the same topic, and the child must find some way to reconcile them. Conflicting views of this type are thought by some theorists to be especially important in the case of peer or sibling discourse since the child is not inclined in these cases to simply defer to the authority of the other's expressed view (as often happens with adults), but rather seeks to find some rational way to deal with the discrepancy (e.g., Piaget, 1932; Damon, 1983; Dunn, 1988).

Second, in naturally occurring discourse between children and adults it happens often that an adult says something that the child does not understand, and vice versa, due to its linguistic formulation. The listener then asks for clarification with such things as "What?" "What did you say?" "You put the bird where?" "You put what in the cage?" and so forth, aimed at one or more of the linguistic forms in the utterance. Clarification requests of this type express in more or less detail precisely what the listener did and did not comprehend of the speaker's utterance. Ideally, then, a repair takes place in which the original speaker repeats or reformulates her utterance in a way that takes account of the fact that—and perhaps even the reason why—the listener was unsuccessful in comprehending it the first time. A number of studies of children's responses to adult clarification requests have established such facts as: (a) two-year-olds respond appropriately to adult clarification requests (Wilcox and Webster, 1980); (b) two- and three-year-olds respond differently to more general clarification requests ("What?" "Huh?") than to specific clarification requests ("Put it where?") (Anselmi, Tomasello, and Acunzo, 1986); and (c) two-year-olds repair general clarification requests for their mothers most often by repeating their utterance, whereas with less familiar adults they most often reformulate the utterance—presumably indicating their understanding that their mothers know their language and thus very likely did not hear them whereas the unfamiliar adult may need a new wording (Tomasello, Farrar, and Dines, 1983). Children at this age also know enough to ask adults for repairs in many situations (Golinkoff, 1993; see Baldwin and Moses, 1996, for a review). Also, falling into this same category are misunderstandings, for example, when a child comes home from school and says "He hit me," and her interlocutor responds with "Who?" (or else assumes it was Jimmy when it was not), signaling her limited knowledge of the situation. In all of these cases, the content of discourse signals to the child that one of the interactive partners understands a situation or utterance in a way that the other does not.

Third, a related but different kind of discourse (actually meta-discourse) occurs when the child expresses some view of a situation and another person then expresses a view about that view. For example, the child may express the view that there is more water in the beaker that is taller, to which an adult may reply that she understands why the child might think that, because taller usually means more, but in this case the great width of the other beaker compensates. Or the child may say that she is going to start to solve a puzzle by looking for pieces of the depicted tree, and the adult may respond by telling her that that is a reasonable strategy, but it will lead to confusion so perhaps she should look first for the corner pieces regardless of the picture. In this case, the child is not confronted with an equal and complementary view, she is presented with a critique of her view, and from an authority figure at that. Consequently, in comprehending the adult's communicative intentions in these kinds of exchanges, the child must understand the adult's expressed view on her own expressed view. This kind of discourse about previous discourse is very special because as the child comprehends it she is led to examine her own thinking from the perspective of the other. Internalizing the view of the other on her own view then leads the child to the kinds of dialogical cognitive representations with which Vygotsky (1978) was primarily concerned, and, eventually, as she generalizes this process, to the ability to self-monitor her own cognitive processes. Because the meta-views thus expressed are couched in the very same natural language terms as the original view, reflection can help the child to create coherence and systematicity in thinking and theorizing about things in the world and perspectives on the world all in a single representational medium (also known as representational redescription; see below).

Children engage on a daily basis in these three kinds of discourse, each of which requires them to take the perspective of another person in a way that goes beyond the perspective-taking inherent in comprehending individual linguistic symbols and constructions. And the situation sometimes requires that they try to reconcile discrepant perspectives as well. That is, they must try to resolve discrepant views that are explicitly expressed; try to identify the parts of their linguistic expression that others fail to understand and reformulate them; and try to understand, and sometimes coordinate, their own perspective and that of someone else who is commenting on that perspective. In combination with the two other general types of social and cultural influence on early cognitive development—the transmission of knowledge via linguistic and other symbols and the structuring role of language—these three kinds of discourse play a very important role, indeed a constitutive role in my opinion, in the development of dialogical and self-reflective cognitive representations in early childhood.

Social and Physical Knowledge

During the early childhood period children gain many kinds of knowledge about specific phenomena in specific cognitive domains, depending on the cultural and educational settings in which they grow up. But it is not so easy to identify distinct and separate domains of cognition in human ontogeny, and different theorists have come up with wildly different catalogues of human cognitive domains (compare, e.g., Fodor, 1983; Karmiloff-Smith, 1992; Carey and Spelke, 1994). My procedure here will thus be to take the same approach I took to infancy; that is, I will focus not on domains of knowledge but on objects of knowledge—the two most fundamental being social-psychological objects and physical objects, which obviously operate in very different ways. Human social-psychological objects are animate (self-moving) and operate intentionally and morally, whereas physical objects are inanimate (non-self-moving) and operate in terms of causal and quantitative relations (with animals and artifacts, as argued in Chapter 3, falling into a very interesting middle ground).

In examining children's understanding of social and physical objects and how this changes during early childhood, I will focus on the social-cultural-linguistic processes involved in these changes. I will not argue that these processes are sufficient to account for the ontogenetic changes that occur, since clearly a number of other cognitive processes are involved. But I will argue that they are necessary, an argument that few theorists are willing to make explicitly. In both the social and physical domains of knowledge, I will argue that engaging with other minds dialogically via symbols and discourse over a several-year period works to transform one- to two-year-old children's cognitive skills, which differ in only a few important ways from those of other primates, into cognitive skills and forms of cognitive representation that differ in myriad ways from those of other primates. Without this dialogic engagement with other minds, this transformation would not occur. In each case I will focus on the three types of social-cultural processes just elaborated: knowledge transmission, the structure of language, and perspective-taking in discourse.

Understanding Social and Moral Agency

If young children understand other persons as intentional agents by about one year of age, an important question is why it takes another two to four years, until they are three to five years of age, before they understand other persons as mental agents who have beliefs about the world that may differ from their own. And children of all cultures do seem to come to this understanding of others as mental agents at very roughly the same age—although only a few non-Western cultures have been studied and although the variability within cultures has yet to be fully explored (Lillard, 1997). To explain the shift in children's social understanding at approximately four years of age, there are of course the usual contingent of theorists who think that the understanding of beliefs is an innate module that simply ripens on its own independent maturational timetable (e.g., Baron-Cohen, 1995). Other theorists believe that understanding the mental states of other persons results from a process of theory formation basically identical to the process as it operates in the physical domain; for example, a child may see a peer looking under a sofa when she knows that the ball he just lost is under the chair. To explain his searching under the sofa she comes to attribute to him the "belief" that the ball is under the sofa (Gopnik, 1993; Wellman, 1990). Through whatever process, this theory-formation ability and the experience with other persons that serves as its data simply reach their necessary degree of power at around four years of age.

The alternative to these views is simulation theory, as espoused most prominently by Harris (1991, 1996) and as invoked to explain infant social cognition in Chapter 3. The main point is that we are concerned here with social-psychological knowledge, which differs in important ways from physical knowledge. In attempting to understand other persons, children can exploit their first-person experience of their own psychological states, which involves unique sources of information such as the internal experience of goals and their attainment or nonattainment, the internal experience of thoughts and beliefs, and so forth—which are not available when observing another person or an inanimate object. In this view, when a child sees a peer searching under the sofa, she knows what it feels like to be looking for something in vain, and she also knows what it feels like to then find it in another location—and so, since she identifies with the other child, she understands his behavior in these same terms. As Harris has pointed out, this simulation of the experience of other persons is not a straightforward process, and the child often has to juggle the simulation with such things as her knowledge of the real situation from her own first-person point of view, that is, that the ball is really under the chair. Interestingly in this connection, Perner and Lopez (1997) found that young children were better at predicting what another person would see in a particular situation if they had actually been in that situation first themselves. So, as a continuous thread with my invocation of processes of simulation at nine months of age to explain infants' coming to understand others as intentional agents, I again invoke simulation to explain young children's coming to understand other persons as mental agents. But this requires that the child come to some new way of understanding her own thoughts and beliefs at around four years of age, which immediately raises the issue of how this might come about.

I do not believe that anything dramatic happens at precisely four years of age that enables children to suddenly understand their own minds more deeply than before. Rather, what happens is that gradually over the early childhood period children gain experience with the interplay between their own mind and that of others, mostly through various kinds of discourse interactions. Indeed, many manifestations of the understanding of the mental states of others are apparent in children's natural interactions at three years of age (Dunn, 1988), and there is much variability in the age at which children pass the false-belief task, with a substantial portion of children not passing until after five years of age. Several theorists have hypothesized that language may play an important role in children's coming gradually to view other persons as mental agents (e.g., Harris, 1996). However, most of the empirical work either concerns very general relationships (e.g., Happé, 1995; Charman and Shmueli-Goetz, 1998; Jenkins and Astington, 1996) or else looks at the content of children's language with specific reference to the use of mental-state terms such as *think, want,* and *believe* (Bartsch and Wellman, 1995). My own view is that, while the content of talk about the mind is important, also important is the process of linguistic communication itself. To comprehend the linguistic communications of others, children must in some sense simulate the perspective of other persons as they are expressing themselves linguistically, and so the back-and-forth of discourse involves the child in a constant shifting of perspectives from her own to those of others and back again.

It is thus not surprising that Appleton and Reddy (1996) found that engaging young children in discourse about the false-belief task itself helped them to understand the mental acts that comprise that task, or that Call and Tomasello (1999) found that nonverbal great apes were unable to pass a nonverbal false-belief task. Perhaps of special importance, Peterson and Siegal (1995) and Russell et al. (1998) have found that deaf children perform very poorly on false-belief tasks. Most of these children have hearing parents, and so have had relatively few opportunities for extended discourse interactions during early childhood. Interestingly, deaf children born to deaf parents, who can converse with them in sign language, have no particular difficulties on false-belief tasks (Peterson and Siegal, 1997), and virtually all deaf adolescents do well on these tasks—perhaps because by this age they have had sufficient discourse experience.

One especially important form of discourse for understanding the relationship between one's own mental states and those of others is disagreements and misunderstandings. Dunn (1988) has documented something of the wide range of disputes and conflicts, as well as cooperative interactions, in which children of the same family participate on a daily basis (see also Dunn, Brown, and Beardsall, 1991). Perhaps of special importance, siblings have conflicting wants and needs with dismaying regularity as they both desire the same toy or wish to engage in the same activity at the same time. In addition to this conflict of goals or desires, they also have conflicts involving beliefs, as one expresses the view that X is the case and the other disputes this and claims that Y is the case. Or, similarly, they have a clear difference of knowledge or beliefs, as when one makes a presupposition that the other does not hold in kind (e.g., the presupposition of shared knowledge in using *he* or *it*), or the same thing may happen in reverse as the sibling makes unwarranted presuppositions about shared knowledge and beliefs. It is thus possible that discourse with other persons, perhaps especially siblings, is a prime mover in a child's coming to think of them as beings with desires, thoughts, and beliefs similar to her own but still different from hers—even when the discourse has no specifically mental terms in it at all. Supportive of this general view is the finding that Western middle-class children with siblings tend to understand other persons in terms of their beliefs at a younger age than children without siblings (Perner, Ruffman, and Leekham, 1994).

There is also another kind of discourse that may be important in children's coming to understand others as mental agents, and that is the process of communicative breakdown and repair. As children begin to engage in discourse with adults at two to three years of age, it happens with some regularity that someone does not understand what they say. Golinkoff (1993) documents some cases in which even very young infants engage in a process of what she calls "the negotiation of meaning" in which the child says something unintelligible, the adult guesses at its meaning, and the infant either accepts or rejects the interpretation. As children get older they experience both (a) misinterpretations, in which the adult interprets the child's utterance in a way that she did not intend, and (b) clarification requests, in which the child says something that the adult does not understand and so the adult asks for clarification. These kinds of discourse—which occur frequently for virtually all young children learning a natural language—put children in the situation in which they formulate an utterance with some more or less coherent hypothesis of the informational needs of the listener, and then that hypothesis is demonstrated to be either accurate or faulty. These situations lead the child to try to discern why the adult does not comprehend the utterance—perhaps she did not hear it, perhaps she is not familiar with this specific linguistic formulation, and so forth. And of course it may happen that the child does not understand the adult's utterance and so asks her for clarification as well. In all, it would seem that these kinds of misunderstandings and repairs are an extremely rich source of information about how one's own understanding of a linguistically expressed perspective on a situation may differ from that of others.

A legitimate question at this point is how exactly to characterize the child's emerging understanding of mental agents: what is the understanding of beliefs (or having a "theory of mind") anyway? I argued in Chapter 3 that human one- and two-year-olds understand other persons as intentional agents, which, while it is an advance over neonates' understanding of others as animate agents, is still something short of older children's understanding of others as mental agents. One problem in current discussions of older children's understanding of others as mental agents (i.e., their "theories of mind") is that an unorganized mix of mental-state terms is used. My view is that the panoply of mental-state terms that apply to the social understanding of preschool children may be cast into a simple framework involving (a) perception or input, (b) behavior or output, and (c) goal or reference state. Table 6.1 shows the progression of each of these components from neonates to older infants and from toddlers to young children. The basic progression over ontogeny—in the case of each of the three components—is the gradual distancing of the component from concrete action. Animacy is only expressed in behavior; intentionality is expressed in behavior but at the same time is somewhat divorced from behavior since it may on occasion be unexpressed or expressed in different ways; but mentality concerns desires, plans, and beliefs that have no necessary behavioral reality at all. And so my specific contention about early childhood social cognition is that there is a continuous developmental progression in children's understanding of others, as follows:

- animate agents, in common with all primates (infancy);
- intentional agents, a species-unique way of understanding conspecifics, which includes an understanding of both the goal-directed behavior and the attention of others (one year); and
- mental agents, the understanding that other persons have not just intentions and attention as manifest in their behavior, but also thoughts and beliefs which may or may not be expressed in behavior—and which may differ from the "real" situation (four years).

The specific hypothesis about process is that the transition to an understanding of mental agents derives mainly from the child's use of intentional understanding in discourse with other persons in which there is a continuous need to simulate other persons' perspectives on things, which often differ from the child's. Table 6.1 may thus be seen as a kind of theory of the ontogenetic progression of young children's social-cognitive skills (their "theory of mind").

There is one other uniquely human aspect of social understanding that begins to make itself felt at the end of the early childhood period, and that concerns moral understanding. In the account of Piaget (1932), moral reasoning is not about following authoritative

Table 6.1 Three levels in the human understanding of social-psychological beings, expressed in terms of the three main components needing to be understood: input (perception), output (behavior), and goal states.

	Understanding of perceptual input	Understanding of behavioral output	Understanding of goal state
Understanding others as animate beings (young infants)	Gaze	Behavior	[Direction]
Understanding others as intentional agents (9-month-olds)	Attention	Strategies	Goals
Understanding others as mental agents (4-year-olds)	Beliefs	Plans	Desires

rules, but rather it is about empathizing with other persons and being able to see and feel things from their point of view. Piaget argued that discourse interactions were of crucial importance for children's skills of moral reasoning, but only (or mostly) if they occurred with peers. He argued that although children may learn some rules governing their social behavior from adult injunctions (e.g., "Share your toys"), moral reasoning is not really transmitted or fostered by such rules. Moral reasoning derives from children's empathetic engagement with others as they, in a sense, put themselves in the place of the other and "feel his pain." Rules carrying rewards and punishments from adults do not foster this experience, and indeed in many ways impede it. It is in social interaction and discourse with others who are equal in terms of knowledge and power that children are led to go beyond rule-following and to engage with other moral agents who have thoughts and feelings like their own (see also Damon, 1983). Note again that it is not the content of the language that is crucial—although some of children's moral development surely does consist of explicit and verbalized principles passed to them from others—but the process of engaging another mind in discourse dialogically.

Of crucial importance in the development of moral reasoning is reflective discourse in which children make comments or ask questions involving the beliefs and desires of others or themselves, for example, "Does she think that I like X?" "I don't want her to want my X." Kruger (1992; see also Kruger and Tomasello, 1986) provided support for this hypothesis in a study of seven- and eleven-year-old children. The children were initially assessed in terms of their moral reasoning skills as measured by the complexity and sophistication of their argumentation about a story in which there was a question about how to divide up rewards among a group of people who had made different contributions to a task. Then some of the children had further discussions with a peer, and others had further discussions with their mothers—after which their moral reasoning skills were again assessed. Children who had intervening discussions with peers showed greater gains in moral reasoning skills than those who had intervening discussions with their mothers. Crucially, Kruger found that in the peer groups much more reflective discourse—discourse in which one participant talked about the view expressed by the other—took place and that this was correlated with the progress individual children made. A very important finding that helps to explain Kruger's result is that of Foley and Ratner (1997), who found that when young children collaborate with a partner in an activity and are later asked to recall which partner performed which actions, they often recall themselves as having done an action that was really done by the other. Foley and Ratner's conclusion is that "young children recode the actions of other people's as their own while thinking about what another person has done or will do" (p. 91). This again demonstrates that, at bottom, what we are talking about is a process of simulation, and linguistic discourse is an especially rich locus for complex and sophisticated simulations.

To summarize, the basic hypothesis is that children have the ability to begin participating in discourse with others from soon after they understand them as intentional agents at one year of age. They only come to understand other persons as mental agents some years later because to understand that other persons have beliefs about the world that differ from their own, children need to engage them in discourse in which these different perspectives are clearly apparent—either in a disagreement, a misunderstanding, a request for clarification, or a reflective dialogue. This does not rule out other forms of interaction with others and observation of their behavior as important in the child's construction of a "theory of mind" as well; it is just that linguistic discourse provides a particularly rich source of information about other minds. It should also be noted that as ontogeny proceeds during later childhood wide variations in the way that different cultures invoke internal mental causes of behavior—perhaps as expressed in the way they use specific mental-state terms—begin to show themselves in children's social-psychological reasoning. In a review and analysis of the cross-cultural evidence, Lillard (1997) proposes that very young children are highly similar across all cultures in their social cognition, for example, in understanding the basic intentions and mental states of other persons, but that beyond these initial universals children are prepared to learn a wide variety of different systems of psychological explanation, including not just individual thoughts and beliefs but also more collectivist social explanations and even outside intervention by witchcraft and the like. And so it is clear that once the universal cognitive competence is in place—deriving from intentional understanding as practiced in linguistic discourse—children in different cultures can learn to use this competence in constructing a wide variety of different systems of explanation depending on the system they are exposed to in their particular language and culture, that is, depending on the content of what is (mostly linguistically) "transmitted" in their particular culture.

Understanding Causal and Quantitative Relations

Sometime near their first birthdays infants begin to use tools in ways that evidence a dawning understanding of the causal powers of their own sensory-motor actions (Piaget, 1954). However, when the causal analysis of interactions among external objects and events is involved (i.e., independent of the child's own action), children perform very poorly for several years after this—even on tasks that adults would see as fairly simple (e.g., Piaget and Garcia, 1974; Schultz, 1982). As in the social-psychological domain, therefore, the question arises as to why this developmental process is so slow.

As argued in Chapters 2 and 3, I believe that children's earliest causal understanding of physical events derives from their intentional understanding of external social-psychological events. This is the foundation for causal understanding that emerges mostly during the second year of life. But beyond these basics, most of children's early causal understanding of specific events derives in one way or another from the three types of social-cultural processes I have singled out in this chapter. That is, although young children may on occasion discover the causes of some particular phenomena through their own observation and experimentation, most often they hear adults explaining causal relations to them, and they attempt to understand this discourse. There are several levels at which this attempted understanding of causal discourse contributes to children's causal understanding. Most fundamental is the fact that in all of the languages of the world causality plays an important structuring role. A large portion of the canonical linguistic constructions of all the world's languages are transitive, or even causative, in one or another form (Hopper and Thompson, 1980). This presumably reflects the fact that causality is such a fundamental aspect of human cognition, and so it is clear that the structure of language is a historical result, not a cause, of causal understanding. But what this means ontogenetically is that children constantly hear descriptions of specific events in causal terms that they would be incapable of constructing by themselves. Thus, even the very simplest change-of-state utterances like *You broke the glass* or *He cleaned his room* assign a cause, or at least a causal agent, to the resulting change of state. This kind of discourse at the very least draws children's attention with regularity to the possibility of causal agents as being responsible for many different kinds of physical events.

In addition, of course, adults and children talk about causes more explicitly, and many, though certainly not all, of children's specific causal explanations are derived via "transmission" from their discourse with adults. But even in the cases of children's creative causal explanations of events, each culture has its own modes of explanation that children soon learn. Thus, among the Jalaris peoples of rural India, illnesses and natural disasters are prototypically explained through an interaction of spirits and human misdeeds (Nuckolls, 1991), and the Azande from central Africa attribute many kinds of unfortunate events to witchcraft (Evans-Pritchard, 1937). It is thus not surprising that Western middle-class children engage in the kinds of explanations they do, once they have caught on to the types of explanations that adults normally give and value. For example, in a study of the earliest causal explanations that young children give in the two- to three-year age period, Bloom and Capatides (1987) found that the majority of children's causal talk was not about events happening independent of themselves, but rather about social-cultural situations and how they might negotiate them—what Bloom and Capatides called "subjective causality." Many of these situations involved "arbitrary" rules and conventions, and so the child's only way to have learned the causal structure was through discourse with adults (see also Hood, Fiess, and Aron, 1982; Callanan and Oakes, 1992). For example:

(1) CHILD: It can't go. (picture of train at stoplight)
    ADULT: It can't go?
    CHILD: No, because that sign doesn't say go.

(2) ADULT: Why do you have him (guinea pig)? Did you take him home from school?
    CHILD: Yeah, 'cause they don't belong in school.

(3) ADULT: I want to go home now.
    CHILD: Wait Mommy comes.
    ADULT: Why?
    CHILD: Because I will be lonely.

Bloom and Capatides note:

The children could not have discovered such relationships as these between events, and the feelings, personal judgments, or cultural beliefs that were causally associated with the events, by acting on the environment. Someone must have told them that red means stop and green means go, that guinea pigs do not belong in school, and so on. Much of what the children knew about subjective causality must have come when adults supplied them with beliefs, reasons, and justifications in past discourse. (p. 389)

This is not to deny that children learn about some causal sequences on their own, or that causal thinking in some sense precedes language both phylogenetically and ontogenetically. But it would nevertheless seem that acquiring the adult-like modes of causal explanations in a particular cultural setting depends in large part on children's attempts during ontogeny to understand adult causal explanations as they participate with them in discourse interactions. This process is also a very important part of how preschool children learn to structure their telling of stories and narratives in extended discourse in a way that gives them causal coherence (Trabasso and Stein, 1981). And interestingly, these adult-like explanations, from the cultural line of development, may sometimes conflict with the child's natural tendency to explain physical events in intentional terms. Thus, Kelemen (1998) documents the "promiscuous teleology" of young American children in providing intentional explanations for natural phenomena (presumably in contrast to the adult causal theories they are hearing around them), for instance, that rocks are pointy so that animals will not sit on them and break them.

A special form of knowledge about objects in the physical world concerns quantity. Mathematical knowledge and reasoning are especially interesting in the current context because nothing seems less social than mathematics. And indeed many nonlinguistic organisms—from birds to primates to prelinguistic infants—can discriminate small quantities from one another (Davis and Perusse, 1988; Starkey, Spelke, and Gelman, 1990). The ontogenetic puzzle, once again, is that prelinguistic human infants have some quantitative skills, but it is only from four to five years of age that children can understand that a quantity, including number, is something that is conserved across various physical transformations, and only after this can they engage in arithmetical operations such as adding and subtracting.

There is no question that arithmetic operations depend crucially on the symbolic media available, whether number words in language or graphic numerals. There are profound differences in how different human cultures perform arithmetic operations depending on what they use to keep track of the counting process as it unfolds (e.g., Saxe, 1981), and there have been radical changes within Western culture in how arithmetic operations are performed, especially with the introduction of Arabic numerals and the place-value system (including the numeral for zero). In all, it is clear that arithmetic as a set of practical activities for helping people to do such things as measure land and keep track of the ownership of things would simply not be possible without symbols of some type. Mathematics is thus the prototype of the cultural ratchet effect, as argued in Chapter 2, in that new procedures are created by adults either individually or collaboratively and then children are later exposed to these products and learn to use them. Although the situation may differ for different mathematical operations, it is almost certainly the case that the majority of human children could not learn the more complex of these procedures (e.g., the division of large numbers into one another) without explicit instruction, that is, "transmission," from more skillful adults.

Interestingly, however, an even more radical argument could be made that the fundamental concept of number is itself dependent on social-cultural cognition. The question, once again, is why young children, who have had some understanding of quantity since they were neonates, wait until they are five to six years old to fully understand number. Individual learning through direct experience and interaction with quantities does not seem like a plausible mechanism (Wallach, 1969), and although some studies have found that children's conservation concepts, including number, may be facilitated through direct instruction from adults, there are serious limits to the youngest age that may be reached via such training (Gelman and Baillargeon, 1983). One possibility is that the understanding of conservation concepts in general, including number, depends on the co-

ordination of perspectives in a way that derives, either directly or indirectly, from social interaction and discourse. Evidence for this
view comes from research by Doise and Mugny (1979), Mugny and
Doise (1978), and Perret-Clermont and Brossard (1985), who found
that many children who initially failed conservation tasks improved
significantly in their performance just from discussing the problem
with another child, even though that partner knew no more than
they did. Presumably the mechanism of change in these cases was
the child's dialogic interaction with the partner in which the partner
expressed some view of the problem that complemented the child's
perspective or otherwise led her to rethink her previously incorrect
formulations. For instance, a child who thought that the taller beaker
had more water because the water reached higher levels might have
been paired with a child who thought that the wider beaker contained more water because the water covered more surface area; and
putting these two perspectives together provides a sufficient solution to the problem. In a recent variation on this theme, Siegler
(1995) found that asking a child to explain an adult experimenter's
mature judgment about a problem led young children to more
adult-like solutions to a conservation of number problem than did
various other kinds of more traditional training and instruction.

Indeed, in some views mathematics may be seen as the epitome of
perspective-taking and perspective-changing skills, and so it derives
ultimately from processes of social cognition and discourse. As
Piaget pointed out, number rests on two fundamental nonsocial concepts: (a) classification concepts (cardination) in which all groups of
objects with the same numerosity are treated as "the same"; and
(b) relational concepts (seriation) in which one item in a series is
seen as simultaneously larger than the preceding and smaller than
the succeeding item. It is not an accident, I would argue, that these
are the same fundamental concepts that structure much of language:
forming categories and classes of items (paradigmatics) and relating
them to one another serially (syntagmatics). It is not that engaging in
linguistic communication creates basic abilities of classification and
relational thinking, since these are present in rudimentary form in
nonhuman primates, but rather that, as argued above, the compre-

hension, acquisition, and use of language requires the exercise of these skills in some unique and very powerful ways. So one part of the answer for why children take so long to come to an adult-like understanding of number is that such an understanding requires extensive exercise and practice with classificational and relational skills of the type required by natural language acquisition and use. It may be relevant in this regard that many deaf children, who experience significant delays in language development during early childhood (presumably due to lack of fluent sign language partners for large parts of their days), also experience significant delays in passing number conservation tasks ranging from two to more than six years beyond the norm (see Mayberry, 1995, for a review).

Following this same line of reasoning, when it comes to arithmetical operations, Von Glasersfeld (1982) points out that the operation of addition relies on the ability to keep simultaneously in mind the items and the group; that is, the calculator must hold in mind not only the item being counted but also the running tally that determines the numerosity of the whole—exemplified by the man who, in a half-asleep state, heard the church bell ring and was unsure whether he had heard the bell ring four, or whether he had heard it ring one four times. The concept of four as the sum of $1 + 1 + 1 + 1$ both keeps the perspective of the items as items and also takes the perspective of a coherent grouping in which they all participate. Multiplying and dividing simply ratchet up this process, for example, counting by threes or by sixes instead of by units of one. It is at least possible that to engage in this kind of simultaneous multiple perspective-taking containing hierarchical ordering, children have to have experienced first at least some of the classifying and relational operations inherent in the process of linguistic communication.

To summarize, children's understanding of the physical world rests on the secure foundation of primate cognition. Two of the most important skills of physical cognition that are both uniquely human and universally human involve causal understanding and certain forms of quantitative reasoning. Causal understanding is the cognitive glue that gives coherence to human cognition in all types of specialized content domains, and number and mathematics underlie many important human activities from money to architecture to business to science. Neither of these cognitive skills has its ultimate origin in social-cultural life, but both of them are what they are today because children encounter them in a cultural and linguistic matrix in which (a) they are given specific pieces of knowledge and models of thinking and explaining via language directly (transmission of knowledge); (b) they operate with the structures of language, including both causal structures and classification-relational structures (the structuring role of language); and (c) they engage in discourse with others about the physical world and its workings in ways that induce the kinds of perspective-taking on which some of these concepts depend (discourse and perspective-taking).

Early Childhood Cognition

I reiterate one more time: social and cultural processes during ontogeny do not create basic cognitive skills. What they do is turn basic cognitive skills into extremely complex and sophisticated cognitive skills. Thus, children's ability to comprehend communicative intentions and language allows for the "transmission" of knowledge and information to them via language, sometimes so much information that they may have to reorganize it on their own to keep track of it by changing what are considered basic-level categories (Mervis, 1987). Moreover, their continuing use of the language conventional in their culture leads children to construe the world in terms of the categories and perspectives and relational analogies embodied in that language, and perhaps to use these highly exercised skills of categorization, analogizing, and perspective-taking in other domains such as mathematics. In addition, in their linguistic discourse with others young children experience myriad conflicting beliefs and points of view about things, a process which is almost certainly an essential ingredient in their coming to see other persons as beings with minds similar to, but different from, their own.

In all, we might imagine, once again, a solitary child on a desert island: in this case placed there at one year of age, cognitively normal, able to comprehend intentional and causal relations, ready for language acquisition, but having been exposed to no people or symbols. This child most certainly would gather information, and would categorize and see causal and other relations in the world to some degree on her own. But:

- she would not experience any information gathered by others, or receive any instruction from others, about causality in the physical world or mentality in the social-psychological world (i.e., no "transmission" of information);
- she would not experience all of the many complex forms of categorization, analogy, causality, and metaphor-making embodied in an historically evolved natural language; and
- she would not experience differing views, or conflicting views, or views expressed about her own views, in dialogical interaction with other persons.

And so my hypothesis is that this child at some later stage would engage in very little causal thinking, very little mathematical thinking, very little reasoning about other people's mental states, and very little moral reasoning. That is because all of these types of thinking and reasoning come about either mainly in or only in the child's dialogical discourse interactions with other persons.

Metacognition and Representational Redescription

In both the physical and social domains of cognitive development, I have outlined several kinds of discourse that lead children to understand and take new perspectives on a situation. The third type discussed was reflective meta-discourse, in which someone comments on or evaluates the verbally expressed thoughts or beliefs of others (often in instructional situations). But there is a special application of this kind of discourse, hinted at above, that needs elaboration because of the special role it plays in cognitive development during the transition from early childhood to childhood cognition. The main idea, as Vygotsky and others have hypothesized, is that children internalize the discourse in which adults instruct them or regulate their behavior (i.e., they culturally or imitatively learn it), and this leads them to examine and reflect on their own thoughts and beliefs in the same way the adult has been doing. The result is a variety of skills of self-regulation and metacognition that first show themselves at the end of the early childhood period, and, perhaps, in processes of representational redescription that result in dialogical cognitive representations.

Self-Regulation and Metacognition

Around the world children five to seven years of age are seen as entering a new phase of development. Virtually all societies in which there is formal schooling begin at this age, and quite often children are given new responsibilities (Cole and Cole, 1996). At least part of the reason for adults' newfound confidence is children's growing ability to internalize various kinds of rules that adults give them and to follow them even in the absence of the rule-making adult, that is, their growing ability to self-regulate. Another reason is that children of this age are able to talk about their own reasoning and problem-solving activities in a way that makes them much more easily educable in many problem-solving activities; that is to say, they are capable of certain kinds of especially useful metacognition.

Without going into a full review of a very large developmental and educational literature, the following are some major domains of metacognitive activity in which children begin to engage at the end of the early childhood period:

- They begin to be able to learn and to follow specific rules that adults have taught them to help in solving an intellectual problem, and they do this in a relatively independent (self-regulated) manner (Brown and Kane, 1988; Zelazo, in press).
- They begin to be able to use social and moral rules in a self-regulating manner to inhibit their behavior, to guide their social interactions, and to plan for future activities (Palincsar and Brown, 1984; Gauvain and Rogoff, 1989).

- They begin to actively monitor the social impression they are making on other people and so to engage in active impression-management activities reflecting their understanding of others' views of them (Harter, 1983).
- They begin to understand and use embedded mental-state language such as "She thinks that I think X" (Perner, 1988).
- They begin to show skills of meta-memory that enable them to formulate planful strategies in memory tasks that, for example, require them to use mnemonic aids (Schneider and Bjorkland, 1997).
- They begin to display literacy skills that depend to a large extent on meta-linguistic skills that allow them to talk about language and how it works (Snow and Ninio, 1986).

Although there is not as much direct evidence as one would like, there is some evidence that these kinds of self-regulatory and metacognitive skills are related to adults using reflective meta-discourse with children—with the children then internalizing this discourse for use in regulating their own behavior independently. The idea is that as the adult regulates the child's behavior in some cognitive task or behavior, the child attempts to comprehend that regulation from the adult's point of view (to simulate the adult's perspective). And then, in many cases, the child later reenacts the adult's instructions overtly in regulating her own behavior in that same or a similar situation in various kinds of performance monitoring, metacognitive strategies, or self-regulating speech.

There are several kinds of evidence supporting this view. First, in a series of classic studies Luria (1961) found that two- and three-year-old children were not able to use speech to regulate their problem-solving activities, as demonstrated by their repeated disregard of their own self-directed speech (they were just mimicking adult speech). But from around their fourth or fifth birthdays the children in Luria's studies did demonstrate an ability to use their speech to actually regulate their own behavior by coordinating their self-regulating speech with their task behavior in a dialogic manner. Second, several studies have found evidence that children's self-regulating speech does indeed derive from adults' regulating and instructional speech specifically. Ratner and Hill (1991), for example, found that children of this age are able to reproduce the instructor's role in a teaching situation weeks after the original pedagogy (see also Foley and Ratner, 1997). There is also evidence of a correlation between instructor and learner behavior that suggests this same conclusion. For example, Kontos (1983) found that children who were instructed in a problem by their mothers showed increases in the amount of self-regulating speech in their subsequent individual problem solving (relative to children who were not instructed). And there is even some experimental evidence that manipulating the style of adult instruction may lead to changes in the amounts of self-regulating speech that children use in their subsequent individual attempts in the same problem situation (Goudena, 1987). Third, it is also interesting that it is during this same age range that informal observations reveal children first showing evidence of spontaneous efforts to teach or regulate the learning of other children, behaviors of relevance here because self-regulation is, in a sense, teaching oneself (see also Ashley and Tomasello, 1998).

Children thus show relatively clear evidence of internalizing adults' regulating speech, rules, and instructions as they are reaching the later stages of the early childhood period. What is internalized is, as Vygotsky emphasized, a dialogue. In the learning interaction the child comprehends the adult instruction (simulates the adult's regulating activity), but she does so in relation to her own understanding—which requires a coordinating of the two perspectives. The cognitive representation that results, therefore, is a representation not just of the instructions but of the intersubjective dialogue (Fernyhough, 1996). One hypothesis is that the adult regulations that are most likely to be appropriated by the child into an internal dialogue are those that come at difficult points in the task, that is, when the child and adult are not both focused on the same aspect of the task (just as happens with other types of imitation). This discrepancy becomes apparent to the child through her attempts to understand the adult's instructions, so that the attempt to reinstate a common understanding takes the form of a dialogue—either acted out or internalized. At least some evidence for this hypothesis is provided by the finding that self-regulating speech is indeed used most often by children at difficult points in problem-solving tasks (Goodman, 1984). It should also be stressed that what children internalize in the case of instruction and regulation is perhaps best thought of as the "voice" of another person (Bakhtin, 1981; Wertsch, 1991)—the important point being that a voice is more than a bloodless point of view, but rather actually directs the child's cognition or behavior with more or less authority. Internalizing an instructional directive from an adult thus includes both a conceptual perspective and a moral injunction: "You should look at it in this way." Bruner (1993, 1996), in particular, has been insistent that to give a full accounting of human culture we must not overlook this "deontic" dimension of culture and cultural learning.

Representational Redescription

Karmiloff-Smith (1992) asks the question: Given that human beings are biological organisms and thus, like other animals, have many specialized domains of cognitive competence, what distinguishes human cognition from that of other species? Her conclusion, based on many types of research, is that it is the process of representational redescription in which humans construct ever more abstract and widely applicable cognitive skills:

> My claim is that a specifically human way to gain knowledge is for the mind to exploit internally the information it has already stored (both innate and acquired), by redescribing its representations or, more precisely, by iteratively re-presenting in different representational formats what its internal representations represent. (p. 15)

This process is important because as individuals re-present knowledge to themselves in different formats—each more encompassing than the previous—they become able to use their knowledge in more flexible ways in a wider array of relevant contexts; that is, their cognition becomes more "systematic," as in the construction of deep generalizations in mathematics and abstract grammatical constructions in language.

There are thus two basic levels of knowledge and understanding in Karmiloff-Smith's model (actually there are some sublevels, but they are not relevant here). First is the kind of knowledge that humans share with other animals, although they undoubtedly have their own species-specific version. This is implicit, procedural knowledge that is built upon innate foundations, but then uses external data to gain behavioral mastery in a particular domain. For example, learning to stack objects on top of one another or to use a language begins as the subject attempts to master the task procedurally, with little explicit knowledge of what she is doing. The second level derives from a representational redescription of this procedural knowledge and results in explicit, consciously and verbally accessible, declarative knowledge. After a person has reached a certain level of mastery in a task, she begins to reflect on the reasons for this success and so to isolate features of her performance relevant to that success (although of course this process is not perfectly accurate itself). Representational redescription does not occur across all domains of knowledge, but takes place within particular domains as the individual reaches mastery in that particular domain. Systems of thought emerge from this reflective activity because self-observation employs all of the categorization and analytic skills that are employed in perceiving, understanding, and categorizing the outside world—in effect the subject perceives, understands, and categorizes her own cognition facilitated by the fact that it is expressed externally in language. The result is thus the construction of more efficient and more abstract cognitive systems as ontogeny proceeds.

Karmiloff-Smith's (1992) explanation for the process of representational redescription is essentially that this is just how the system works; this is the way that humans, but not other animals, are built:

The process of representational redescription is posited to occur spontaneously as part of an internal drive toward the creation of intra-domain and inter-domain relationships. Although I stress the endogenous nature of representational redescription, clearly the process may at times be triggered by external influences. (p. 18)

This is a very reasonable hypothesis. However, I must say that from an evolutionary point of view it is difficult to imagine the ecological conditions that would have selected for such a generalized "drive" in human beings but not in closely related animal species.

An alternative account of the process of representational redescription is that it results from an individual taking an outsider's perspective on its own behavior and cognition: the child behaves, and then observes that behavior and the cognitive organization it makes manifest, as if she were observing another person's behavior. This reflective process has its origins in the kind of reflective metadialogues discussed above, especially in those in which adults instruct children, who then internalize those instructions. What I am positing here is that, as with many cognitive skills, children become more skillful at this internalization process so that they are able to generalize it and consequently to reflect on their own behavior and cognition *as if* they were another person looking at it. Thus, systematizing basic mathematical concepts most likely happens as subjects reflect on their own rudimentary mathematical activities (Piaget, 1970). And it is likely that in language acquisition children construct their more complex grammatical structures (e.g., subject of a sentence in those languages that use this structure) as they reflect on their productive use of abstract linguistic constructions (Tomasello, 1992b; Tomasello and Brooks, 1999). As stressed above, this reflecting on one's own behavior and cognition employs basic skills of categorization, schematization, analogy, and so forth, that are used in dealing with the outside world, so that the child may categorize, organize, and schematize her own cognitive skills in the same way that she does these things with external phenomena. Presumably the fact that this all takes place in the same linguistic format—that is, both the child's comment about the world and the adult's comment about the child's comment are normal linguistic expressions—facilitates the process by which children are able to utilize their basic cognitive skills in reflective activities.

The speculation is thus that the evolutionary adaptations aimed at the ability of human beings to coordinate their social behavior with one another—to understand one another as intentional beings—may also, after much ontogenetic elaboration, underlie the ability of human beings to reflect on their own behavior and so to create systematic structures of explicit knowledge, such as scientific theories (see also Humphrey, 1983). The human system-making ability may be, in Gould's (1982) terms, an exaptation from humans' reflective abilities, which derive, ultimately, from their social-cognitive abilities.

The Internalization of Perspectives

Everyone who has thought much about these things recognizes that culture plays an indispensable role in human cognitive development during the early childhood period. Much of the specific knowledge that children of this age are expected to learn, or are explicitly taught, or seek out on their own, comes to them via culturally conventional symbols or direct instruction from others. Becoming an expert in a domain entails learning what others have learned and then, perhaps, adding some small novelties oneself. And the ready-made categories of language cannot be overlooked either, as they provide the child with a starting point for conceptually grouping and interrelating entities of various types to one another. Cultural transmission of this type, of course, is only possible because children have primate skills of perception, memory, categorization, and the like, but uniquely human cultural learning skills enable them to use these individually based skills to benefit from the knowledge and skills of others in their social group in uniquely powerful ways.

Very few researchers, however, have gone beyond this recognition of the powerful role of culture in the content of children's cognition to consider the role of culture in the *process* of cognitive development. Although children's ability to take the perspective of others is a well recognized fact, it is typically considered as a separate skill—a skill of social cognition only. My view—which is in many ways reminiscent of some views expressed by Piaget (1928) in his early work—is that, especially during the early childhood period, the process of perspective-taking begins to permeate all aspects of children's cognitive development. The two key manifestations are:

- children's growing ability to view an entity from two or more perspectives simultaneously (as in hierarchical categorization, metaphors, analogies, number, etc.); and
- children's growing ability to reflect on their own intentional behavior and cognition so as to representationally redescribe them and so make them more "systematic."

These processes very well may take place only within fairly well-defined domains of cognitive activity somewhat independently of one another, each depending on a certain "critical mass" of specific experiential material before they can do their work in any given domain (Hirschfield and Gelman, 1994). However, one of the hallmarks of mature human cognition is precisely the way diverse types of skills and knowledge may be related to one another.

It is possible that human beings have some specialized biological adaptation for certain kinds of cognition or social cognition that allow them to take multiple simultaneous perspectives and to reflect on their own cognition in the absence of any social interaction, and that these abilities simply emerge during the early to middle childhood periods of human ontogeny. But if that is so, it is somewhat puzzling why these skills should take so long to emerge ontogenetically. My own view is that these very powerful cognitive functions emerge as late as they do because they depend on the exercise of the basic human adaptation for social cognition and culture in real-life social interaction over a several-year period. The acquisition and use of a conventional language are especially integral to the process because of the different perspectives a language embodies, because of the rich kind of discourse it enables, and because of the common representational format it provides for reflective acts of metacognition and representational redescription. And it would seem evolutionarily odd, to me at least, if there were some very general cognitive functions, not related to any specific cognitive domain or content, that would just emerge in the middle of cognitive ontogeny with virtually no prefiguring in other primate species. Much more plausible is the view that these new functions are of a piece with the earlier-emerging uniquely human cognitive skills of understanding others as intentional agents and culturally learning things from and through them—it is just that in this case what children learn about from and through others is different ways of looking at and thinking about things, including their own cognition.

Many cultural psychologists have talked about some of these same themes, but they do not wish to talk about the child as an individual in the process (e.g., Lave, 1988; Rogoff, 1990; Rogoff, Chavajay, and Mutusov, 1993). As an advocate of the more psychologically based wing of Cultural Psychology, I think we do need to talk about the individual child, and this means the process of internalization (see also Greenfield, in press). The child understands that the views expressed by other people are indeed external to herself—they are often views she would never have generated herself—and if she wants to "make them her own" for future use in a new situation, she will have to appropriate or "internalize" them. As I have expressed on previous occasions (Tomasello, Kruger, and Ratner, 1993), the process of internalization is not some mysterious additional cognitive or learning process alien to current theoretical formulations. When the child hears an adult express a view on a topic, or even on her own cognition, internalization means simply that she learns that view toward that topic in the same way she learns other perspectivally based things. We could even call the process cultural or imitative learning in the sense that the child imitatively learns to adopt the perspective of the other on a topic in just the way she learns to adopt the emotion of another toward a novel object (social referencing) or the behavior of another toward an object (imitative learning of instrumental activities). It is just that, when this view is expressed in language, the child imitatively learns the symbolic (intersubjective) formulation—sometimes even directed toward herself.

And so it seems that in this case as well human ontogeny really matters. Children's biological inheritance for cultural inheritance prepares them to engage in certain kinds of social interactions, but it is these social interactions themselves that actually do the work of leading the child to take multiple perspectives on things and on herself. An apt analogy might be such culturally specific activities as chess or basketball. Of course culture does not create the individual's cognitive or sensory-motor abilities that are required to play these games. But there is no way to become skillful at them without some time—many years in fact—of actually playing the games with others and having the experience of precisely what works well, what does not, and what the partner is likely to do in certain situations. Human children inherit much both biologically and culturally; but there is still much work to be done.

7

CULTURAL COGNITION

We may say that thinking is essentially the activity of operating with signs.

—Ludwig Wittgenstein

We have no power of thinking without signs.

—Charles Sanders Peirce

Only in terms of gestures as significant symbols
is the existence of mind or intelligence possible.

—George Herbert Mead

Thought is not merely expressed in words; it comes into existence through them.

—Lev Vygotsky

Human cognition is a specific, in the literal meaning of the word, form of primate cognition. Human beings share the majority of their cognitive skills and knowledge with other primates—including both the sensory-motor world of objects in their spatial, temporal, categorical, and quantitative relations and the social world of behaving conspecifics in their vertical (dominance) and horizontal (affiliative) relationships. And all primate species use their skills and knowledge to formulate creative and insightful strategies when problems arise in either the physical or the social domain. Naturally, however, any one species of primate may have additional cognitive skills on top of those shared with other members of the order, and humans are no exception. In the current hypothesis human beings do indeed possess a species-unique cognitive adaptation, and it is in many ways an especially powerful cognitive adaptation because it changes in fundamental ways the *process* of cognitive evolution.

This adaptation arose at some particular point in human evolution, perhaps fairly recently, presumably because of some genetic and natural selection events. This adaptation consists in the ability and tendency of individuals to identify with conspecifics in ways that enable them to understand those conspecifics as intentional agents like the self, possessing their own intentions and attention, and eventually to understand them as mental agents like the self, possessing their own desires and beliefs. This new mode of understanding other persons radically changed the nature of all types of social interactions, including social learning, so that a unique form of cultural evolution began to take place over historical time, as multiple generations of developing children learned various things from their forebears and then modified them in a way that led to an accumulation of these modifications—most typically as embodied in some material or symbolic artifact. The "ratchet effect" thus produced radically changed the nature of the ontogenetic niche in which human children develop so that, in effect, modern children encounter and interact with their physical and social worlds almost totally through the mediating lenses of preexisting cultural artifacts, which embody something of the inventors' and users' intentional relations to the world when using them. Developing children are thus growing up in the midst of the very best tools and symbols their forebears have invented for negotiating the rigors of their physical and social worlds. Moreover, as children internalize these tools and symbols—as they learn to use them through basic processes of cultural learning—they create in the process some powerful new forms of cognitive representation based in the intentional and mental perspectives of other persons.

And so, from a meta-theoretical perspective, my claim is that we cannot fully understand human cognition—at least not its uniquely human aspects—without considering in detail its unfolding in three distinct time frames:

- in phylogenetic time, as the human primate evolved its unique ways of understanding conspecifics;
- in historical time, as this distinctive form of social understanding led to distinctive forms of cultural inheritance involving material and symbolic artifacts that accumulate modifications over time; and

- in ontogenetic time, as human children absorb all that their cultures have to offer, developing unique modes of perspectivally based cognitive representation in the process.

To conclude, I will offer a few more thoughts on the processes involved in each of these time frames, along with a few brief reflections on some of the major theoretical paradigms that offer competing accounts of these processes.

Phylogeny

A dominant paradigm in the modern study of human behavior and cognition posits that human beings possess a number of different and distinct innate cognitive modules. This approach had its origins in the pronouncements of philosophers such as Chomsky (1980) and Fodor (1983), but has since made its way into a number of empirical paradigms, among them neo-nativism in developmental psychology and sociobiology and evolutionary psychology in evolutionary anthropology (e.g., Spelke and Newport, 1997; Tooby and Cosmides, 1989; Pinker, 1997). The major problem for modularity theories has always been: What are the modules and how might we go about identifying them? In the absence of any commonly recognized methodology, the majority of theorists simply focus on those they consider to be the clearest cases, although even these differ considerably in different accounts. Among the most commonly hypothesized modules are (a) knowledge of objects, (b) knowledge of other persons, (c) knowledge of number, (d) knowledge of language, and (e) knowledge of biology. Even within domains, however, there are controversies about whether there exist constitutive mini-modules. For example, Baron-Cohen (1995) posits that the early knowledge of other persons is actually constituted by four very specific mini-modules, and many Chomskian linguists believe that the language faculty also comprises a number of distinct linguistic mini-modules. Searching for answers in the brain, as suggested by some modularists, is far from straightforward, as localization of function in the brain may result from many different developmental processes not involving genetic specification of epistemological content; for example, a particular part of the brain might process particularly complex information and the first emerging developmental function that needs such computing power might simply localize there (Bates, in press; Elman et al., 1997).

The second major problem for modularity theorists, as outlined in Chapter 1, is the problem of time. For human cognitive functions shared with other mammals and primates, there has been plenty of time for biological evolution to have worked its wonders. But for uniquely human cognitive functions, there has been insufficient time for the evolution of a whole host of these—only 6 million years at most, but much more likely only one-quarter of a million years. A much more plausible view is thus one that focuses on processes that work much more quickly—in historical and ontogenetic time, for example—and searches for the ways in which these processes actually go about creating and maintaining uniquely human cognitive functions. There are certainly human cognitive functions for which historical and ontogenetic processes play only a minor role, for example, basic processes of perceptual categorization. But such things as linguistic symbols and social institutions are socially constituted and so could not conceivably have emerged full blown all at once in human evolution; social-interactive processes must have played some role in their creation and maintenance. In general, the basic problem with genetically based modularity approaches—especially when they address uniquely human and socially constituted artifacts and social practices—is that they attempt to skip from the first page of the story, genetics, to the last page of the story, current human cognition, without going through any of the intervening pages. These theorists are thus in many cases leaving out of account formative elements in both historical and ontogenetic time that intervene between the human genotype and phenotype.

My attempt is to find a single biological adaptation with leverage, and thus I have alighted upon the hypothesis that human beings evolved a new way of identifying with and understanding conspecifics as intentional beings. We do not know the ecological pressures that might have favored such an adaptation, and we can hypothesize any number of adaptive advantages it might have conferred. My own view is that any one of many adaptive scenarios might have led to the same evolutionary outcome for human social cognition, because if an individual understands conspecifics as intentional beings for whatever reason—whether for purposes of cooperation or competition or social learning or whatever—this understanding will not then evaporate when that individual interacts with conspecifics in other circumstances. In other words, such things as communication, cooperation, and social learning are not different modules or domains of knowledge, but rather are different domains of activity, each of which would be equally profoundly transformed by a new way of understanding conspecifics, that is, a new form of social cognition. The point is that the new form of social cognition would have profound effects whenever individuals interacted with one another—during historical time, transforming things social into things cultural, and during ontogenetic time, transforming skills of primate cognition and cognitive representation into uniquely human skills of cultural learning and perspectival cognitive representation.

It is important to emphasize that this uniquely human form of social cognition does not just concern the understanding of others as animate sources of motion and power, as hypothesized by Piaget (1954) and Premack (1990), which is a type of understanding seemingly possessed by all primates. Rather, this new form of social cognition concerns the understanding that others make choices in their perception and action and that these choices are guided by a mental representation of some desired outcome, that is, a goal. This is much more than an understanding of simple animacy. On the other hand, many other theorists have implied that what distinguishes human cognition from that of other animals is a "theory of mind," which is appropriate if that term is used generically to mean social cognition in general. But if the term is meant to focus narrowly on the understanding of false beliefs, it should be noted that this is something human children do not do until they are four years of age, but human cognition begins to differ in important ways from nonhuman primate cognition at around one to two years of age with joint attention, language acquisition, and other forms of cultural learning. Thus, as I have said before, the understanding of false beliefs is simply icing on the human social-cognitive cake, which is composed most fundamentally of the understanding of intentionality.

I must also say at this point that anthropomorphizing or romanticizing the cognitive abilities of other animal species will not help us to answer these difficult questions. By this I do not mean to imply that researchers should only look for differences between human and nonhuman primate cognition. On the contrary, if we are going to identify what is uniquely human, as well as what is uniquely chimpanzee or uniquely capuchin, it is crucial that scientists look for both similarities and differences. But the many popular accounts based on anecdotal observations of animal behavior, along with a healthy dose of the human penchant for seeing other beings as identical to themselves, are not, in my opinion, helpful to the enterprise. It is indeed ironic that the very ability whose virtues I have been extolling—the ability to see others as intentional beings like the self—can for some intellectual purposes be a tendency that is more harmful than helpful. I also do not think that searching for modules by itself is the answer. It is true that some of the more evolutionarily urgent problems like incest avoidance (leading to a very specific and inflexible mechanism that may be the same in many animal species) and the need to be assured that one's genes are passed on (leading to various forms of sexual jealousy that seem especially pronounced in humans because of the way the mating system works) may be good candidates for adaptive specializations unrelated to other adaptive specializations (Buss, 1994). But truly cognitive adaptations, almost by definition, are more flexible than this. Although they may have arisen to solve one specific adaptive problem, they are quite often used for a wide array of related problems (e.g., cognitive maps that help in finding food, water, home bases, mates, offspring, predators, and so forth). I thus do not see the point of trying to modularize human cognition, and the many different proposals for what the human module menu looks like attest to the practical difficulties of doing this as well.

History

In general, in my opinion, many theorists are much too quick to explain uniquely human cognitive skills in terms of specific genetic adaptations—typically without any genetic research, it should be added. It is a popular procedure mainly because it is so quick, easy, and unlikely to be immediately refuted by empirical evidence. But another important reason for many theorists' tendency to posit innate cognitive modules as a method of first resort is a lack of appreciation of the workings of human cultural-historical processes, that is, processes of sociogenesis, both in the sense of their direct generative powers and in the sense of their indirect effects in creating a new type of ontogenetic niche for human cognitive development. And, importantly, historical processes work on a completely different time scale than evolutionary processes (Donald, 1991).

Let us take as an example the game of chess. The children who learn to play this game do so in interaction with mature players, and some of them develop quite sophisticated cognitive skills in the context of this game, many of which would seem to be domain specific in the extreme. A cognitive psychologist can only marvel at the complex plannings and imaginations required for orchestrating a king side attack in which the opposing king's pawn protectors are first eliminated by means of a bishop sacrifice, and then the king's movements are restricted and the attack is consummated with the coordination of knight, rook, and queen. Despite the cognitive complexities involved, and despite the domain specificity of the cognitive skills involved, I have never seen anyone posit an innate chess-playing module. The reason is that chess is a very recent product of human history, and there are even books with pictures that trace its historical development. Chess was originally a simpler game, but as the players came to some mutual understandings of things that would make the game better, they modified rules or added new ones until they produced the modern game—for which children today can, over the course of a few years of play and practice, develop quite impressive cognitive skills. Of course chess does not create in children basic cognitive skills such as memory, planning, spatial reasoning, categorization—the game could evolve only because human beings already possessed these skills—but it does channel basic cognitive processes in new directions, helping to create some new and very specialized cognitive skills as a result.

My contention is simply that cognitive skills of language and complex mathematics are like chess: they are the products of both historical and ontogenetic developments working with a variety of pre-existing human cognitive skills, some of which are shared with other primates and some of which are uniquely human. These are easiest to see in the case of mathematics because—and this is somewhat like chess—(a) we can trace much of the historical development of modern mathematics in the last 2,000 years, (b) in many cultures the only mathematical operations used are very simple counting procedures (and their arithmetic variants), and (c) within cultures using complex mathematics many individuals only learn some simple procedures. These facts thus constrain the possibilities, so that modularity theorists can posit as a mathematics module something that contains only the most basic of quantitative concepts. In the case of language, however, (a) we know very little of its history (only the relatively recent history of the few languages that have been written down), (b) all cultures have complex languages, and (c) all typically developing children within a culture acquire basically equivalent linguistic skills. These facts make it clear that language is different from mathematics and chess, but they do not specify the reason for this difference. It may just be that language, for whatever reason, began its historical development first—early in the evolution of modern humans some 200,000 years ago—and so reached something near its current level of complexity before modern languages began to diverge from this prototype. If we may use ontogeny as any guide to cognitive complexity, modern children begin using natural languages with much sophistication well before they master complex mathematics or chess strategics. Perhaps the reason that language is cognitively primary is that it is such a direct manifestation of the human symbolic ability, which itself derives so directly from the joint attentional and communicative activities that the understanding of others as intentional agents engenders. The point is thus that language is special, but not so special.

And so my account for how a single human cognitive adaptation could result in all of the many differences in human and nonhuman primate cognition is that this single adaptation made possible an evolutionarily new set of processes, that is, processes of sociogenesis, that have done much of the actual work and on a much faster time scale than evolution. Perhaps this single novelty changed the way human beings interacted with one another, and with much effort over much historical time these new ways of interacting transformed such basic primate phenomena as communication, dominance, exchange, and exploration into the human cultural institutions of language, government, money, and science—without any additional genetic events. The transformations in the different domains of human activity as a result of this new adaptation clearly were not instantaneous. For example, human beings were already communicating with one another in complex ways when they began to understand one another as intentional agents, and so it took some time, perhaps many generations, for this new understanding of others to make itself felt and thus for symbolic forms of communication to emerge. The same would have held true for the other domains of activity—such as various forms of cooperation and social learning—as this new kind of social understanding gradually enabled new kinds of social interactions and artifacts. Table 7.1 presents an oversimplified and certainly not exhaustive listing of some domains of human activity and how they might have been transformed by the uniquely human adaptation of social cognition as it worked itself into various social interactive processes over many generations of human history.

Ideally we should know much more than we do about the process of sociogenesis in different domains of activity in human history. Cultural psychologists, who should be concerned with this problem, have mostly not spent great effort in empirical investigations of the historical processes by means of which particular cultural institutions in particular cultures have taken shape—for example, processes of grammaticization in the history of particular languages

Table 7.1 Some domains of social activity transformed over historical time into domains of cultural activity by the uniquely human way of understanding conspecifics.

Domain	Social	Cultural
Communication	Signals	Symbols (intersubjective, perspectival)
Gaze of others	Gaze follow	Joint attention (intersubjectivity)
Social learning	Emulation, ritualization	Cultural learning (reproducing intentional acts)
Cooperation	Coordination	Collaboration (role taking)
Teaching	Facilitation	Instruction (mental states of others)
Object manipulation	Tools	Artifacts (intentional affordances)

or processes of collaborative invention in the history of the mathematical skills characteristic of a particular culture. Perhaps the most enlightening investigations of these processes are studies by intellectual historians concerned with such things as the history of technology, the history of science and mathematics, and language history (see Chapter 2). But these scholars are mostly not concerned with cognitive or other psychological processes per se, and so the information to be gleaned by psychologists is decidedly indirect. And there are perhaps some relevant facts to be gleaned from studies of cooperation in which two partners who are naive to a problem domain manage to collaboratively invent some new artifact or strategy—in a manner analogous to processes of cultural creation in historical time (see Ashley and Tomasello, 1998).

In all, we may underscore the power of sociogenesis by proposing a variation on our recurrent theme of a wild child on a desert island. In this case, let us suppose that a giant X-ray comes down from outer space and makes all human beings over one year of age profoundly autistic—so much so that they cannot intentionally communicate with one another or with the infants (although, miraculously, they are able to provide the infants with sustenance and protection). So the one-year-olds are left to their own devices to interact with one another (*Lord of the Flies* style), with the hulking infrastructure of modern technology rusting in the background (*Mad Max* style). The question is: How long would it take for the children to re-create, or perhaps to create different but equivalent, social practices and institutions such as language, mathematics, writing, governments, and so on? I am certain that there are scholars who think it would take place almost immediately, especially in the case of language, but I believe that this is a naive view that seriously underestimates the historical work that has gone into these institutions as they have ratcheted up in complexity over many generations historically. (And studies of children creating gestural signs in interaction with language-proficient adults, or with one another in the context of a school for the deaf, though relevant, do not address the question directly since there are in these cases many ways in which the fully functioning cultures in which these children live facilitate the process of cultural creation.) Language may be somewhat special because of its intimate connection to the uniquely human social-cognitive adaptation in question—as outlined above—but the social conventions that comprise a natural language can only be created in certain kinds of social interaction, and some linguistic constructions can only be created after others have first been established. My own guess, then, is that the creation of something resembling modern natural languages would take many generations to evolve, and undoubtedly many more still would be needed for such things as writing, complex mathematics, and governmental and other institutions.

Ontogeny

Ontogeny is a very different process for different animal species. For some species it is important that their young be almost fully functional from the time they encounter the outside world, to maximize their chances of surviving to the age of reproduction, whereas for other species a long ontogeny, with much individual learning, is the life-history strategy of choice. Learning is thus a product of evolution—one of its strategies, if we may anthropomorphize the process a bit—as are culture and cultural learning as special cases of the "extended ontogeny" evolutionary strategy. There is thus no question of opposing nature versus nurture; nurture is just one of the many forms that nature may take. The question for developmentalists is therefore only how the process takes place, how the different factors play their different roles at different points in development. At birth human infants are poised to become fully functioning adult human beings: they have the genes they need and they are living in a pre-structured cultural world ready to facilitate their development and actively teach them things as well. But they are not at that point adults; there is still more work to be done.

It is important to note that human cognitive ontogeny is not a replay of chimpanzee ontogeny with a "terminal addition" on the end. As I argued in Chapter 3, human cognitive ontogeny is unique from very early on, perhaps from birth, as human neonates do various things that demonstrate a special form of identification with conspecifics (e.g., neonatal mimicking and protoconversations). This is the uniqueness from which all else flows, as it enables infants to exploit a novel source of information about other persons: the analogy to the self. At around nine months of age, analogizing self and other persons enables infants to attribute to other persons the same kinds of intentionality in which they themselves are just beginning to engage (and they may also analogize to the self, somewhat inappropriately, in their causal reasoning about why inanimate objects behave as they do). The new and powerful forms of social cognition that result open up the cultural line of human development in the sense that children are now in a position to participate with other persons in joint attentional activities and so to understand and attempt to reproduce their intentional actions involving various kinds of material and symbolic artifacts. And, indeed, this tendency to imitatively learn the actions of other persons is a very strong one, as young children sometimes imitate adult actions with objects even when they would do better to ignore them, and in language acquisition they have a long period where they essentially reproduce exactly the relational structure of the adult utterances they are hearing. This is the cultural line of development at its strongest, and it is the reason why four-year-olds in different cultures are so different from one another in terms of the specific behaviors in which they engage. But throughout this early period, and even more strongly later, children are also making individual judgments, decisions, categorizations, analogies, and evaluations—more or less from the individual line of development—and these interact in interesting ways with children's tendencies in the cultural line of development to do what the other persons around them are doing.

Children's mastery of one very special cultural artifact—language—has transforming effects on their cognition. Language does not create new cognitive processes out of nothing, of course, but when children interact with other persons intersubjectively and adopt their communicative conventions, this social process creates a new form of cognitive representation—one that has no counterpart in other animal species. The novelty is that linguistic symbols are both intersubjective and perspectival. The intersubjective nature of human linguistic symbols means that they are socially "shared" in a way that animal signals are not, and this forms the pragmatic matrix within which many inferences about the communicative intentions of other people may be made—why they chose one symbol rather than another that they also share with the listener, for example. The perspectival nature of linguistic symbols means that as children learn to use words and linguistic constructions in the manner of adults, they come to see that the exact same phenomenon may be construed in many different ways for different communicative purposes depending on many factors in the communicative context. The linguistic representations thus formed are free of the immediate perceptual context not just in the sense that with these symbols children can communicate about things removed in space and time, but also in the sense that even the exact same perceptually present entity can be linguistically symbolized in innumerable different ways. It is perhaps paradoxical, in this age of computers and in this "decade of the brain," that this radically new and powerful form of cognitive representation emanates not from any new storage facilities or computing power inside the human brain, but rather from the new forms of social interaction, enabled by new forms of social cognition, that take place between individuals inside human cultures.

Language is also structured to symbolize in various complex ways events and their participants, and this is instrumental in leading children to "slice and dice" their experience of events in many complex ways. Abstract linguistic constructions may then be used to view experiential scenes in terms of one another in various analogical and metaphorical ways. Narratives add more complexity still, as they string together simple events in ways that invite causal and intentional analysis, and indeed explicitly symbolized causal or intentional marking, to make them coherent. And extended discourse and other kinds of social interactions with adults lead children into even more esoteric cognitive spaces, as they enable them to understand conflicting perspectives on things that must be reconciled in some way. Finally, the kind of interaction in which adults comment on children's cognitive activities, or instruct them explicitly, leads children to take an outsider's perspective on their own cognition in acts of metacognition, self-regulation, and representational redescription, resulting in more systematic cognitive structures in dialogical formats. Whether or not different languages do these things differently, as in classic arguments about "linguistic determinism," learning a language or some comparable form of symbolic communication—as opposed to not learning one at all—seems to be an essential ingredient in human intersubjectivity and perspectival cognition, event representation, and metacognition.

I believe that this is what all of the thinkers quoted at the beginning of this chapter, each in his own way and with different specifics than are in the current argument, were attempting to articulate when they made their various claims to the effect that human thinking is essentially operating with symbols. Human beings can of course think without symbols if by thinking we mean perceiving, remembering, categorizing, and acting intelligently in the world in ways similar to other primates (Piaget, 1970; Tomasello and Call,

1997). But the uniquely human forms of thinking—for example, those in which I am engaged as I formulate this argument and attempt to anticipate the dialogic responses it will elicit from other thinkers (and perhaps my response to those responses)—do not just depend on, but in fact derive from, perhaps even are constituted by, the interactive discourse that takes place through the medium of intersubjective and perspectival linguistic symbols, constructions, and discourse patterns. And it is not unimportant that an individual can gain mastery in the use of such symbols and their concomitant ways of thinking only over a period of several years of virtually continuous interaction with mature symbol users.

And so, like evolution and history, ontogeny really matters. Human beings have evolved in such a way that their normal cognitive ontogeny depends on a certain kind of cultural environment for its realization. The importance of biological inheritance in the ontogenetic process is underscored by the problems of children with autism, who do not have in its full-fledged form the human biological adaptation for identifying with other persons, and so do not end up as normally functioning cultural agents. The importance of cultural inheritance in the ontogenetic process is underscored by the many cognitive differences that exist among the peoples of different cultures and by the unfortunate cases of neglected or abused children brought up in culturally deficient circumstances, but it is highlighted even more if we imagine the cognitive development of children growing up without any culture or language at all. A child raised on a desert island without human companions would not come out as Rousseau envisioned, a "natural" human being free of the constraints of society, but rather would come out as Geertz envisioned, something of a monster, something other than a fully human intentional and moral agent.

Focus on Process

We are, as Wittgenstein (1953) and Vygotsky (1978) saw so clearly, fish in the water of culture. As adults investigating and reflecting on human existence, we cannot take off our cultural glasses to view the world aculturally—and so compare it to the world as we perceive it culturally. Human beings live in a world of language, mathematics, money, government, education, science, and religion—cultural institutions composed of cultural conventions. The sound "tree" stands for what it does because, and only because, we think it does; men and women are married because, and only because, we think they are; I can obtain a car in exchange for a piece of paper because, and only because, we think the paper is worth as much as the car (Searle, 1996). These kinds of social institutions and conventions are created and maintained by certain ways of interacting and thinking among groups of human beings. Other animal species simply do not interact and think in these ways.

But the human cultural world is not thereby free of the biological world, and indeed human culture is a very recent evolutionary product, having existed in all likelihood for only a few hundred thousand years. The fact that culture is a product of evolution does not mean that each one of its specific features has its own dedicated genetic underpinnings; there has not been enough time for that. A more plausible scenario is that all human cultural institutions rest on the biologically inherited social-cognitive ability of all human individuals to create and use social conventions and symbols. However, these social conventions and symbols do not wave a magic wand and turn nonhuman primate cognition into human cognition on the spot. Modern adult cognition of the human kind is the product not only of genetic events taking place over many millions of years in evolutionary time but also of cultural events taking place over many tens of thousands of years in historical time and personal events taking place over many tens of thousands of hours in ontogenetic time. The desire to avoid the hard empirical work necessary to follow out these intermediate processes that occur between the human genotype and phenotype is a strong one, and it leads to the kinds of facile genetic determinism that pervade large parts of the social, behavioral, and cognitive sciences today. Genes are an essential part of the story of human cognitive evolution, perhaps even from some points of view the most important part of the story since they are what got the ball rolling. But they are not the whole story, and the ball has rolled a long way since it got started. In all, the tired old philosophical categories of nature versus nurture, innate versus learned, and even genes versus environment are just not up to the task—they are too static and categorical—if our goal is a dynamic Darwinian account of human cognition in its evolutionary, historical, and ontogenetic dimensions.

REFERENCES

Acredolo, L. P., and Goodwyn, S. W. 1988. Symbolic gesturing in normal infants. *Child Development 59*, 450–466.

Akhtar, N., Carpenter, M., and Tomasello, M. 1996. The role of discourse novelty in children's early word learning. *Child Development 67*, 635–645.

Akhtar, N., Dunham, F., and Dunham, P. 1991. Directive interactions and early vocabulary development: the role of joint attentional focus. *Journal of Child Language 18*, 41–50.

Akhtar, N., and Tomasello, M. 1996. Twenty-four month old children learn words for absent objects and actions. *British Journal of Developmental Psychology 14*, 79–93.

——— 1997. Young children's productivity with word order and verb morphology. *Developmental Psychology 33*, 952–965.

Anselmi, D., Tomasello, M, and Acunzo, M. 1986. Young children's responses to neutral and specific contingent queries. *Journal of Child Language 13*, 135–144.

Appleton, M., and Reddy, V. 1996. Teaching three-year-olds to pass false belief tests: A conversational approach. *Social Development 5*, 275–291.

Ashley, J., and Tomasello, M. 1998. Cooperative problem solving and teaching in preschoolers. *Social Development 17*, 143–163.

Baillargeon, R. 1995. Physical reasoning in infancy. In M. Gazzaniga, ed., *The cognitive neurosciences*, 181–204. Cambridge, MA: MIT Press.

Bakhtin, M. 1981. *The dialogic imagination.* Austin: University of Texas Press.

Baldwin, D. 1991. Infants' contributions to the achievement of joint reference. *Child Development 62*, 875–890.

—— 1993. Infants' ability to consult the speaker for clues to word reference. *Journal of Child Language 20*, 395–418.

Baldwin, D., and Moses, L. 1994. The mindreading engine: Evaluating the evidence for modularity. *Current Psychology of Cognition 13*, 553–560.

——1996. The ontogeny of social information gathering. *Child Development 67*, 1915–39.

Baron-Cohen, S. 1988. Social and pragmatic deficits in autism: Cognitive or affective? *Journal of Autism and Developmental Disorders 18*, 379–401.

—— 1993. From attention-goal psychology to belief-desire psychology: The development of a theory of mind and its dysfunction. In S. Baron-Cohen, H. Tager-Flusberg, and D. J. Cohen, eds., *Understanding other minds: Perspectives from autism.* New York: Oxford University Press.

—— 1995. *Mindblindness: An essay on autism and theory of mind.* Cambridge, MA: MIT Press.

Barresi, J., and Moore, C. 1996. Intentional relations and social understanding. *Behavioral and Brain Sciences 19*, 107–154.

Barsalou, L. 1992. *Cognitive psychology: An overview for cognitive scientists.* Hillsdale, NJ: Erlbaum.

Bartsch, K., and Wellman, H. 1995. *Children talk about the mind.* New York: Oxford University Press.

Basalla, G. 1988. *The evolution of technology.* Cambridge: Cambridge University Press.

Bates, E. 1979. *The emergence of symbols: Cognition and communication in infancy.* New York: Academic Press.

—— In press. Modularity, domain specificity, and the development of language. *Journal of Cognitive Neuroscience.*

Bauer, P., and Fivush, R. 1992. Constructing event representations: Building on a foundation of variation and enabling relations. *Cognitive Development 7*, 381–401.

Bauer, P., Hestergaard, L., and Dow, G. 1994. After 8 months have passed: Long term recall of events by 1- to 2-year-old children. *Memory 2*, 353–382.

Berman, R., and Armon-Lotem, S. 1995. How grammatical are early verbs? Paper presented at the Colloque International de Besançon sur l'Acquisition de la Syntaxe, Besançon, France.

Berman, R., and Slobin, D. 1995. *Relating events in narrative.* Mahwah, NJ: Erlbaum.

Bishop, D. 1997. *Uncommon understanding: Development and disorders of language comprehension in children.* London: Psychology Press.

Bloom, L., and Capatides, J. 1987. Sources of meaning in the acquisition of complex syntax: The sample case of causality. *Journal of Experimental Child Psychology 43*, 112–128.

Bloom, L., Tinker, E., and Margulis, C. 1993. The words children learn: Evidence for a verb bias in early vocabularies. *Cognitive Development 8*, 431–450.

Boesch, C. 1991. Teaching among wild chimpanzees. *Animal Behavior 41*, 530–532.

――― 1993. Towards a new image of culture in wild chimpanzees? *Behavioral and Brain Sciences 16*, 514–515.

――― 1996. The emergence of cultures among wild chimpanzees. In W. Runciman, J. Maynard-Smith, and R. Dunbar, eds., *Evolution of social behaviour patterns in primates and man*, 251–268. Oxford: Oxford University Press.

――― In press. *The chimpanzees of the Tai Forest*. Oxford: Oxford University Press.

Boesch, C., Marchesi, P., Marchesi, N., Fruth, B., and Joulian, F. 1994. Is nut cracking in wild chimpanzees a cultural behavior? *Journal of Human Evolution 26*, 325–338.

Boesch, C., and Tomasello, M. 1998. Chimpanzee and human culture. *Current Anthropology 39*, 591–614.

Bolinger, D. 1977. *Meaning and form*. New York: Longmans.

Bourdieu, P. 1977. *Outline of a theory of practice*. Cambridge: Cambridge University Press.

Bowerman, M. 1982. Reorganizational processes in lexical and syntactic development. In L. Gleitman and E. Wanner, eds., *Language acquisition: The state of the art*. Cambridge: Cambridge University Press.

Boyd, R., and Richerson, P. 1985. *Culture and the evolutionary process*. Chicago: University of Chicago Press.

――― 1996. Why culture is common but cultural evolution is rare. *Proceedings of the British Academy 88*, 77–93.

Braine, M. 1963. The ontogeny of English phrase structure. *Language 39*, 1–14.

――― 1976. Children's first word combinations. *Monographs of the Society for Research in Child Development 41* (1).

Brooks, P., and Tomasello, M. In press. Young children learn to produce passives with nonce verbs. *Developmental Psychology*.

Brown, A., and Kane, M. 1988. Preschool children can learn to transfer: Learning to learn and learning from example. *Cognitive Psychology 20*, 493–523.

Brown, P. In press. The conversational context for language acquisition: A Tzeltal (Mayan) case study. In M. Bowerman and S. Levinson, eds., *Language acquisition and conceptual development*. Cambridge: Cambridge University Press.

Brown, R. 1973. *A first language: The early stages*. Cambridge, MA: Harvard University Press.

Bruner, J. 1972. The nature and uses of immaturity. *American Psychologist* 27, 687–708.

———— 1975. From communication to language. *Cognition 3*, 255–287.

———— 1983. *Child's talk*. New York: Norton.

———— 1986. *Actual minds, possible worlds*. Cambridge, MA: Harvard University Press.

———— 1990. *Acts of meaning*. Cambridge, MA: Harvard University Press.

———— 1993. Commentary on Tomasello et al., "Cultural Learning." *Behavioral and Brain Sciences 16*, 515–516.

———— 1996. *The culture of education*. Cambridge, MA: Harvard University Press.

Bullock, D. 1987. Socializing the theory of intellectual development. In M. Chapman and R. Dixon, eds., *Meaning and the growth of understanding*. Berlin: Springer-Verlag.

Buss, D. 1994. *The evolution of desire*. New York: Basic Books.

Byrne, R. W. 1995. *The thinking ape*. Oxford: Oxford University Press.

Byrne, R. W., and Whiten, A. 1988. *Machiavellian intelligence: Social expertise and the evolution of intellect in monkeys, apes, and humans*. New York: Oxford University Press.

Call, J., and Tomasello, M. 1996. The role of humans in the cognitive development of apes. In A. Russon, ed., *Reaching into thought: The minds of the great apes*. Cambridge: Cambridge University Press.

———— 1998. Distinguishing intentional from accidental actions in orangutans, chimpanzees, and human children. *Journal of Comparative Psychology 112*, 192–206.

———— 1999. A nonverbal false belief task: The performance of chimpanzees and human children. *Child Development 70*, 381–395.

Callanan, M., and Oakes, L. 1992. Preschoolers' questions and parents' explanations: Causal thinking in everyday activity. *Cognitive Development 7*, 213–233.

Carey, S. 1978. The child as word learner. In M. Halle, J. Bresnan, and G. Miller, eds., *Linguistic theory and psychological reality*. Cambridge, MA: MIT Press.

Carey, S., and Spelke, E. 1994. Domain-specific knowledge and conceptual change. In L. Hirschfeld and S. Gelman, eds., *Mapping the mind: Domain specificity in cognition and culture*. New York: Cambridge University Press.

Carpenter, M., Akhtar, N., and Tomasello, M. 1998. Fourteen-through 18-month-old infants differentially imitate intentional and accidental actions. *Infant Behavior and Development 21* (2), 315–330.

Carpenter, M., Nagell, K., and Tomasello, M. 1998. Social cognition, joint attention, and communicative competence from 9 to 15 months of age. *Monographs of the Society for Research in Child Development 63.*

Carpenter, M., and Tomasello, M. In press. Joint attention, cultural learning, and language acquisition: Implications for children with autism. In A. Wetherby and B. Prizant, eds., *Communication and language issues in autism.* New York: Brooks.

Carpenter, M., Tomasello, M., and Savage-Rumbaugh, E. S. 1995. Joint attention and imitative learning in children, chimpanzees and enculturated chimpanzees. *Social Development 4,* 217–237.

Charman, T., and Shmueli-Goetz, Y. 1998. The relationship between theory of mind, language, and narrative discourse: An experimental study. *Cahiers de Psychologie Cognitive 17,* 245–271.

Chomsky, N. 1980. Rules and representations. *Behavioral and Brain Sciences 3,* 1–61.

Clark, E. 1987. The principle of contrast: A constraint on language acquisition. In B. MacWhinney, ed., *Mechanisms of language acquisition,* 1–33. Hillsdale, NJ: Erlbaum.

———— 1988. On the logic of contrast. *Journal of Child Language 15,* 317–336.

———— 1997. Conceptual perspective and lexical choice in acquisition. *Cognition 64,* 1–37.

Clark, H. 1996. *Uses of language.* Cambridge: Cambridge University Press.

Cole, M. 1996. *Cultural psychology: A once and future discipline.* Cambridge, MA: Harvard University Press.

Cole, M., and Cole, S. 1996. *The development of children.* San Francisco: Freeman.

Comrie, B., ed. 1990. *The world's major languages.* Oxford: Oxford University Press.

Croft, W. 1998. Syntax in perspective: Typology and cognition. Presentation at DGFS, Mainz, Germany.

Csibra, G., Gergeley, G., Biró, S., and Koos, O. In press. The perception of pure reason in infancy. *Cognition.*

Custance, D., Whiten, A., and Bard, K. 1995. Can young chimpanzees imitate arbitrary actions? *Behaviour 132,* 839–858.

Damerow, P. 1998. Prehistory and cognitive development. In J. Langer and M. Killen, eds., *Piaget, evolution, and development.* Mahwah, NJ: Erlbaum.

Damon, W. 1983. *Social and personality development.* New York: Norton.

Danzig, T. 1954. *Number: The language of science.* New York: Free Press.

Dasser, V. 1988a. A social concept in Java monkeys. *Animal Behaviour 36,* 225–230.

———— 1988b. Mapping social concepts in monkeys. In R. W. Byrne and A. Whiten, eds., *Machiavellian intelligence: Social expertise and the evolution of intellect in monkeys, apes, and humans,* 85–93. New York: Oxford University Press.

Davis, H., and Perusse, R. 1988. Numerical competence in animals: Definitional issues, current evidence and a new research agenda. *Behavioral and Brain Sciences 11,* 561–615.

Decasper, A. J., and Fifer, W. P. 1980. Of human bonding: Newborns prefer their mothers' voices. *Science 208,* 1174–76.

DeLoache, J. S. 1995. Early understanding and use of symbols: The model model. *Current Directions in Psychological Science 4,* 109–113.

de Waal, F. B. M. 1986. Deception in the natural communication of chimpanzees. In R. W. Mitchell and N. S. Thompson, eds., *Deception: Perspectives on human and nonhuman deceit,* 221–244. Albany: SUNY Press.

Doise, W., and Mugny, G. 1979. Individual and collective conflicts of centrations in cognitive development. *European Journal of Psychology 9,* 105–108.

Donald, M. 1991. *Origins of the modern mind.* Cambridge, MA: Harvard University Press.

Dryer, M. 1997. Are grammatical relations universal? In J. Bybee, J. Haiman, and S. Thompson, eds., *Essays on language function and language type.* Amsterdam: John Benjamins.

Dunham, P., Dunham, F., and Curwin, A. 1993. Joint attentional states and lexical acquisition at 18 months. *Developmental Psychology 29,* 827–831.

Dunn, J. 1988. *The beginnings of social understanding.* Oxford: Blackwell.

Dunn, J., Brown, J., and Beardsall, L. 1991. Family talk about feeling states and children's later understanding about others' emotions. *Developmental Psychology 27,* 448–455.

Durham, W. 1991. *Coevolution: Genes, culture, and human diversity.* Stanford: Stanford University Press.

Elman, J., Bates, E., Karmiloff-Smith, A., Parisi, D., Johnson, M., and Plunkett, K. 1997. *Rethinking innateness.* Cambridge, MA: MIT Press.

Evans-Pritchard, E. 1937. *Witchcraft, oracles, and magic among the Azande.* Oxford: Clarendon Press.

Eves, H. 1961. *An introduction to the history of mathematics.* New York: Holt, Rinehart and Winston.

Fantz, R. L. 1963. Pattern vision in newborn infants. *Science 140*, 296–297.

Fernyhough, C. 1996. The dialogic mind: A dialogic approach to the higher mental functions. *New Ideas in Psychology 14*, 47–62.

Fillmore, C. 1985. Syntactic intrusions and the notion of grammatical construction. *Berkeley Linguistic Society 11*, 73–86.

——— 1988. Toward a frame-based lexicon. In A. Lehrer and E. Kittay, eds., *Frames, fields, and contrast*. Hillsdale, NJ: Erlbaum.

Fillmore, C. J., Kay, P., and O'Conner, M. C. 1988. Regularity and idiomaticity in grammatical constructions: The case of *let alone*. *Language 64*, 501–538.

Fisher, C. 1996. Structural limits on verb mapping: The role of analogy in children's interpretations of sentences. *Cognitive Psychology 31*, 41–81.

Fisher, C., Gleitman, H., and Gleitman, L. R. 1991. On the semantic content of subcategorization frames. *Cognitive Psychology 23*, 331–392.

Fodor, J. 1983. *The modularity of mind*. Cambridge, MA: MIT Press.

Foley, M., and Ratner, H. 1997. Children's recoding in memory for collaboration: A way of learning from others. *Cognitive Development 13*, 91–108.

Foley, R., and Lahr, M. 1997. Mode 3 technologies and the evolution of modern humans. *Cambridge Archeological Journal 7*, 3–36.

Franco, F., and Butterworth, G. 1996. Pointing and social awareness: declaring and requesting in the second year. *Journal of Child Language 23*, 307–336.

Frye, D. 1991. The origins of intention in infancy. In D. Frye and C. Moore, eds., *Children's theories of mind*, 101–132. Hillsdale, NJ: Erlbaum.

Galef, B. 1992. The question of animal culture. *Human Nature 3*, 157–178.

Gauvain, M. 1995. Thinking in niches: Sociocultural influences on cognitive development. *Human Development 38*, 25–45.

Gauvain, M., and Rogoff, B. 1989. Collaborative problem solving and children's planning skills. *Developmental Psychology 25*, 139–151.

Gelman, R., and Baillargeon, R. 1983. A review of some Piagetian concepts. In P. Mussen, ed., *Carmichael's manual of child psychology*, 167–230. New York: Wiley.

Gentner, D., and Markman, A. 1997. Structure mapping in analogy and similarity. *American Psychologist 52*, 45–56.

Gentner, D., and Medina, J. 1997. Comparison and the development of cognition and language. *Cognitive Studies 4*, 112–149.

Gentner, D., Rattermann, M. J., Markman, A., and Kotovsky, L. 1995. Two forces in the development of relational similarity. In T. J. Simon and G. S. Halford, eds., *Developing cognitive competence: New approaches to process modeling*, 263–313. Hillsdale, NJ: Erlbaum.

Gergely, G., Nádasdy, Z., Csibra, G., and Biró, S. 1995. Taking the intentional stance at 12 months of age. *Cognition 56*, 165–193.

Gibbs, R. 1995. *The poetics of mind: Figurative thought, language, and understanding.* Cambridge: Cambridge University Press.

Gibson, E., and Rader, N. 1979. Attention: The perceiver as performer. In G. Hale and M. Lewis, eds., *Attention and cognitive development,* 6–36. New York: Plenum.

Gibson, J. J. 1979. *The ecological approach to visual perception.* Boston: Houghton Mifflin.

Givón, T. 1979. *On understanding grammar.* New York: Academic Press.

——— 1995. *Functionalism and grammar.* Amsterdam: John Benjamins.

Gleitman, L. 1990. The structural sources of verb meaning. *Language Acquisition 1,* 3–55.

Goldberg, A. 1995. *Constructions: A construction grammar approach to argument structure.* Chicago: University of Chicago Press.

Goldin-Meadow, S. 1997. The resilience of language in humans. In C. Snowdon and M. Hausberger, eds., *Social influences on vocal development,* 293–311. New York: Cambridge University Press.

Golinkoff, R. 1993. When is communication a meeting of the minds? *Journal of Child Language 20,* 199–208.

Gómez, J. C., Sarriá, E., and Tamarit, J. 1993. The comparative study of early communication and theories of mind: Ontogeny, phylogeny, and pathology. In S. Baron-Cohen, H. Tager-Flusberg, and D. J. Cohen, eds., *Understanding other minds: Perspectives from autism,* 397–426. New York: Oxford University Press.

Goodall, J. 1986. *The chimpanzees of Gombe: Patterns of behavior.* Cambridge, MA: Harvard University Press.

Goodman, J., McDonough, L., and Brown, N. 1998. The role of semantic context and memory in the acquisition of novel nouns. *Child Development 69,* 1330–44.

Goodman, S. 1984. The integration of verbal and motor behavior in preschool children. *Child Development 52,* 280–289.

Gopnik, A. 1993. How we know our minds: The illusion of first-person knowledge about intentionality. *Behavioral and Brain Sciences 16,* 1–14.

Gopnik, A., and Choi, S. 1995. Names, relational words, and cognitive development in English and Korean speakers: Nouns are not always learned before verbs. In M. Tomasello and W. E. Merriman, eds., *Beyond names for things: Young children's acquisition of verbs,* 63–80. Hillsdale, NJ: Erlbaum.

Gopnik, A., and Meltzoff, A. 1997. *Words, thoughts, and theories.* Cambridge, MA: MIT Press.

Goudena, P. P. 1987. The social nature of private speech of preschoolers during problem solving. *International Journal of Behavioral Development 10*, 187–206.

Gould, S. J. 1982. Changes in developmental timing as a mechanism of macroevolution. In J. Bonner, ed., *Evolution and development*. Berlin: Springer-Verlag.

Greenfield, P. In press. Culture and universals: Integrating social and cognitive development. In L. Nucci, G. Saxe, and E. Turiel, eds., *Culture, thought, and development*. Mahwah, NJ: Erlbaum.

Greenfield, P., and Lave, J. 1982. Cognitive aspects of informal education. In D. Wagner and H. Stevenson, eds., *Cultural perspectives on child development*. San Francisco: Freeman.

Grice, P. 1975. Logic and conversation. In P. Cole and J. Morgan, eds., *Speech acts, syntax, and semantics*. New York: Academic Press.

Haith, M., and Benson, J. 1997. Infant cognition. In D. Kuhn and R. Siegler, eds., *Handbook of child psychology*, vol. 2. New York: Wiley.

Happé, F. 1995. *Autism: An introduction to psychological theory*. Cambridge, MA: Harvard University Press.

Harris, P. 1991. The work of the imagination. In A. Whiten, ed., *Natural theories of mind*, 283–304. Oxford: Blackwell.

——— 1996. Desires, beliefs, and language. In P. Carruthers and P. Smith, eds., *Theories of theories of mind*, 200–222. Cambridge: Cambridge University Press.

Harter, S. 1983. Developmental perspectives on the self system. In P. Mussen, ed., *Carmichael's manual of child psychology*, vol. 4, 285–386. New York: Wiley.

Hayes, K., and Hayes, C. 1952. Imitation in a home-raised chimpanzee. *Journal of Comparative and Physiological Psychology 45*, 450–459.

Heyes, C. M. 1993. Anecdotes, training, trapping and triangulating: Do animals attribute mental states? *Animal Behaviour 46*, 177–188.

Heyes, C. M., and Galef, B. G. Jr., eds. 1996. *Social learning in animals: The roots of culture*. New York: Academic Press.

Hirschfield, L., and Gelman, S., eds. 1994. *Mapping the mind: Domain specificity in cognition and culture*. Cambridge: Cambridge University Press.

Hobson, P. 1993. *Autism and the development of mind*. Hillsdale, NJ: Erlbaum.

Hockett, C. 1960. Logical considerations in the study of animal communication. In W. Lanyon and W. Tavolga, eds., *Animal sounds and communication*. Washington: American Institute of Biological Sciences, no. 7.

Hood, L., Fiess, K., and Aron, J. 1982. Growing up explained: Vygot-skians look at the language of causality. In C. Brainerd and M. Pressley, eds., *Verbal processes in children.* Berlin: Springer-Verlag.

Hopper, P., and Thompson, S. 1980. Transitivity in grammar and dis-course. *Language 56,* 251–291.

———— 1984. The discourse basis for lexical categories in universal gram-mar. *Language 60,* 703–752.

Hopper, P., and Traugott, E. 1993. *Grammaticalization.* Cambridge: Cam-bridge University Press.

Humphrey, N. 1976. The social function of intellect. In P. Bateson and R. A. Hinde, eds., *Growing points in ethology,* 303–321. Cambridge: Cambridge University Press.

Humphrey, N. 1983. *Consciousness regained.* Oxford: Oxford University Press.

Hutchins, E. 1995. *Cognition in the wild.* Cambridge, MA: MIT Press.

James, W. 1890. *The principles of psychology.* New York: Holt.

Jarrold, C., Boucher, J., and Smith, P. 1993. Symbolic play in autism: A review. *Journal of Autism and Developmental Disorders 23,* 281–308.

Jenkins, J., and Astington, J. 1996. Cognitive factors and family structure associated with theory of mind development in children. *Develop-mental Psychology 32,* 70–78.

Johnson, M. 1987. *The body in the mind.* Chicago: University of Chicago Press.

Karmiloff-Smith, A. 1992. *Beyond modularity: A developmental perspective on cognitive science.* Cambridge, MA: MIT Press.

Kawai, M. 1965. Newly-acquired pre-cultural behavior of the natural troop of Japanese monkeys on Koshima Islet. *Primates 6,* 1–30.

Kawamura, S. 1959. The process of sub-culture propagation among Japanese macaques. *Primates 2,* 43–60.

Kelemen, D. 1998. Beliefs about purpose: On the origins of teleological thought. In M. Corballis and S. Lea, eds., *The evolution of the hominid mind.* Oxford: Oxford University Press.

Keller, H., Schölmerich, A., and Eibl-Eibesfeldt, I. 1988. Communication patterns in adult-infant interactions in western and non-western cultures. *Journal of Cross-Cultural Psychology 19,* 427–445.

Killen, M., and Uzgiris, I. C. 1981. Imitation of actions with objects: The role of social meaning. *Journal of Genetic Psychology 138,* 219–229.

King, B. J. 1991. Social information transfer in monkeys, apes, and ho-minids. *Yearbook of Physical Anthropology 34,* 97–115.

King, M., and Wilson, A. 1975. Evolution at two levels in humans and chimpanzees. *Science 188,* 107–116.

Klein, R. 1989. *The human career: Human biological and cultural origins.* Chicago: University of Chicago Press.

Kontos, S. 1983. Adult-child interaction and the origins of metacognition. *Journal of Educational Research 77,* 43–54.

Kruger, A. 1992. The effect of peer and adult-child transactive discussions on moral reasoning. *Merrill-Palmer Quarterly 38,* 191–211.

Kruger, A., and Tomasello, M. 1986. Transactive discussions with peers and adults. *Developmental Psychology 22,* 681–685.

———— 1996. Cultural learning and learning culture. In D. Olson, ed., *Handbook of education and human development: New models of teaching, learning, and schooling,* 169–187. Oxford: Blackwell.

Kummer, H., and Goodall, J. 1985. Conditions of innovative behaviour in primates. *Philosophical Transactions of the Royal Society of London B308,* 203–214.

Lakoff, G. 1987. *Women, fire, and dangerous things: What categories reveal about the mind.* Chicago: University of Chicago Press.

Lakoff, G., and Johnson, M. 1980. *Metaphors we live by.* Chicago: University of Chicago Press.

Langacker, R. 1987a. *Foundations of cognitive grammar,* vol. 1. Stanford: Stanford University Press.

———— 1987b. Nouns and verbs. *Language 63,* 53–94.

———— 1991. *Foundations of cognitive grammar,* vol. 2. Stanford: Stanford University Press.

Lave, J. 1988. *Cognition in practice.* Cambridge: Cambridge University Press.

Legerstee, M. 1991. The role of person and object in eliciting early imitation. *Journal of Experimental Child Psychology 51,* 423–433.

Leonard, L. 1998. *Children with specific language impairment.* Cambridge, MA: MIT Press.

Leslie, A. 1984. Infant perception of a manual pick up event. *British Journal of Developmental Psychology 2,* 19–32.

Levinson, S. 1983. *Pragmatics.* Cambridge: Cambridge University Press.

Lewis, M., and Brooks-Gunn, J. 1979. *Social cognition and the acquisition of self.* New York: Plenum.

Lewis, M., Sullivan, M., Stanger, C., and Weiss, M. 1989. Self-development and self-conscious emotions. *Child Development 60,* 146–156.

Lieven, E., Pine, J., and Baldwin, G. 1997. Lexically-based learning and early grammatical development. *Journal of Child Language 24,* 187–220.

Lillard, A. 1997. Other folks' theories of mind and behavior. *Psychological Science 8,* 268–274.

Lock, A. 1978. The emergence of language. In A. Lock, ed., *Action, gesture, and symbol: The emergence of language*. New York: Academic Press.

Loveland, K. 1993. Autism, affordances, and the self. In U. Neisser, ed., *The perceived self*, 237–253. Cambridge: Cambridge University Press.

Loveland, K., and Landry, S. 1986. Joint attention in autism and developmental language delay. *Journal of Autism and Developmental Disorders 16*, 335–349.

Loveland, K., Tunali, B., Jaedicke, N., and Brelsford, A. 1991. Rudimentary perspective taking in lower functioning children with autism and Down syndrome. Paper submitted to Society for Research in Child Development, Seattle.

Lucy, J. 1992. *Grammatical categories and cognition*. New York: Cambridge University Press.

Luria, A. 1961. *The role of speech in the regulation of normal and abnormal behavior*. New York: Boni and Liveright.

Mandler, J. 1992. How to build a baby, II: Conceptual primitives. *Psychological Review 99*, 587–604.

Marchman, V., and Bates, E. 1994. Continuity in lexical and morphological development: A test of the critical mass hypothesis. *Journal of Child Language 21*, 339–366.

Markman, E. 1989. *Categorization and naming in children*. Cambridge, MA: MIT Press.

——— 1992. Constraints on word learning: Speculations about their nature, origins, and word specificity. In M. Gunnar and M. Maratsos, eds., *Modularity and constraints in language and cognition*. Hillsdale, NJ: Erlbaum.

Mayberry, R. 1995. The cognitive development of deaf children: Recent insights. In S. Segalowitz and I. Rapin, eds., *Handbook of neuropsychology*, vol. 7, 51–68. Amsterdam: Elsevier.

McCrae, K., Ferretti, T., and Amyote, L. 1997. Thematic roles as verb-specific concepts. *Language and Cognitive Processes 12*, 137–176.

McGrew, W. 1992. *Chimpanzee material culture*. Cambridge: Cambridge University Press.

——— 1998. Culture in nonhuman primates? *Annual Review of Anthropology 27*, 301–328.

Meltzoff, A. 1988. Infant imitation after a one-week delay: Long-term memory for novel acts and multiple stimuli. *Developmental Psychology 24*, 470–476.

——— 1995. Understanding the intentions of others: Re-enactment of intended acts by 18-month-old children. *Developmental Psychology 31*, 838–850.

Meltzoff, A., and Gopnik, A. 1993. The role of imitation in understanding persons and developing a theory of mind. In S. Baron-Cohen, H. Tager-Flusberg, and D. J. Cohen, eds., *Understanding other minds: Perspectives from autism,* 335–366. New York: Oxford University Press.

Meltzoff, A., and Moore, K. 1977. Imitation of facial and manual gestures by newborn infants. *Science 198,* 75–78.

——— 1989. Imitation in newborn infants: Exploring the range of gestures imitated and the underlying mechanisms. *Developmental Psychology 25,* 954–962.

——— 1994. Imitation, memory, and the representation of persons. *Infant Behavior and Development 17,* 83–99.

Mervis, C. 1987. Child basic categories and early lexical development. In U. Neisser, ed., *Concepts and conceptual development.* Cambridge: Cambridge University Press.

Moore, C. 1996. Theories of mind in infancy. *British Journal of Developmental Psychology 14,* 19–40.

Moore, C., and Dunham, P., eds. 1995. *Joint attention: Its origins and role in development.* Hillsdale, NJ: Erlbaum.

Mugny, G., and Doise, W. 1978. Sociocognitive conflict and the structure of individual and collective performances. *European Journal of Social Psychology 8,* 181–192.

Muir, D., and Hains, S. 1999. Young infants' perception of adult intentionality: Adult contingency and eye direction. In P. Rochat, ed., *Early social cognition.* Mahwah, NJ: Erlbaum.

Mundinger, P. 1980. Animal cultures and a general theory of cultural evolution. *Ethology and Sociobiology 1,* 183–223.

Mundy, P., Sigman, M., and Kasari, C. 1990. A longitudinal study of joint attention and language development in autistic children. *Journal of Autism and Developmental Disorders 20,* 115–128.

Murray, L., and Trevarthen, C. 1985. Emotional regulation of interactions between two-month-olds and their mothers. In T. M. Field and N. A. Fox, eds., *Social perception in infants,* 177–197. Norwood, NJ: Ablex.

Myowa, M. 1996. Imitation of facial gestures by an infant chimpanzee. *Primates 37,* 207–213.

Nadel, J., and Tremblay-Leveau, H. 1999. Early perception of social contingencies and interpersonal intentionality: dyadic and triadic paradigms. In P. Rochat, ed., *Early social cognition.* Mahwah, NJ: Erlbaum.

Nagell, K., Olguin, K., and Tomasello, M. 1993. Processes of social learning in the tool use of chimpanzees (*Pan troglodytes)* and human children (Homo sapiens). Journal of Comparative Psychology 107, 174–186.

Neisser, U. 1988. Five kinds of self-knowledge. Philosophical Psychology 1, 35–59.

———— 1995. Criteria for an ecological self. In P. Rochat, ed., The self in infancy: Theory and research. Amsterdam: Elsevier.

Nelson, K. 1985. Making sense: The acquisition of shared meaning. New York: Academic Press.

———— 1986. Event knowledge: Structure and function in development. Hillsdale, NJ: Erlbaum.

————, ed. 1989. Narratives from the crib. Cambridge, MA: Harvard University Press.

———— 1996. Language in cognitive development. New York: Cambridge University Press.

Nelson, K. E. 1986. A rare event cognitive comparison theory of language acquisition. In K. E. Nelson and A. van Kleeck, eds., Children's language, vol. 6. Hillsdale, NJ: Erlbaum.

Nishida, T. 1980. The leaf-clipping display: A newly discovered expressive gesture in wild chimpanzees. Journal of Human Evolution 9, 117–128.

Nuckolls, C. 1991. Culture and causal thinking. Ethos 17, 3–51.

Palincsar, A., and Brown, A. 1984. Reciprocal teaching of comprehension-fostering and monitoring activities. Cognition and Instruction 1, 117–175.

Perner, J. 1988. Higher order beliefs and intentions in children's understanding of social interaction. In J. Astington, P. Harris, and D. Olson, eds., Developing theories of mind. Cambridge: Cambridge University Press.

Perner, J., and Lopez, A. 1997. Children's understanding of belief and disconfirming visual evidence. Cognitive Development 12, 367–380.

Perner, J., Ruffman, T., and Leekham, S. 1994. Theory of mind is contagious: You catch it from your sibs. Child Development 65, 1228–38.

Perret-Clermont, A.-N., and Brossard, A. 1985. On the interdigitation of social and cognitive processes. In R. A. Hinde, A.-N. Perret-Clermont, and J. Stevenson-Hinde, eds., Social relationships and cognitive development. Oxford: Clarendon Press.

Peters, A. 1983. The units of language acquisition. Cambridge: Cambridge University Press.

Peterson, C., and Siegal, M. 1995. Deafness, conversation, and theory of mind. Journal of Child Psychology and Psychiatry 36, 459–474.

———— 1997. Domain specificity and everyday thinking in normal, autistic, and deaf children. In H. Wellman and K. Inagaki, eds., New directions in child development, no. 75. San Francisco: Jossey-Bass.

Piaget, J. 1928. *The development of logical thinking in childhood*. London: Kegan Paul.

—— 1932. *The moral judgment of the child*. London: Kegan Paul.

—— 1952. *The origins of intelligence in children*. New York: Basic Books.

—— 1954. *The construction of reality in the child*. New York: Basic Books.

—— 1970. Piaget's theory. In P. Mussen, ed., *Manual of child development*, 703–732. New York: Wiley.

Piaget, J., and Garcia, R. 1974. *Understanding causality*. New York: Norton.

Pine, J. M., and Lieven, E. V. M. 1993. Reanalysing rote-learned phrases: Individual differences in the transition to multi-word speech. *Journal of Child Language 20*, 551–571.

Pinker, S. 1989. *Learnability and cognition: The acquisition of verb-argument structure*. Cambridge, MA: Harvard University Press.

—— 1994. *The language instinct: How the mind creates language*. New York: Morrow.

—— 1997. *How the mind works*. London: Penguin.

Pizutto, E., and Caselli, C., 1992. The acquisition of Italian morphology. *Journal of Child Language 19*, 491–557.

Povinelli, D. 1994. Comparative studies of animal mental state attribution: A reply to Heyes. *Animal Behaviour 48*, 239–241.

Povinelli, D., and Cant, J. 1996. Arboreal clambering and the evolutionary origins of self-conception. *Quarterly Review of Biology 70*, 393–421.

Povinelli, D., Nelson, K., and Boysen, S. 1990. Inferences about guessing and knowing by chimpanzees *(Pan troglodytes)*. *Journal of Comparative Psychology 104*, 203–210.

Povinelli, D., Perilloux, H., Reaux, J., and Bierschwale, D. 1998. Young chimpanzees' reactions to intentional versus accidental and inadvertent actions. *Behavioural Processes 42*, 205–218.

Premack, D. 1983. The codes of man and beasts. *Behavioral and Brain Sciences 6*, 125–167.

—— 1986. *Gavagai!* Cambridge, MA: MIT Press.

—— 1990. The infant's theory of self-propelled objects. *Cognition 36*, 1–16.

Premack, D., and Woodruff, G. 1978. Does the chimpanzee have a theory of mind? *Behavioral and Brain Sciences 4*, 515–526.

Quine, W. 1960. *Word and object*. Cambridge, MA: Harvard University Press.

Ratner, H., and Hill, L. 1991. Regulation and representation in the development of children's memory. Paper presented to the Society for Research in Child Development, Seattle.

Reaux, J. 1995. Explorations of young chimpanzees' *(Pan troglodytes)* comprehension of cause-effect relationships in tool use. Master's thesis, University of Southwestern Louisiana.

Rochat, P., and Barry, L. 1998. Infants reaching for out-of-reach objects. Paper presented at the International Conference for Infant Studies, Atlanta.

Rochat, P., and Morgan, R. 1995. Spatial determinants of leg movements by 3-to-5-month-old infants. *Developmental Psychology 31*, 626–636.

Rochat, P., Morgan, R., and Carpenter, M. 1997. The perception of social causality in infancy. *Cognitive Development 12*, 537–562.

Rochat, P., and Striano, T. 1999. Social cognitive development in the first year. In P. Rochat, ed., *Early social cognition*. Mahwah, NJ: Erlbaum.

Rogoff, B. 1990. *Apprenticeship in thinking*. Oxford: Oxford University Press.

Rogoff, B., Chavajay, P., and Mutusov, E. 1993. Questioning assumptions about culture and individuals. *Behavioral and Brain Sciences 16*, 533–534.

Rollins, P., and Snow, C. 1999. Shared attention and grammatical development in typical children and children with autism. *Journal of Child Language 25*, 653–674.

Rubino, R., and Pine, J. 1998. Subject-verb agreement in Brazilian Portuguese: What low error rates hide. *Journal of Child Language 25*, 35–60.

Russell, J. 1997. *Agency: Its role in mental development*. Cambridge, MA: MIT Press.

Russell, P., Hosie, J., Gray, C., Scott, C., Hunter, N., Banks, J., and Macaulay, D. 1998. The development theory of mind in deaf children. *Journal of Child Psychology and Psychiatry 39*, 905–910.

Russon, A., and Galdikas, B. 1993. Imitation in ex-captive orangutans. *Journal of Comparative Psychology 107*, 147–161.

Samuelson, L., and Smith, L. 1998. Memory and attention make smart word learning: An alternative account of Akhtar, Carpenter, and Tomasello. *Child Development 69*, 94–104.

Savage-Rumbaugh, E. S., McDonald, K., Sevcik, R. A., Hopkins, W. D., and Rubert, E. 1986. Spontaneous symbol acquisition and communicative use by pygmy chimpanzees *(Pan paniscus)*. *Journal of Experimental Psychology: General 115*, 211–235.

Savage-Rumbaugh, E. S., Rumbaugh, D. M., and Boysen, S. T. 1978. Sarah's problems in comprehension. *Behavioral and Brain Sciences 1*, 555–557.

Saxe, G. 1981. Body parts as numerals: A developmental analysis of numeration among a village population in Papua New Guinea. *Child Development 52*, 306–316.

Scarr, S., and McCarthy, K. 1983. How people make their own environments: A theory of genotype-environment effects. *Child Development 54*, 424–435.

Schieffelin, B., and Ochs, E. 1986. *Language socialization across cultures.* Cambridge: Cambridge University Press.

Schneider, W., and Bjorkland, D. 1997. Memory. In D. Kuhn and R. Siegler, eds., *Handbook of child psychology*, vol. 2. New York: Wiley.

Schultz, T. 1982. Rules of causal attribution. *Monographs of the Society for Research in Child Development 47.*

Scollon, R. 1973. *Conversations with a one year old.* Honolulu: University of Hawaii Press.

Searle, J. 1996. *The social construction of reality.* New York: Pergamon.

Siegler, R. 1995. How does change occur: A microgenetic study of number conservation. *Cognitive Psychology 28*, 225–273.

Sigman, M., and Capps, L. 1997. *Children with autism: A developmental perspective.* Cambridge, MA: Harvard University Press.

Slobin, D. 1985. The language making capacity. In D. Slobin, ed., *The cross-linguistic study of language acquisition*, 1157–1256. Hillsdale, NJ: Erlbaum.

———— 1991. Learning to think for speaking: Native language, cognition, and rhetorical style. *Pragmatics 1*, 7–26.

———— 1997. The origins of grammaticalizable notions: Beyond the individual mind. In D. Slobin, ed., The *cross-linguistic study of language acquisition.* Mahwah, NJ: Erlbaum.

Smith, C. B., Adamson, L. B., and Bakeman, R. 1988. Interactional predictors of early language. *First Language 8*, 143–156.

Smith, D., and Washburn, D. 1997. The uncertainty response in humans and animals. *Cognition 62*, 75–97.

Smith, L. 1995. Self-organizing processes in learning to use words: Development is not induction. *Minnesota symposium on child psychology*, vol. 28. Mahwah, NJ: Erlbaum.

Snow, C., and Ninio, A. 1986. The contracts of literacy: What children learn from learning to read books. In W. Teale and E. Sulzby, eds., *Emergent literacy: Writing and reading.* Norwood, NJ: Ablex.

Spelke, E. 1990. Principles of object perception. *Cognitive Science 14*, 29–56.

Spelke, E., Breinliger, K., Macomber, J., and Jacobson, K. 1992. Origins of knowledge. *Psychological Review 99*, 605–632.

Spelke, E., and Newport, E. 1997. Nativism, empiricism, and the development of knowledge. In R. Lerner, ed., *Handbook of child psychology*, vol. 1. New York: Wiley.

Sperber, D. and Wilson, D. 1986. *Relevance: Communication and cognition.* Cambridge, MA: Harvard University Press.

Starkey, P., Spelke, E. S., and Gelman, R. 1990. Numerical abstraction by human infants. *Cognition 36*, 97–128.

Stern, D. 1985. *The interpersonal world of the infant*. New York: Basic Books.

Striano, T., Tomasello, M., and Rochat, P. 1999. Social and object support for early symbolic play. Manuscript.

Stringer, C., and McKie, R. 1996. *African exodus: The origins of modern humanity*. London: Jonathon Cape.

Talmy, L. 1996. The windowing of attention in language. In M. Shibatani and S. Thompson, eds., *Grammatical constructions: Their form and meaning*. Oxford: Oxford University Press.

Thomas, R. K. 1986. Vertebrate intelligence: A review of the laboratory research. In R. J. Hoage and L. Goldman, eds., *Animal intelligence: Insights into the animal mind*, 37–56. Washington: Smithsonian Institution Press.

Tomasello, M. 1987. Learning to use prepositions: A case study. *Journal of Child Language 14*, 79–98.

——— 1988. The role of joint attentional process in early language development. *Language Sciences 10*, 69–88.

——— 1990. Cultural transmission in the tool use and communicatory signaling of chimpanzees? In S. Parker and K. Gibson, eds., *Language and intelligence in monkeys and apes: Comparative developmental perspectives*. Cambridge: Cambridge University Press.

——— 1992a. The social bases of language acquisition. *Social Development 1* (1), 67–87.

——— 1992b. *First verbs: A case study in early grammatical development*. Cambridge: Cambridge University Press.

——— 1993. The interpersonal origins of self concept. In U. Neisser, ed., *The perceived self: Ecological and interpersonal sources of self knowledge*, 174–184. Cambridge: Cambridge University Press.

——— 1994. The question of chimpanzee culture. In R. W. Wrangham, W. C. McGrew, F. B. M. de Waal, and P. G. Heltne, eds., *Chimpanzee cultures*, 301–317. Cambridge, MA: Harvard University Press.

——— 1995a. Joint attention as social cognition. In C. Moore and P. Dunham, eds., *Joint attention: Its origins and role in development*, 103–130. Hillsdale, NJ: Erlbaum.

——— 1995b. Understanding the self as social agent. In P. Rochat, ed., *The self in early infancy: Theory and research*, 449–460. Amsterdam: North Holland-Elsevier.

——— 1995c. Pragmatic contexts for early verb learning. In M. Tomasello and W. Merriman, eds., *Beyond names for things: Young children's acquisition of verbs*. Mahwah, NJ: Erlbaum.

—— 1995d. Language is not an instinct. *Cognitive Development 10*, 131–156.

—— 1996a. Do apes ape? In B. G. Galef Jr. and C. M. Heyes, eds., *Social learning in animals: The roots of culture*, 319–346. New York: Academic Press.

—— 1996b. Chimpanzee social cognition. Commentary for *Monographs of the Society for Research in Child Development 61* (3).

—— 1998. One child's early talk about possession. In J. Newman, ed., *The linguistics of giving*. Amsterdam: John Benjamins.

—— 1999a. The cultural ecology of young children's interactions with objects and artifacts. In E. Winograd, R. Fivush, and W. Hirst, eds., *Ecological approaches to cognition: Essays in honor of Ulric Neisser*. Mahwah, NJ: Erlbaum.

—— 1999b. Do young children operate with adult syntactic categories? Manuscript.

—— In press. Perceiving intentions and learning words in the second year of life. In M. Bowerman and S. Levinson, eds., *Language acquisition and conceptual development*. Cambridge: Cambridge University Press.

Tomasello, M., and Akhtar, N. 1995. Two-year-olds use pragmatic cues to differentiate reference to objects and actions. *Cognitive Development 10*, 201–224.

Tomasello, M., Akhtar, N., Dodson, K., and Rekau, L. 1997. Differential productivity in young children's use of nouns and verbs. *Journal of Child Language 24*, 373–387.

Tomasello, M., and Barton, M. 1994. Learning words in non-ostensive contexts. *Developmental Psychology 30*, 639–650.

Tomasello, M., and Brooks, P. 1998. Young children's earliest transitive and intransitive constructions. *Cognitive Linguistics 9*, 379–395.

—— 1999. Early syntactic development. In M. Barrett, ed., *The development of language*. London: Psychology Press.

Tomasello, M., and Call, J. 1994. Social cognition of monkeys and apes. *Yearbook of Physical Anthropology 37*, 273–305.

—— 1997. *Primate cognition*. New York: Oxford University Press.

Tomasello, M., Call, J., and Gluckman, A. 1997. The comprehension of novel communicative signs by apes and human children. *Child Development 68*, 1067–81.

Tomasello, M., Call, J., Nagell, K., Olguin, K., and Carpenter, M. 1994. The learning and use of gestural signals by young chimpanzees: A trans-generational study. *Primates 35*, 137–154.

Tomasello, M., Call, J., Warren, J., Frost, T., Carpenter, M., and Nagell, K. 1997. The ontogeny of chimpanzee gestural signals: A comparison across groups and generations. *Evolution of Communication 1*, 223–253.

Tomasello, M., and Farrar, J. 1986. Joint attention and early language. *Child Development 57*, 1454–63.

Tomasello, M., Farrar, J., and Dines, J. 1983. Young children's speech revisions for a familiar and an unfamiliar adult. *Journal of Speech and Hearing Research 27*, 359–363.

Tomasello, M., George, B., Kruger, A., Farrar, J., and Evans, E. 1985. The development of gestural communication in young chimpanzees. *Journal of Human Evolution 14*, 175–186.

Tomasello, M., Gust, D., and Frost, G. T. 1989. The development of gestural communication in young chimpanzees: A follow up. *Primates 30*, 35–50.

Tomasello, M., and Kruger, A. 1992. Joint attention on actions: Acquiring verbs in ostensive and non-ostensive contexts. *Journal of Child Language 19*, 311–334.

Tomasello, M., Kruger, A. C., and Ratner, H. H. 1993. Cultural learning. *Behavioral and Brain Sciences 16*, 495–552.

Tomasello, M., Mannle, S., and Kruger, A. C. 1986. Linguistic environment of 1- to 2-year-old twins. *Developmental Psychology 22*, 169–176.

Tomasello, M., Mannle, S., and Werdenschlag, L. 1988. The effect of previously learned words on the child's acquisition of words for similar referents. *Journal of Child Language 15*, 505–515.

Tomasello, M., and Merriman, W., eds. 1995. *Beyond names for things: Young children's acquisition of verbs*. Mahwah, NJ: Erlbaum.

Tomasello, M., Savage-Rumbaugh, E. S., and Kruger, A. C. 1993. Imitative learning of actions on objects by children, chimpanzees, and enculturated chimpanzees. *Child Development 64*, 1688–1705.

Tomasello, M., Striano, T., and Rochat, P. In press. Do young children use objects as symbols? *British Journal of Developmental Psychology*.

Tomasello, M., Strosberg, R., and Akhtar, N. 1996. Eighteen-month-old children learn words in non-ostensive contexts. *Journal of Child Language 22*, 1–20.

Tomasello, M., and Todd, J. 1983. Joint attention and lexical acquisition style. *First Language 4*, 197–212.

Tooby, J., and Cosmides, L. 1989. Evolutionary psychology and the generation of culture, part I. *Ethology and Sociobiology 10*, 29–49.

Trabasso, T., and Stein, N. 1981. Children's knowledge of events: A causal analysis of story structure. *Psychology of Learning and Motivation 15*, 237–282.

Traugott, E., and Heine, B. 1991a, 1991b. *Approaches to grammaticalization*, vols. 1 and 2. Amsterdam: John Benjamins.

Trevarthen, C. 1979. Instincts for human understanding and for cultural cooperation: Their development in infancy. In M. von Cranach, K. Foppa, W. Lepenies, and D. Ploog, eds., *Human ethology: Claims and limits of a new discipline.* Cambridge: Cambridge University Press.

——— 1993a. Predispositions to cultural learning in young infants. *Behavioral and Brain Sciences 16*, 534–535

——— 1993b. The function of emotions in early communication and development. In J. Nadel and L. Camaioni, eds., *New perspectives in early communicative development,* 48–81. New York: Routledge.

Trueswell, J., Tanenhaus, M., and Kello, C. 1993. Verb-specific constraints in sentence processing. *Journal of Experimental Psychology: Learning, Memory, and Cognition 19*, 528–553.

van Valin, R., and LaPolla, R. 1996. *Syntax: Structure, meaning, and function.* Cambridge: Cambridge University Press.

Visalberghi, E., and Fragaszy, D. M. 1990. Food-washing behaviour in tufted capuchin monkeys, *Cebus apella,* and crab-eating macaques, *Macaca fascicularis. Animal Behaviour 40,* 829–836.

Visalberghi, E., and Limongelli, L. 1996. Acting and understanding: Tool use revisited through the minds of capuchin monkeys. In A. E. Russon, K. A. Bard, and S. T. Parker, eds., *Reaching into thought,* 57–79. Cambridge: Cambridge University Press.

von Glasersfeld, E. 1982. Subitizing: The role of figural patterns in the development of numerical concepts. *Archives de Psychologie 50,* 191–218.

Vygotsky, L. 1978. *Mind in society: The development of higher psychological processes.* Ed. M. Cole. Cambridge, MA: Harvard University Press.

Wallach, L. 1969. On the bases of conservation. In D. Elkind and J. Flavell, eds., *Studies in cognitive development.* Oxford: Oxford University Press.

Want, S., and Harris, P. 1999. Learning from other people's mistakes. Manuscript.

Wellman, H. 1990. *The child's theory of mind.* Cambridge, MA: MIT Press.

Wellman, H., and Gelman, S. 1997. Knowledge acquisition in foundational domains. In D. Kuhn and R. Siegler, eds., *Handbook of child psychology,* vol. 2. New York: Wiley.

Wertsch, J. 1991. *Voices of the mind: A sociocultural approach to mediated action.* Cambridge, MA: Harvard University Press.

Whiten, A., Custance, D. M., Gómez, J. C., Teixidor, P., and Bard, K. A. 1996. Imitative learning of artificial fruit processing in children *(Homo sapiens)* and chimpanzees *(Pan troglodytes). Journal of Comparative Psychology 110,* 3–14.

Wilcox, J., and Webster, E. 1980. Early discourse behaviors: Children's response to listener feedback. *Child Development 51,* 1120–25.

Winner, E. 1988. *The point of words: Children's understanding of metaphor and irony.* Cambridge, MA: Harvard University Press.

Wittgenstein, L. 1953. *Philosophical investigations.* New York: Macmillan.

Wolfberg, P., and Schuler, A. 1993. Integrated play groups: A model for promoting the social and cognitive dimensions of play in children with autism. *Journal of Autism and Developmental Disorders 23,* 467–489.

Wood, D., Bruner, J., and Ross G. 1976. The role of tutoring in problem solving. *Journal of Child Psychology and Psychiatry 17,* 89–100.

Woodruff, G., and Premack, D. 1979. Intentional communication in the chimpanzee: The development of deception. *Cognition 7,* 333–362.

Woodward, A. 1998. Infants selectively encode the goal object of an actor's reach. *Cognition 69,* 1–34.

Wrangham, R. W., McGrew, W. C., de Waal, F. B. M., and Heltne, P. G. 1994. *Chimpanzee cultures.* Cambridge, MA: Harvard University Press.

Zelazo, P. In press. Self-reflection and the development of consciously controlled processing. In P. Mitchell and K. Riggs, eds., *Children's reasoning and the mind.* London: Psychology Press.

INDEX